The Music of Everyday Speech

The Music of Everyday Speech

Prosody and Discourse Analysis

ANN WENNERSTROM

UNIVERSITY PRESS

2001

OXFORD
UNIVERSITY PRESS

Oxford   New York
Athens   Auckland   Bangkok   Bogotá   Buenos Aires   Cape Town
Chennai   Dar es Salaam   Delhi   Florence   Hong Kong   Istanbul   Karachi
Kolkata   Kuala Lumpur   Madrid   Melbourne   Mexico City   Mumbai   Nairobi
Paris   São Paulo   Shanghai   Singapore   Taipei   Tokyo   Toronto   Warsaw

and associated companies in
Berlin   Ibadan

Published by Oxford University Press, Inc.
198 Madison Avenue, New York, New York 10016

Oxford is a registered trademark of Oxford University Press

Library of Congress Cataloging-in-Publication Data
Wennerstrom, Ann K.
The music of everyday speech : prosody and discourse
analysis / Ann Wennerstrom.
    p.   cm.
Includes bibliographical references and index.
ISBN 0-19-514321-3; ISBN 0-19-514322-1 (pbk.)
1. Prosodic analysis (Linguistics)   2. Discourse analysis.
3. Speech acts (Linguistics)   I. Title.
P224 .W46 2001
414'.6—dc21   00-066548

9 8 7 6 5 4 3 2 1

Printed in the United States of America
on acid-free paper

For my mother,

Mona Jeanne Hart Wennerstrom Loomer

PREFACE

The more I have worked with discourse, the more it has become clear that prosody—intonation, timing, and volume—is central to the interpretation of spoken language, but that, unfortunately, it is often ignored in actual analyses of discourse. Moreover, I have perceived a certain frustration among discourse analysts who have attempted to approach the subject of prosody. This may be due in part to the fact that much of the phonological work on prosody is highly technical and difficult to read unless one has a background in phonology. Therefore, an analyst who wishes to discuss the prosodic features in a text is faced with either wading into a technical body of phonological literature or describing those features in an ad hoc way.

Those brave souls who choose the former then encounter another problem: phonologists' conceptions of prosody are far from settled. At a recent conference of the American Association of Applied Linguistics, I noted that three very different models of intonation—those of Pierrehumbert, Brazil, and Halliday—were invoked by different presenters for different purposes. Aspects of the same prosodic phenomenon are being discussed under different theoretical assumptions. For the audience, the result may be a blind-men-and–the-elephant understanding of prosody. Although this metaphor is probably no longer politically correct, I find it apt to describe the situation a discourse analyst may confront in the attempt to incorporate prosody into an analysis. It is not always obvious how one aspect of prosody functions in the larger system or how the models of prosody described in the literature relate to each other.

The purpose of this book then is to demonstrate the centrality of prosody in the interpretation of spoken texts, to draw together a set of theoretical assumptions about prosody common to much of the phonological literature, and to provide an overview of prior analyses of discourse that have taken prosody into account. I argue that discourse analysis as a field would do well to regard prosody not as some extraneous flourish but as a central, meaningful component of the grammar of the text. Moreover, the kind of meaning conveyed by prosody can best be understood at the discourse level rather than through the analysis of isolated utterances. Thus, those with a discourse analysis perspective are in the most appropriate position to further our understanding of the functions of prosody in the coherence of communication.

The list of sources I cite is necessarily very broad. My intent has been to include, rather than exclude, a variety of work whenever possible. Although my own background is most closely influenced by the work of Pierrehumbert, and, more broadly, prosodic phonology, I have attempted to draw in extensive research on prosody, in order to point out common features and common goals even among diverse approaches. Thus, I devote a good deal of page space in early theoretical chapters to comparing and contrasting others' treatments of prosody in the belief that they are essentially describing much of the same real-world phenomena.

The audience for this book I also envision as broad. I hope it will be a useful resource for discourse analysts of many stripes who are interested in incorporating prosody into their research. For those who do have a background in phonology and phonetics, especially in prosody, I hope that the book will encourage a more discourse-oriented approach to prosodic analysis. I expect the book to be used in graduate courses in discourse analysis, ethnography, second-language acquisition, and conversation analysis. It can also serve as a text for courses in applied phonology and sociophonetics.

In order to address such a wide audience, I have covered several approaches to discourse analysis. After the initial theoretical chapters on the phonology and phonetics of prosody, the remainder of the book centers around discourse topics (rather than topics of prosody). Within each chapter, I have categorized prior research based on its discourse focus, regardless of its authors' theoretical assumptions about prosody. In this way, I hope to bring together work on prosody that shares common goals from a discourse analyst's perspective. Each chapter begins with an overview of the basic principles behind a particular approach to discourse analysis. This initial introduction will doubtless be unnecessary for some readers, but I decided to include the material in order to quickly orient those less familiar with discourse analysis.

In another attempt to broaden the appeal of the book, I decided to include sample analyses by guest contributors. This idea may be credited in part to Deborah Schiffrin, whose 1994 book effectively incorporates sample analyses to illustrate the material of each chapter with a concrete application. Moreover, by featuring other authors' work, I hope to demonstrate that discourse analysts from a range of backgrounds have already fruitfully incorporated prosody into their work. The guest authors also bring different perspectives on discourse analysis, different genres of discourse, different data with different dynamics of interaction, and different research methodologies, all of which has, I hope, added variety to the book.

It is also necessary to say a word about the computer figures used to illustrate points about prosody in this book. Although I could have created all the figures in a soundproof booth using my own voice to produce "perfect" illustrations, I chose instead to draw my examples from natural contexts. With a few exceptions, the figures in this volume are taken from tapes of discourse collected for other purposes in past projects. I then played these tapes into a computerized speech laboratory, made TIFF files of the appropriate screens, and added text and prosodic coding with other software. Two consequences of this decision need to be mentioned. First, those readers accustomed to seeing the clean figures produced in much phonetics research will find my figures "messy." Natural speech is fast, the vowels are often reduced, there is overlap between speakers, there is background noise, and speakers may move away from the microphone during the recording, affecting the volume. Therefore, there are gaps in my pitch tracks and many extraneous dots. Nevertheless, I stand by my commitment to show how real people actually behave in their use of prosody.

Second, since the purpose of figures is to illustrate specific aspects of prosody, I have taken the liberty of erasing at least some of this "noise" when I consider it to distract from the phenomenon being discussed. Erasures include nonhuman background sounds, such as chairs squeaking and cars going past; certain human sounds, in some cases another speaker's contribution that obscures the pitch of the featured speaker; and artifacts of the computer program, as in the high F_0 often manifest in aspirated and fricative consonants. This will no doubt displease some readers who prefer to see every detail of the context. However, given the limitation of two-dimensional diagrams in the representation of the pitch of speech, I have chosen clarity over completeness. In a computerized graph of pitch, any sound is represented by one or more dots. I understand my role as the illustrator to illuminate dots that are meaningful in the context of the discussion at hand and bring them to readers' attention. Thus, I have judged certain erasures to be for the greater good.

Another decision related to the presentation of data involves my use of other scholars' transcripts. Authors such as Tannen, Gumperz, Schegloff, and Eggins and Slade regularly incorporate prosodic features into their transcripts, using a variety of symbols that do not always correspond to mine. In citing their work, I had to choose between directly reproducing their coding systems or adapting their transcripts to my system. With a few exceptions, I have made the latter choice in the interests of consistency of transcription within this volume. To the best of my ability, I have made adaptations true to their authors' original arguments. In addition, I have provided notes for each transcript to indicate how specific conversions were made. I believe that the result is preferable to its alternative—the wholesale adoption of others' transcription codes, which would require *for every system* an explanation of the theoretical assumptions behind the codes and definitions of the terminology.

Finally, no discussion of this book's rationale would be complete without a comment on the varieties of language covered. In general, this book is about the prosody of English. I made this choice because by far the majority of prior work on prosody and discourse analysis has been conducted on English data. Also, the language of my own research has always been English, and therefore the data corpora I have at hand are largely in English. Although I have reviewed some studies of other Germanic languages for which I believe the findings are generalizable, the majority of the examples involve English. Moreover, let me be the first to admit that I have focused on the variety of English with which I am most familiar, Standard American English, or what some have called "The Northern Cities Dialect." Where possible, I have tried to combat this bias by including other scholars' excerpts of other varieties of English—analyses of Australian, African American Vernacular, and certain varieties of British English have been included, but they are admittedly sporadic. Having said this, however, I will add my belief that many of the prosodic phenomena described in this book are gross features, common to many varieties of English. I strongly urge others to test this claim; comparative work on prosody across dialects of English cries out to be done.

In thinking about and writing this book, I have relied on many people for ideas, inspiration, and advice. It is my pleasure to acknowledge a number of colleagues and friends for their contributions. First, I'd like to thank Peter Ohlin, Julia Balestracci, Lila Shahani, and Robin Miura from Oxford University Press for their straightforward and helpful approach to the publication process. I would also like to thank the guest authors in this volume, Kathleen Ferrara, Susan Fiksdal, Philip Gaines, and Heidi Riggenbach, not only for providing a fresh perspective through their data analyses but also for their enthusiasm and encouragement for the project.

In the academic community, several colleagues from various areas of expertise read or discussed different parts of the manuscript with me during its creation. Although any shortcomings in the manuscript are my own responsibility, the strongest ideas surely developed through these interactions. The contributions of the following people, listed in alphabetical order, are greatly appreciated: Anne Curzan, George Dillon, Cecile Ford, Ellen Kaisse, Robert Ladd, Carol Myers-Scotton, Fritz Newmeyer, Toni Prothero, Heidi Riggenbach, Sandra Silberstein, and Jim Tollefson. I also thank three other anonymous reviewers.

In addition, I wish to acknowledge the members of the University of Washington phonetics laboratory group for creating a stimulating and nurturing atmosphere for the exchange of ideas in their weekly meetings. Many thanks to Richard Wright, who directs the laboratory, and to regular participants: Robert Hagiwara, Zev Handel, Sharon Hargus, Ellen Kaisse, Soohee Kim, Misha Preston, and Alicia Beckford Wassink.

On a more personal level, I'd like to thank several other friends, colleagues, and fellow travelers for their enthusiasm and personal support behind the scenes. My sincere appreciation to Heidi Riggenbach, Suzanne LePeintre, Laurie Stephan, Phil Gaines, Alice Taff, Lucy Pickering, John Hellermann, Anis Bawarshi, Patty Heiser, Cherie Lenz-Hackett, Bill Harshbarger, and Kate Monahan.

On the home front, I want to thank my family for tolerating, and often even encouraging, the writing of this book. My warmest thanks to Andrew Siegel, Bonnie Wennerstrom, Clara Siegel, Michael Wennerstrom, Jeanne Loomer, and Mildred Siegel. In addition, I'd like to thank Steve Teig, one of my favorite musicians, for coming up with the title for the book, Paulette Booker for hours and hours of child care, and Paul Stanton, the "Coffee Grandpa" at my local Starbucks, for never failing to ask how the book was coming along.

CONTENTS

GUEST CONTRIBUTORS

Dr. Kathleen W. Ferrara is Associate Professor and Coordinator of Linguistics at Texas A & M University. She holds a Ph.D. in Linguistics from the University of Texas at Austin. Ferrara is the author of *Therapeutic Ways with Words* (Oxford University Press, 1994) and multiple articles on discourse analysis and sociolinguistic variation.

Dr. Susan Fiksdal is a member of the faculty at The Evergreen State College, where she teaches linguistics and French. Author of *The Right Time and Pace* (Ablex, 1990), her research interests focus on conversation, particularly rapport, metaphor, and gender.

Dr. Philip Gaines is an Assistant Professor and Coordinator of Composition in the Department of English at Montana State University. His areas of specialization include linguistics, discourse analysis, legal language, and composition studies. He is currently at work on a book examining the discourses of Anglo-American adversarial trial practice.

Dr. Heidi Riggenbach, Associate Professor of Applied Linguistics, teaches primarily in the University of Washington English department's Teaching English to Speakers of Other Languages (TESOL) program. She has taught ESOL and teacher education in the United States, China, Malaysia, and Zimbabwe. Author of *Discourse Analysis in the Language Classroom* (University of Michigan, 1999), her research is in the areas of spoken discourse, intercultural communication, and second-language acquisition.

TRANSCRIPTION SYMBOLS AND ABBREVIATIONS

Intonation Symbols

H*	high pitch accent
L*	low pitch accent
L+H*	steeply rising high pitch accent
L*+H	steeply rising low pitch accent
↑	high-rising pitch boundary
↗	low-rising pitch boundary
→	plateau pitch boundary
↘	partially falling pitch boundary
↓	low pitch boundary
-	cut-off speech with no intonation boundary
⇑	high paratone
⇓	low paratone
↱	high key
↳	low key
→	mid key
L-	low phrase accent (Pierrehumbert, 1980)
H-	high phrase accent (Pierrehumbert, 1980)
L%	low boundary tone (Pierrehumbert, 1980)
H%	high boundary tone (Pierrehumbert, 1980)

Textual Symbols for Stress and Intonation

á	primary word stress
à	secondary word stress
CÁPITALS	high pitch accent (H*)
SÚBSCRIPTED CÁPITALS	low pitch accent (L*)
ÚNDERLINED CÁPITALS	steeply rising high pitch accent (L+H*)
SÚBSCRIPTED ÚNDERLINED CÁPITALS	steeply rising low pitch accent (L*+H)

Paralinguistic Symbols

((coughs))	information about the interaction
(xxx)	can't be transcribed
⁺yikes⁺, ⁺⁺yikes⁺⁺, etc.	extremely high pitch
° let's go	quiet speech or whisper
h, hn, huh, hah	syllables of laughter are transcribed as [h] or to approximate their actual sound
>> hurry up	tempo speeds up
<< slow down	tempo slows down
/ beat / beat /	rhythmic beats
(.)	brief unmeasured pause
(1.1)	pause measured in seconds
ma:::n	elongated syllable
⌈speech ⌊speech	overlapping speech
I've got it =	latch from one speaker to the next
= great.	without pause

Other Abbrieviations

X	a weight marker on a metrical grid
*	ungrammatical
#	pragmatically odd
ADJ	adjective
ADV	adverb
BEV	Black English Vernacular
CA	Conversation Analysis
CSL	Computerized Speech Lab
Db	Decibel

ESL	English as a second language
GR	grammaticalization
Hz	Hertz
INS	Immigration and Naturalization Service
ITA	international teaching assistant
LL	language learner
NNS	nonnative speaker
NP	noun phrase
NS	native speaker
SPEAK	Spoken English Assessment Kit
TESOL	Teachers of English to Speakers of Other Languages
TSE	Test of Spoken English

The Music of Everyday Speech

1

INTRODUCTION

Prosody and Spoken Discourse

It may be readily observed that prosody plays a central role in the coherence of discourse in spoken English, beyond the sentence level. Let us consider, for example, a brief exchange from a conversation about weight gain and loss. (from Corpus 2; see Appendix for description of data corpora). The participants are a group of friends who have been discussing the fact that one member of the group has just recovered from an illness during which he lost a lot of weight. Now that he is better, he is eating more than usual to gain it back. A female member of the group remarks:

> M God how WÓNDERFUL to be so SKÍNNY you could just
> STUFF yourself↓ ((pause))
> And <u>WÁNNA</u> <small>GAIN WEIGHT</small>↓ ((pause))

Another rejoins:

> C But how <u>TÉRRIBLE</u> to be <u>SICK</u> to GET that way↓[1]

To briefly comment on the role of prosody in this exchange, intonation reinforces the contrastive relationship between the words *wonderful* and *terrible*. This occurs across turns—the use of a contrastive pitch by C comes in reaction to a notion introduced by M. Further cohesion is provided by M's low pitch on *gain weight*, which indicates that the topic of

3

weight gain is already under discussion. In the same utterance, M associates a contrastive pitch with *wanna*. To an ethnographer studying modern American culture, the notion that one normally does *not* want to gain weight, conveyed in this intonation, might be of interest. The turn-taking between these conversants also depends in part on their prosody. All three utterances end with a low pitch, followed by a pause, offering an optional place for a transition to a new speaker's turn. Moreover, the high-pitched syllables are rhythmically aligned, providing an additional cue for one speaker to anticipate the completion of the other's turn. All of these prosodic signals, and others as well, are integrated among the many language features that play a role in communication, whether participants are conscious of them or not.

As this example begins to illustrate, prosody is a general term encompassing intonation, rhythm, tempo, loudness, and pauses, as these interact with syntax, lexical meaning, and segmental phonology in spoken texts. In the field of discourse analysis, there has been an increasing awareness of the central role of these aspects of language. Although most discourse analysts recognize the importance of prosody, often prosodic issues are regarded as separate from "mainstream" discourse analyses, touched on in isolated examples or not at all. There are several good reasons for prosody's sideline status in discourse analysis. First, with the exception of punctuation and certain occasional special fonts, prosodic features are not readily available in English orthography. Thus, the convention in the field of converting spoken discourse to written transcripts usually results in some loss of prosodic detail. Whereas conversation analysts (such as Jefferson, 1984) have included prosodic components in their transcription coding systems, not all transcribers consistently use the codes. Once spoken discourse is committed to a transcript, that transcript tends to take on a life of its own in place of the original interaction. Future analyses of that transcript then lack the original prosody.

In addition, much of the current work on prosody, particularly intonation and rhythm, is written by and for phonologists and phoneticians and therefore tends to be difficult for those who lack this background. My own initial foray into the intonation literature as a new graduate student of phonology was to read Janet Pierrehumbert's dissertation (1980), arguably the most influential document on intonation written since Halliday (1967a). Yet it proved to be extremely difficult reading for the nonspecialist, as I was at the time. Furthermore, many phonological treatments of intonation in the tradition of generative phonology rely on constructed utterances out of context for their illustrative examples. While I have found instances in my own work when a constructed example can quickly illustrate a point, the sole reliance on such data, typical of many phonological approaches to intonation, leads to certain limitations for the discourse analyst. One problem is that constructed examples tend to be single utterances, leaving the role of prosody in extended discourse inaccessible. In addition, conclusions based on a "citation form" of an utterance may be missing some of the evidence that a full analysis of data in context would provide. Often, "out-of-the-blue" utterances actually entail a context that enters into an interpretation, whether readers are aware of it or not. Since there is a strong relationship between intonation and presupposition, a presupposed context may influence the intonation of a citation form. For example, Cruttendon (1986, p. 83), a scholar of intonation, uses the following constructed out-of-the-blue utterance to illustrate a case of "nuclear pitch accent" (the most intonationally prominent point of an utterance) occurring in utterance-medial position:

Watch out! That CHÍMNEY'S falling down.

He presents this as an exception to the widely held belief that nuclear accent goes in sentence-final position except in cases of contrast (Halliday, 1967a; Chomsky & Halle, 1968). He then proposes that a special semantic category, "event sentences," have the highest pitch prominence on their grammatical subjects. However, I submit that an alternative analysis can be constructed once we realize that if this utterance were heard in a natural context, certain facts would be presupposed. From the warning *Watch out!* it is evident that the speaker sees a danger that he supposes the hearer does not yet see. After this phrase, the hearer is on the alert, looking for something amiss. The word *that* conveys the deictic structure of the situation: a particular chimney must be visible, at some distance from the speaker and hearer, but near enough to pose a danger, hence the warning. The present progressive tense in *is falling* indicates that some change in the chimney must already be visible at the time of the utterance for the hearer to perceive. Therefore, it could be argued that since low pitch tends to be associated with information already presumed accessible to a hearer (Chafe, 1994), the lack of prominence on *falling down* is due to its redundancy after the combination of the warning, the utterance of the word *chimney,* and the visibility of the chimney's changing state. (What else could a chimney be doing in this context?)[2] My point is not necessarily to disagree with Cruttendon's semantic interpretation of this data but rather to point out that sentences out of context, standard examples among phonologists, always include presuppositions that might in themselves affect the prosody and, hence, the theoretical claims. Given the trend that prosodic theory has traditionally been in the domain of phonology rather than discourse analysis, a discourse analyst who wishes to investigate prosody faces a choice between the task of interpreting abstract phonological treatments, on one hand, or opting for a non-systematic account of the prosody, on the other.

Finally, and ironically, for some discourse analysts the recent developments in computerized speech technology have been a *deterrent* to the study of prosody. They have, at the very least, introduced a new set of methodological decisions about how to proceed. On one hand, speech technology has opened up a wealth of possibilities for the acoustic analysis of discourse data. On the other, because computer technology has been expensive and may require special training for use, its existence may actually diminish the likelihood that a nonspecialist will attempt a prosodic analysis. It is tempting to fall prey to the discouraging belief that the real "truth" can be found only in precise measurements made by instruments and that without a high-tech background one should abandon any thought of working on prosody.

To synthesize this discussion, despite the essential role of prosody in oral communication, barriers deter nonphonologists who wish to incorporate prosody into their analyses of spoken discourse. In view of these barriers, we arrive at the purpose of this book: to provide discourse analysts with an accessible account of the prosody of English, which is systematically based on phonological theory but understandable to those without a background in phonology or phonetics. Discussions will center on contextualized examples drawn from natural discourse. My approach is to cover a variety of topics within the field of discourse analysis and to include sample analyses for each in which I show how prosody can be incorporated to enhance and expand previously held theoretical frameworks. I will argue that since prosody is always present in spoken discourse, it is not merely an added flourish or superimposed feature but central to a full understanding of any spoken text. Moreover, I believe that since prosodic meaning is manifest at the discourse level, discourse analysis as a field is poised to make an important contribution to the understanding of prosodic meaning. This book is an attempt to make prosody more manageable in the hope that discourse researchers will further develop its potential as a meaningful component of communication.

What Is Prosody?

Prosody includes a number of speech characteristics traditionally considered "suprasegmental" or separate from segmental phonology. Of these, the main aspects treated in this volume are intonation, rhythm, and the distribution and length of pauses. Volume, tempo, and voice quality are also discussed where appropriate. Prosody has universal and language-specific functions, both considered in the chapters that follow. Universally, prosodic features can convey emotional priorities (Bolinger, 1978) and tend to differ from one genre of speech to another for stylistic and pragmatic reasons (Tench, 1991). For example, regardless of one's language background, level of pitch and volume are likely to be more extreme in warning cries than in intimate conversation. Rhythm is also manifest in all cultures, not only in language but also in music, poetry, and other art forms (Couper-Kuhlen, 1993; Liberman, 1975). These universal facts about prosody are central to the thinking behind this volume because I assume that a rhythmic base underlies the phonology of languages and that other prosodic elements interact with rhythm to convey meaning.

On the other hand, not all languages have the same intonation system and distribution of rhythm and pauses because prosodic features associate with particular constituents in discourse in a rule-governed and meaningful way. Starting in chapters 2 and 3, I consider the structure of prosody in English in detail, from the perspective of the theory broadly known as prosodic phonology (Liberman & Prince, 1977; Nespor & Vogel, 1986; Selkirk, 1984; Pierrehumbert, 1980; and numerous other works). I argue that there is an English-specific system of intonation built upon a rhythmic foundation that functions as a "grammar of cohesion." This means that prosody, particularly intonation, contributes information about connections among constituents in discourse, conveying meaning beyond what is provided through lexical and syntactic systems. Some of these connections involve the information structure of the discourse (Halliday, 1967b), as illustrated in the weight-gain example in the beginning of this chapter. In that example, we saw that a contrast could be maintained across turns by virtue of the intonation pattern associated with the lexical items being contrasted. Prosody also serves to link large topic constituents in the organizational structure of the discourse (Brown, 1977; Swerts & Geluykens, 1994; Yule, 1980). Finally, at a more local level, the prosody at the initial and final boundaries of utterances indicates their level of interdependency (Brazil, 1985; Pierrehumbert & Hirschberg, 1990), which is crucial to the turn-taking system. In short, the prosody of English is part of the coherence of texts at the discourse level.

For the most part, the universal and the language-specific aspects of prosody are treated separately in this volume; however, I do not imply that they are entirely independent. Chafe (1994) believes (and I concur) that an iconic relationship exists between prosody and modern grammars. The prosodic features of the cries of our prelinguistic ancestors may have become grammaticalized over the millennia into specific prosodic systems of modern languages. For example, the association between high pitch and increased volume and salient, new information, found in the intonation patterns of many languages, may stem from prelinguistic responses to what is worthy of attention in the environment. Therefore, although each modern language manifests a unique prosodic system, it would not be surprising if certain common features were present.

Organization of the Book

This volume is constructed to show how prosodic analysis can be integrated into different areas of discourse analysis. Part I provides an overview of the model of prosody underlying the subsequent chapters. As I noted before, this is based on the theory of prosodic or, more specifically, metrical phonology, which posits a universal rhythmic structure underlying the syllables and stress systems of languages of the world. Chapter 2 begins with a simple overview of the intonation model used in the rest of the book, illustrated with examples from natural speech. The remainder of the chapter provides the rationale for this model of intonational meaning. The model is an adaptation of work by Pierrehumbert (1980) and Pierrehumbert and Hirschberg (1990) in which meaningful components of intonation, or tones, work together to contribute to an overall interpretation. I have also drawn from Brazil's (1985) model of intonation, which includes the notion that the pitch range, or "key," at the onset of an utterance is an indicator of attitudinal stance among speakers in interaction. Finally, in discussions of prosodic organization at the topic level, I look to Brown (1977) and Yule (1980) for their work on the "paratone."

Chapter 3 continues with an explanation of how the intonation system aligns with rhythm in interaction. Following Halliday (1967a), Hayes (1995), Liberman (1975), and others, I discuss the fundamental role of rhythm in linguistic structure. Further, I present evidence that in interaction, rhythm acts as an organizing resource in the processing of speech and can even be maintained from one speaker to the next (Couper-Kuhlen, 1993; Gumperz, 1982). The discussion of rhythm is followed by an overview of the paralinguistic features of prosody, such as volume, vowel duration, and pitch extremes, and a discussion of how these relate to the phonological systems of prosody. In general, the goal of part I is to single out aspects of the theoretical material on prosody that are most relevant to discourse analysis and to search for common threads in previous work.

Part II, on the application of prosodic analysis to discourse, has six chapters devoted to different approaches to discourse analysis. Each chapter gives a brief introduction to a discourse tradition and then reviews how prosody has been incorporated into that area in previous work. Many examples and diagrams are included to illustrate how prosodic phenomena function in context. Wherever possible, I show that bringing prosodic evidence to bear on earlier discourse analyses can shed light on unresolved theoretical debates. Based on the work that has come before, I provide recommendations for further prosodic analyses and suggestions for how these might be undertaken. Finally, I include a sample of a prosodic analysis applied to the particular area of discourse analysis covered in the chapter. Two of these sample analyses are drawn from my own work and four are contributed by guest authors, writing in their own fields of specialization. The aim of these sample analyses is to provide concrete demonstrations of how discourse data can be analyzed for some aspect of its prosodic structure. The guest authors also introduce a range of perspectives in their interests and approaches to research and provide methodologies that may be replicated in future projects.

Specifically, chapter 4 centers on the role of intonation in the cohesion and coherence of discourse as participants build mental representations of the information structure of a particular speech event. Starting with Halliday and Hasan's (1976) taxonomy of lexical and grammatical devices of cohesion, I explore how intonation interacts with cohesive language. Following Sperber and Wilson (1995), I further suggest that intonation is involved in the retrieval of schemata stored in memory in the interpretation of a text. In addition, I show how intonation performs a deictic function in differentiating foreground from background material in the perception of the physical environment. The sample analysis (my own) investigates a statistics lecture from which I argue that intonation contributes more information about how the audience is to construct a coherent mental representation of the lecture than does the lexicogrammatical structure alone. This sheds light on the lecturer's assumptions about the common knowledge shared among class members and on how new knowledge structures might be acquired by the students.

Moving to a larger scale of discourse structure, chapter 5 considers the interaction of prosody and the global organization of discourse. One type of interaction is between intonation and discourse markers (Schiffrin, 1987), expressions such as *well, you know,* and *oh.* Although they are hard to classify in dictionary terms, Schiffrin amply demonstrates that such items are essential to the organizational structure of discourse. As I show, when certain discourse markers have more than one meaning, often the intonation contour associated with the marker makes the distinction. A second, related contribution of prosody to discourse organization involves topic structure. As Brown (1977) and

Yule (1980) have documented, topic units tend to be delineated with changes in pitch and volume. Borrowing from written genres where topics are arranged into paragraphs, linguists have applied the term "paratone" to a spoken topic unit. In this sense, I argue that prosody itself can be considered a discourse marker. For this chapter, the sample analysis contributed by Kathleen Ferrara shows that the discourse marker *anyway* can be analyzed as having three different meanings, each with its own distinctive intonation contour.

Chapter 6 focuses on speech act theory and the fact that the illocutionary force of an utterance is often closely tied to its prosody. As a simple illustration, when a syntactic statement is uttered with rising, instead of falling, intonation, it may become a question. As Liberman and Sag (1974) have pointed out, certain intonation contours, such as the "contradiction contour," can idiomatically convey a speech act regardless of their lexicogrammatical structure. Because of such facts, and because intonation is a meaningful part of the English language, I question the status of its illocutionary force as "indirect," in opposition to the "direct" force of the lexicogrammatical structure. I explore arguments by Ward and Hirschberg (1985) and others to determine where in a model of speech act theory intonational meaning properly belongs. The sample analysis, by Philip Gaines, shows how intonation contributes to illocutionary force in legal questioning. Here, the role of intonation in speech acts becomes particularly acute, since courtroom discourse affects matters of life and death.

Chapter 7 moves to the analysis of conversation, an area where prosody has already been taken quite seriously. Gumperz (1971, 1982, 1992), for example, has made extended use of prosody in his notion of "contextualization cues" with which speakers continuously adjust and readjust their interpretations of a conversation as it progresses. Likewise, conversation analysts in the tradition of Sacks, Schegloff, and Jefferson (1974) typically take many prosodic features such as pause length, vowel elongation, volume, intonation, and voice quality into account. With such elaborate groundwork already laid, my contribution focuses on drawing connections among certain prosodic analyses already done on conversation data and reinterpreting them within the theoretical framework of this volume. I also discuss areas where I believe more detailed prosodic analysis may be advantageous: the relationship between intonation boundaries and pauses in turn-taking; the contribution of prosody to the coherence of a conversation; the role of pitch in "tone concord," or the extent to which conversants match their pitch across turns (Brazil, 1985); and the functions of rhythm and tempo in interaction. In the sample analysis, Susan Fiksdal makes the case that the rhythmic structure of a conversation can be an indication of the extent of rapport between conversants. When speakers are comfortable, they are likely to synchronize their rhythm; rhythm breaks down, however, during what Fiksdal calls "uncomfortable moments."

In chapter 8 I discuss the paralinguistic aspects of prosody. I consider the contribution of prosody to the telling of narratives with a focus on the role it plays in supporting the structure of the narrative and in displaying emotion. Prosody is clearly an essential element in what Wolfson (1982) calls the "performance features" of storytelling, along with quoted speech, gestures, and other methods tellers use to highlight key components of their stories. The chapter provides many examples in which lexicogrammatical features discussed in the narrative literature as "evaluative" (Labov, 1972) coincide with exaggerated prosodic forms. In addition, the role of prosody in storytelling style is reviewed: prosodic features are often a part of what distinguishes the style of one particular speech community, or of one individual, from another. The sample analysis, my own contribution, emphasizes the relationship between prosody and evaluative language in a corpus of oral narratives. I conclude that prosodic analysis should be a central component of ethnographic and other approaches to the narratives of a culture.

In chapter 9, the topic of second-language discourse is considered. The general argument of the chapter is that descriptions of interlanguage speech and research into its structure and development should not ignore the contribution of prosody. English as a second language materials developers have made a significant contribution in this area; many current pronunciation textbooks devote a good deal of page space to prosody in contexts of communication. The chapter reviews research on interlanguage speech that has focused on intonation, speech rate, pausing, and other prosodic phenomena. The effect of prosody on ratings of accentedness and fluency is also discussed, for these appear to have more influence on raters' judgments than do other aspects of pronunciation (Anderson-Hsieh, Johnson, & Koehler, 1992). Finally, the nature of the acquisition of prosody by learners of English is considered, a topic about which relatively little is known. The sample analysis for the chapter is contributed by Heidi Riggenbach, who shows the effect of pauses and rate of speech on raters' judgments of nonnative speaker fluency. Riggenbach is interested in how fluency is manifest in dialogue rather than monologue, drawing from informal conversations between native and nonnative speakers of English.

In sum, this volume is organized to present features of prosody as components of a coherent system and to demonstrate that discourse analysts from a variety of backgrounds can fruitfully integrate prosody into their research. For each of a number of traditional areas of discourse analysis, I provide examples and diagrams to illustrate prosodic phenomena, an overview of how prosody has already been researched, recommendations for future directions of study, and a sample analysis of some aspect of prosody in discourse.

Computers and Prosodic Analysis

Before concluding this chapter, I would like to say a few words about the computer analysis of speech. There is no doubt that speech technology provides exciting possibilities for the analysis of prosody in spoken discourse. This is demonstrated, for example, in an anthology by Couper-Kuhlen and Selting (1996), a collection of studies of natural discourse data from a variety of languages. In several of these studies, the existence of distinctive prosodic forms in the data is documented through computer measurement tools. Another use of technology is to gather large numbers of measurements of a particular prosodic feature and apply statistical tests in a search for large-scale trends (as Wennerstrom, 1998). Finally, for the purpose of illustration, a computer-generated diagram can be of great value—indeed, I have included many such diagrams throughout this volume to illustrate prosodic features and thereby support my arguments.

I mentioned earlier, however, my fear that the development of speech technology may actually have discouraged some nonspecialists from undertaking the analysis of prosody for lack of access to technological resources. Meanwhile, computer analysis has increasingly become the standard whereas impressionistic analysis might have been considered sufficient in earlier descriptions of prosody. I believe that the purpose of one's research, rather than some arbitrary principle about technology, should determine the methodology and tools one chooses. For some purposes, it may not be necessary to document with speech technology the presence or absence of obvious prosodic features.

Indeed, there is empirical evidence that the ear can be trained to distinguish certain prosodic categories with a good degree of accuracy. In a corpus of naturally occurring conversation data, Schuetze-Coburn, Shapley, and Weber (1991) performed both an auditory and an acoustic analysis to identify a basic constituent of intonation and to determine how closely the two types of analysis would correlate. Auditory analysis was highly consistent with acoustic analysis in the identification of the onset of "declination units"—short units of intonation within which a speaker's pitch gradually declines from beginning to end. A second finding was that the auditory analysis revealed a more deeply embedded unit within the declination unit that was not identified through the instrumental analysis of pitch reset and pause. Their analysis confirms that impressionistic judgments, having a basis in physical signals, can be quite consistent, at least in some categories. They conclude that both auditory and acoustic analysis can play a role in research methodologies.

Furthermore, as Ladd (1996) points out, the difference between instrumental and impressionistic approaches to the study of intonation is theoretical rather than necessarily a matter of thoroughness or correctness.

> [I]t is important to recognise that the impressionistic descriptions involve phonological categories that could *in principle* be related to instrumentally validated acoustic or articulatory parameters. More importantly, critics of impressionistic descriptions often fail to recognise that the instrumental approach also involves theoretical assumptions which can be examined and evaluated, and which do not always stand up to close inspection. (pp. 13–14)

My inclination then is to call for a combination of approaches. Depending on one's research goals, both impressionistic judgments and computer measurement can be effective in the analysis of prosody. Speech technology can be used to check one's intuitions, reinforce one's conclusions, illustrate particular phenomena, or collect measurements in projects that rely on statistical analysis. In addition, I advocate that creative interdisciplinary alliances be forged between phoneticians and speech pathologists, who understand the physics of speech, and discourse analysts, sociolinguists, and others, whose expertise lies in the structure and dynamics of social interaction. Such collaborations could be beneficial to both parties. Indeed, the burgeoning field of sociophonetics attests to the effectiveness of combining these areas of specialization.

As a final comment on this topic, I note that, in a sense, time is on the side of the discourse analyst as corporate money pours into the engineering of new speech software. Trends are quickly moving in the direction of more variety and better quality of technology for the analysis of speech while the tools are becoming increasingly less expensive and easy to use. As an illustration, I will tell the story of a colleague, a sociolinguist, who was recently approached by a major children's toy company asking how to take dialectal variation into account in developing computer toys that recognize children's verbal commands. The company was prepared to devote considerable payment to finding a solution to this problem.[3] At this rate of funding, interest, and development, it will not be long before even the technology-shy and resource-impoverished have easy access to speech analysis instruments.

Summary

In this volume I present phonological and phonetic principles of prosody in an accessible framework for those with an interest in social interaction and language structure at the discourse level. Rather than relying on constructed examples, I apply these principles wherever possible to natural spoken language in context. I hope that discourse analysts will gain new insights into how to incorporate prosodic features into more traditional analytical frameworks. Likewise, phonologists and phoneticians who have previously confined their investigations to constructed sentences or isolated utterances may decide to consider the role of prosody in more extended, natural contexts. Perhaps some day all fields involving human behavior can routinely regard the "music" of speech as a part of the foundation of communication.

I

THEORETICAL
BACKGROUND

2

INTONATIONAL MEANING

Intonation is the pitch or "melody" of the voice during speech. In English, a language that makes extensive use of intonation, speakers can manipulate their pitch on particular words, phrases, or even topic-sized constituents to convey meaning about relationships in discourse. Intonation is not derived automatically from the stress patterns or syntax of an utterance; instead, a speaker decides to associate particular intonation patterns with particular constituents, depending on the discourse context.

One immediate difficulty in consolidating the literature on intonation is the lack of aggreement on terminology. If I wish to talk about syntax, I can feel confident that most audiences will understand words such as "noun" and "verb." However, with intonation, terms such as "stress," "accent," "tone," and "emphasis" may mean different things to different people. Not only are the lay terms different from the linguists' terms, but linguists themselves disagree on terminology. To make matters worse, there are even different schools of thought on what counts as a unit in an intonation analysis. Should the intonation contour of an entire phrase be interpreted as a single, meaning-bearing unit? Is it possible to identify smaller units as meaningful? Where exactly does a unit start and stop? And, for the purpose at hand, to analyze spoken discourse in context, what level of detail is most reasonable?

The task of this chapter is to sort out some of the common threads among these terms and points of view in theorists' discussions and to present and justify a model of intonation for the purpose of discourse analysis. As a basis for the intonation model here, I follow an adaptation of Pierrehumbert's (1980) dissertation on intonation and Pierrehumbert and Hirschberg's (1990) treatment of intonational meaning. According to this school of thought, the intonation of an utterance can be analyzed as a series of high and low tones, each conveying a particular meaning in discourse. Underemphasized in Pierrehumbert's work, however, is the contribution of utterance-initial pitch to intonational meaning. For this, I incorporate Brazil's (1985, 1997) notion of "key," a speaker's choice of pitch at the initiation of an utterance. Finally, at the organizational level, I include a "paratone" component in the model, whereby pitch range marks topic shifts (Brown, 1977; Yule, 1980). The chapter begins with a bare-bones outline of this model with examples of each of its components. For those with further theoretical interest, I follow this with a more detailed rationale for the model and the assumptions behind it. To the extent possible, important concepts are introduced with simple explanations and examples, meant to be accessible to an audience without any specific background in prosody.

Intonational Meaning: An Overview

The model of intonational meaning used in this volume includes four main categories: pitch accents, pitch boundaries, key, and paratones, each of which has a number of subcomponents, or "intonational morphemes." The categories are described briefly below in terms of their discourse functions and are illustrated with examples from naturally occurring speech. Diagrams were obtained from a Computerized Speech Lab (CSL) (Model 4300B, Kay Elemetrics). The descriptions of intonational meaning in this introductory presentation are very general and should not be taken as rigid definitions. The task of this volume as a whole will be to explore many of the subtle meanings that can be attained through this model of intonation and other aspects of prosody in a variety of contexts and genres of discourse.

Pitch Accents

Pitch accents are the various tones associated with lexical items that a speaker decides are especially salient in the information structure of the discourse. A star symbol indicates that the pitch accent is associated with the stressed syllable of the word being accented. In transcriptions of multisyllabic words, the stress is marked with accent symbols on the vowels (é = primary stress; è = secondary stress). *H* pitch accent,* which is transcribed with capital letters, indicates information being added to the discourse as new; *L+H* pitch accent,* transcribed with underlined capital letters, indicates information contrasting with a prior item or idea in the discourse; *L* pitch accent,* transcribed with subscripted capital letters, indicates information that is not to be added to the discourse as new, either because it is already believed to be accessible, or because it is extrapropositional; and *L*+H pitch accent,* transcribed with subscripted and underlined capital letters, indicates that the relevance of an item to the discourse is questioned in contrast to some other item.

The following utterance, from a lecture on international trade (Corpus 1-C), shows the H*, L*, and L+H* pitch accents working together. D, the professor, is discussing the marketing of bicycles in the United States versus China (other transcription codes are provided in the beginning of this volume):

D ... for the BÍCYCLE in (.) in the U.S. versus the ᴮᵢCYCLE in
CHÍNA.

As shown in figure 2.1, H* pitch accents are associated with the words *bicycle* and *U.S.*, which are introduced as new information at the beginning of the utterance; L* pitch accent is associated with the second use of *bicycle,* which is now assumed by the speaker to be accessible to the hearers; the steeply rising L+H* pitch accent is associated with the word

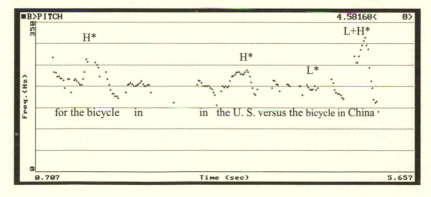

Figure 2.1   The H*, L*, and L+H* pitch accents interact with the information structure of the discourse.

China, which contrasts with *U.S.* The starred, high part of the L+H* pitch accent is associated with the stressed syllable of the word.

The L*+H pitch accent has a scooped shape, also steeply rising, but the starred part, which associates with the stressed syllable of the word, is low. Here is an example of two L*+H pitch accents in a conversation about restaurants in Nepal (Corpus 2):

> T   I ate at this one WÉSTERN place
> M   They have a ᴡᴇ́ꜱᴛᴇʀɴ ʀᴇ́ꜱᴛᴀᴜʀᴀɴᴛ?

As figure 2.2 shows, this pitch accent is associated with the words *western* and *restaurant,* whose relevance is being questioned. It is contrastive in the sense that an alternative might be considered more appropriate. (Nepal may have other types of restaurants, but a western restaurant is surprising). The L*+H pitch accent often conveys a "does this count?" sense (Ward & Hirschberg, 1985, p. 756).

Pitch Boundaries

Pitch boundaries are the pitch configurations at the ends of phrases, accompanied by a lengthening of the final syllables. I use arrow symbols for boundaries to indicate their direction with respect to the speaker's pitch range. Starting from the final pitch accent of the phrase, they rise or fall at various degrees of steepness or remain flat. Following Pierrehumbert and Hirschberg (1990), I consider the interpretation of pitch boundaries to be independent of the interpretation of pitch accents: pitch boundaries indicate how speakers intend each constituent to be hierarchically integrated with the subsequent one. In general, pitch bound-

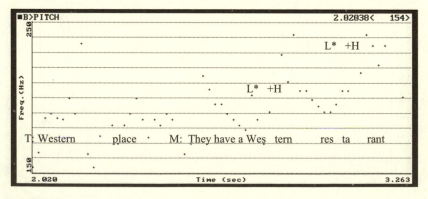

Figure 2.2   L*+H pitch accents are associated with the words *western* and *restaurant.*

aries that terminate above the bottom of the speaker's pitch range convey an interdependency with the following constituent, whereas low boundaries do not convey this interdependency.

High-rising boundaries (↑), which rise upward from the last pitch accent of the phrase, anticipate subsequent discourse for their interpretation, usually from another speaker. These are often used to solicit backchannels—short responses such as "uh huh" or "yeah." They may also be associated with classic yes-no questions, as in the following exchange, also about Nepal (Corpus 2):

  M Did you COMMÚNICÀTE in um ₙₑwÁᵣᵢ all the time↑
  T At the END, but at the <u>BEGÍNNING</u>, NO.

This is shown in figure 2.3.

Low-rising boundaries (↗), which begin low and then rise, also anticipate subsequent discourse for their interpretation, often from the same speaker, as in the following utterance from a lecture in mathematics (Corpus 1-A):

  The QUÉSTION IS↗ (.) WHAT is the ROLE of H?

Figure 2.4 shows how the low-rising boundary after *is* anticipates the subsequent phrase for a complete interpretation.

Partially falling boundaries (↘), which slope downward but stop short of the bottom of the speaker's range, also indicate an interdependency between the phrase that they occupy and the subsequent one, usually within the same speaker's utterance. They are often functionally inter-

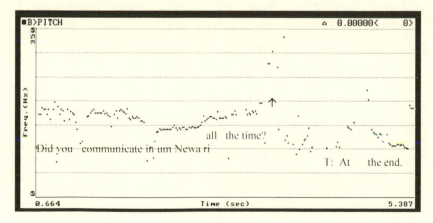

Figure 2.3 The high-rising pitch boundary (↑) occurs at the end of a yes-no question.

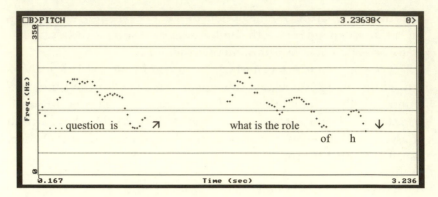

Figure 2.4   The low-rising pitch boundary (↗) at the end of the first phrase anticipates the second phrase for its completion.

changeable with low-rising boundaries, but the connection with the next phrase is usually even closer than the one established by the low rise. We saw an example of a partially falling boundary after *bicycle* in figure 2.1, whose text is reprinted here:

> . . . for the BÍCYCLE↘ in (.) in the U.S.↗ versus the ʙíᴄʏᴄʟᴇ in CHÍNA.

Plateau boundaries (→), which extend from the final pitch accent of the phrase in a flat, level shape, again anticipate subsequent discourse for their interpretation, often in a list or sequence. This boundary is also used in hesitation. The example below (from Corpus 2) contains plateau boundaries after the words *worms* and *amoebas*, elements in a list of parasitic diseases that T unfortunately contracted in Nepal. In the middle of the list, another participant offers an incredulous comment ("Really?") with a high-rising pitch boundary (pause lengths are also given in parentheses):

T	OH maybe TWO or THREE weeks LÁTER it was the TRÍPLE
	WHÁMMY↘ ʏᴏᴜ ᴋɴᴏᴡ↘ (1.1.) WORMS→ 'n =
M	= RRRÉALLY↑ (.2)
T	yeah, A ⎡MÉOBAS→ (.3)
M	⎣ohh ↘
T	hh the WHOLE thing.

Figure 2.5 shows the part of the sequence beginning with *worms.*

Low boundaries (↓), the only pitch boundaries that end at the bottom of the speaker's pitch range, convey no special dependency on the subsequent utterance. We have already seen an example of a low boundary at the end of the utterance in figure 2.1, whose text is reprinted here:

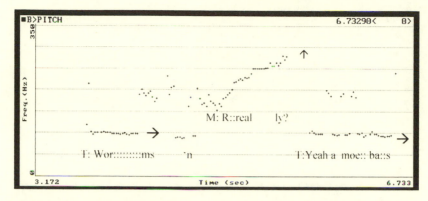

Figure 2.5 The plateau pitch boundary (→) is used in a listing sequence.

um, the <u>PRÍMARY</u> ꜰᴜɴᴄᴛɪᴏɴ for the BÍCYCLE↘ in (.) in the U.S.↗
versus the ʙɪᴄʏᴄʟᴇ in <u>CHÍNA</u>↓

In this case, the low boundary provides closure at the end of a set of interdependent constituents.

No pitch boundary (-), or "cut off intonation," occurs when a speaker
hesitates in midconstituent before completing an utterance. The speech
stream is cut off, usually with a glottal or other stop and no final lengthening. Cutoffs often occur in the middle of syntactic units and after discourse markers such as *like* or *you know*. Returning to the bicycle example,
there is no boundary after the first utterance of the word *in*, represented
this time with a hyphen symbol:

um, the <u>PRÍMARY</u> ꜰᴜɴᴄᴛɪᴏɴ for the BÍCYCLE↘ in- (.) in the U.S.↗
versus the ʙɪᴄʏᴄʟᴇ in <u>CHÍNA</u>↓

Again, this cutoff is visible in figure 2.1, where the pitch of *in* is not especially elongated, nor does it rise or fall.

Key

Key is the choice of pitch a speaker makes at the onset of an utterance to
indicate the attitude or stance toward the prior one. Arrow symbols are
used to show the relative position in the pitch range that a speaker has
chosen to begin an utterance. *High key*(↑), a high onset in the pitch range,
indicates a contrast in attitude with respect to the prior utterance. *Mid
key* (→), having no change in pitch range, indicates a consistent attitudinal stance with respect to the prior utterance. *Low key* (↳), a low onset in
the pitch range, indicates that the utterance does not add anything spe-

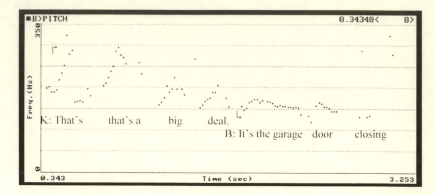

Figure 2.6 A high key (⌐) is met with a low key (└) in this exchange.

cial with respect to the prior one, or as Brazil (1985) says, it is a foregone conclusion. The following excerpt (from Corpus 3) comes from a conversation between two women about the feeling of loss that B associates with reaching the end of her child-bearing years. In the example, B's key remains low while K's is high:

> K ⌐THAT'S- THAT'S a BIG DEAL!
> B └It's the garage DOOR closing.

I interpret this as a difference in emotional stance: K's high key shows her attempt to acknowledge that B's circumstance is not to be dismissed lightly. B, in a face-protective move, maintains a cynical acceptance of the foregone conclusion that her child-bearing years are over; her utterance is delivered in a low key. The exchange appears in figure 2.6.

Paratones

Paratones, the expansion or compression of pitch range, function as a kind of intonational "paragraphing" to mark topical junctures. I use a double arrow symbol to indicate this higher order pitch-range shift at the onset of topic constituents.

High paratone (⇑), an expansion of the speaker's pitch range, begins a new organizational unit of discourse. In the following lecture excerpt (Corpus 1-B), the speaker makes a transition between two explanations of data plots drawn on the blackboard:

> DUCKS that had a <u>LÓWER</u> PLÚMAGE RÁTING TÉNDED ÁLSO TO HAVE A <u>LÓWER BEHÁVIORAL</u> RÁTING. (2.1)
> ⇑ Let's SKIP FOR RIGHT NOW onto the <u>NEXT</u> PLOT · · ·

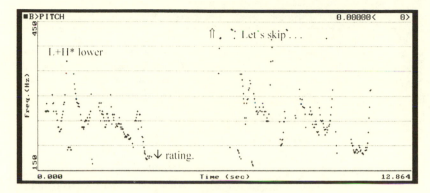

Figure 2.7 At the start of the new topic, the lecturer's pitch expands in a high paratone (⇑).

Figure 2.7 shows the transition. ~~As is typical of high paratones, there is a rather long pause of 2.1 seconds between topics~~.

Low paratone (⇓), a compression of the pitch range, marks an aside, or parenthetical, with respect to the main topic. The following example, taken from the same lecture (Corpus 1-B), contains a parenthetical definition of the term *crossbreeds* as the lecturer describes a genetic study of the interbreeding of two species of ducks, the mallard and the pintail:

> And the QUÉSTION that was being ADDRÉSSED by this
> PARTÍCULAR _{STÚDY}↗ was whether→ CRÓSS_{BREEDS}↗ (.4)
> ⇓so DUCKS that had a- ONE MÁLLARD _{PÁRENT} and ONE PÍNTAIL
> _{PÁRENT}↗(.4)
> ⇑ if you LOOK at _{THEM}↗

Figure 2.8 shows the sequence.

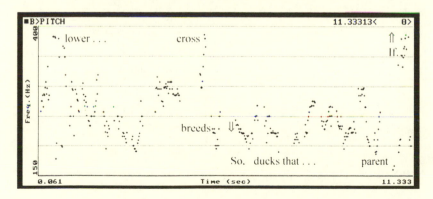

Figure 2.8 A parenthetical definition is uttered with a compressed pitch range, or low paratone (⇓).

TABLE 2.1 Summary of the Discourse Functions of Intonation

Intonation	Symbol	Discourse Function
Pitch accents		*The role of salient lexical items in the information structure*
H*	CÁPITALS	added: new
L+H*	ÚNDERLINED CÁPITALS	added: contrasting
L*	SÚBSCRIPTED CÁPITALS	not added: accessible, extrapropositional, proposition questioned
L*+H	ÚNDERLINED SÚBSCRIPTED CÁPITALS	not added: relevance uncertain in contrast to another item
Pitch boundaries		*The degree of dependency of one phrase on the next*
high-rise	↑	anticipates next constituent (usually from other speaker)
low-rise	↗	anticipates next constituent (often from same speaker)
plateau	→	anticipates next constituent (listing or hesitation)
partially falling	↘	anticipates next constituent (very close connection)
low	↓	independent of next constituent
no boundary (speech cutoff)	-	incomplete thought (usually within turn)
Key		*The stance at the onset of a phrase with respect to the prior*
high key	↱	contrastive
mid key	→	additive
low key	↳	equative; foregone conclusion
Paratone		*The topic organization*
high	⇑	new topic
low	⇓	aside from main topic

Table 2.1 summarizes all of the categories of intonational meaning discussed in this section.

Theoretical Underpinnings

At this point, I turn to the rationale behind the general overview of intonational meaning presented in the previous section. There are, in par-

ticular, three schools of thought whose influence permeates the literature on intonation, especially as it pertains to topics of interest to discourse
analysts. These are Halliday's (1967a, 1967b) works on the intonation of
British English, Pierrehumbert's (1980) dissertation on intonation and
Pierrehumbert and Hirschberg's (1990) subsequent work on interpretation, and Brazil's (1975, 1978, 1985, 1997; Brazil & Coulthard, 1997) research on intonation and communication. It is worth summarizing these
three approaches briefly before discussing the details of intonation
itself.

Halliday, founder of the systemic-functional tradition of linguistics
and himself a discourse analyst, developed a functional description of
the intonation of Standard British English (1967a). The system identifies five distinctive intonation contour shapes, each of which has a holistic interpretation. Halliday's contour system has been influential for
many later theorists treating intonation, such as Bing (1985), Bolinger
(1986, 1989), Gussenhoven (1984), Ladd (1980), and Tench (1996),
all of whom work with an inventory of meaningful contours. It has also
been applied extensively to the analysis of spoken discourse, starting
with Halliday himself, who included an analysis of the text of a natural
conversation in the back of his book (1967a). Halliday (1967b) is also
responsible for contributing to the discussion of intonational focus and
"information systems," the interplay between items being introduced
into the discourse as new and those that are already given in context.
This work on information structure has influenced virtually every later
discussion of the topic (Brown & Yule, 1983; Chomsky, 1971; Ladd, 1980;
Levinson, 1983; Prince, 1981; Werth, 1984, to name a few). Finally, his
recognition of rhythm as an underlying structure in spoken language
is an important contribution whose impact is apparent in much subsequent work.

A second important contributor within the field of intonation is
Pierrehumbert (1980), who developed a tone-based model of intonation for the purpose of speech synthesis and recognition in the United
States. Linked to metrical phonology, the model is part of a larger framework within the theoretical tradition of generative phonology (Chomsky
& Halle, 1968) in the sense that, from a bare-bones underlying representation of meaningful tones, a continuous surface representation is
generated through phonetic principles. Pierrehumbert and Hirschberg
(1990) subsequently developed an application of Pierrehumbert's system to the interpretation of discourse in which level tones within the
intonation contour are individually meaningful: the intonation of particular lexical items provides information about their role in the coherence of the discourse, while the pitch of the intonation boundaries

contributes meaning about how each phrase is interrelated with its neighbors. In my view, Pierrehumbert and Hirschberg's model need not be opposed to Halliday's—it simply recognizes a finer level of meaningful tones underlying larger contours (see Roach, 1994, and Ladd, 1996, p. 82, for comparisons of Pierrehumbert-based and Halliday-based models).

A third major approach to intonation in discourse comes from Brazil (1975, 1978, 1985, 1997) and is also applied and explained in Brazil, Coulthard, and Johns (1980). Brazil, a member of the Birmingham school of discourse analysis, was thoroughly exposed to Halliday's work on intonation; his basic tone constituent includes what I consider a final pitch accent and a pitch boundary. Although there is no evidence that he was especially familiar with Pierrehumbert (1980), a careful scrutiny of his model shows certain similarities. Pierrehumbert's and Brazil's models both analyze smaller units than the intonation contour as meaningful; both agree that unstressed syllables, clitics, and function words need not play a role in intonational meaning; and both have an inventory of four possible final intonation boundary shapes derived from two separate boundary components. One unique contribution of Brazil's model for my purposes is its recognition of the importance of pitch range in interaction. Brazil pays particular attention to the speaker's pitch at the initiation of utterances with his notion of "key," an indicator of attitudinal relationships between one intonation unit and the next.[1] Because of its emphasis on reactions, Brazil's model has great potential for the analysis of interactional dynamics.

In the next sections, I draw extensively from these three approaches to explain the assumptions underlying the model of intonational meaning I use here. To begin, I introduce the notion of the intonational phrase, a fundamental prosodic constituent referred to in virtually every theory of intonation.

The Intonational Phrase

In yet another example of confusing terminology, what I and others call the "intonational phrase" is designated as the "intermediate phrase" by Pierrehumbert (1980), the "tone unit" by Halliday (1967a) and Brazil (1985), and the "intonation unit" by Chafe (1994). All of these terms refer to a more or less continuous pitch contour with, at minimum, an initial key, a number of pitch accents, and a pitch boundary. Ideally, the intonational phrase can be thought of as the intonation unit at which the cognition, syntax, physics, phonetics, and phonology of speech converge.

Even body movements tend to coincide with these units (Acton, 1998; Erickson, 1992).

According to Chafe (1994), the size of the intonational phrase is optimal to occupy "echoic" memory, an immediate, short-term recall system that allows a listener to process each unit of speech as a whole (p. 55). This is consistent with Halliday's (1967b) claim that the tone unit coincides with the "information unit." Likewise, from the speaker's point of view, Levelt (1989) discusses the preplanning, slightly prior to speech, of short linguistic units, each of which is to be articulated as a single intonational phrase. For Levelt, the intonational phrase corresponds to a syntactic clause; however, as we will see in the upcoming discussion, the correspondence between intonation and syntax is by no means absolute. As Sacks, Schegloff, and Jefferson (1974) point out, any subcomponent of a grammatical sentence can be uttered in a single intonational phrase.

Turning to the phonetic characteristics of the intonational phrase, one consequence of the physical requirement of breathing is that speakers often pause between intonational phrases. Chafe (1994) also points out that the tempo of speech is faster at the beginning of an intonational phrase and slows down toward the end. This process is also known as "final lengthening" (Klatt, 1975) because the final syllables of an intonational phrase are elongated. For some speakers, the intonational phrase ends with a change in voice quality as well, such as a creakier or breathier voice.[2] In addition, there is typically a gradual lowering or "declination" of pitch throughout the duration of an intonational phrase as the speaker's air pressure diminishes. At the onset of each new intonational phrase, the pitch is reset back to a higher level. Pierrehumbert (1980) calculates the "baseline" of an intonational phrase based on the slope of the low points of the pitch contour, which decline throughout the phrase. This is important because, although a speaker's pitch may rise and fall to convey discourse meaning, the gradual trend of the phrase is from higher to lower. Thus, pitch accents within the same intonational phrase may perform a similar discourse function even though they do not have the same absolute pitch. For example, the utterance shown in figure 2.9 contains a series of H* pitch accents associated with items newly added to the information structure in a lecture (Corpus 1-A). One can see the downward "stair-step" trend throughout the intonational phrase, regulated by English-based phonetic implementation rules (see Pierrehumbert, 1980). In this figure the speaker associates pitch accents only with those items that contribute to discourse meaning. Meanwhile, unstressed syllables and function words,

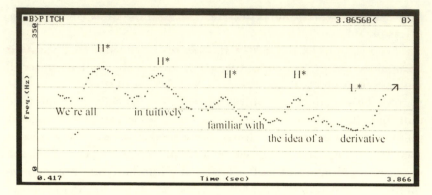

Figure 2.9 A series of H* pitch accents descends gradually throughout the phrase.

such as auxiliary verbs, articles, copulas, pronouns, and complementizers, derive their intonation through a phonetic process of interpolation from the pitch of the neighboring tones. Between two H* pitch accents, the pitch of intervening unstressed syllables will start to dip toward the speaker's baseline and then begin to rise again for the next high tone. Between two L* pitch accents, the pitch of unstressed syllables will remain low (Pierrehumbert, 1980, p. 37). In my system of transcription, the former case is represented in regular type; the latter is transcribed with subscripted capital letters.

For English, the intonational phrase is the domain of certain phonological "fast speech" rules (Kaisse, 1985; Nespor & Vogel, 1986). For example, flapping of /t/ before unstressed noninitial syllables, common in many American dialects of English, is likely to occur across a word boundary within an intonational phrase, but not across an intonational phrase boundary, as shown in the following constructed example:

| Did you get a job↑ | => | Didja ge[ɾ]a job↑ |
| What did you get↓ A job↑ | => | Whadja ge[t]↓ A job↑ |

In the first example, which consists of one intonational phrase, the /t/ at the end of *get* is pronounced as a flap [ɾ] and syllabified with the following article; in the second, the /t/ resides at the end of the first intonational phrase. It does not syllabify with the vowel across the intonation boundary or become a flap.

In summary, the "ideal" intonational phrase coincides with a cluster of linguistic features, any of which may be useful in its identification. It can be uttered within one breath; it is often set off by pauses; it gradually declines in pitch throughout its duration; it ends with final lengthening, slower tempo, and possible changes in voice quality; it forms the domain of certain phonological rules; and it may coincide with syntactic constituents.

In natural discourse, however, the intonational phrase is often less clear cut. Although in some genres, such as news reporting, the canonical intonational phrase I described is appropriate, speakers in conversational genres appear to manipulate the linguistic features of intonational phrases to signal interactional intentions. For example, as a floor-keeping strategy, speakers may pause for breath in the middle of an intonational phrase and then proceed without pause into the next phrase in Schegloff's (1982) "rush-through." Syntactic structure may also be obscured by ellipsis, hesitations, repairs, and other fast-speech phenomena. The following example (from Corpus 2) illustrates the variability in the alignment among intonation, syntax, and pause. Intonational phrase boundaries are delineated by arrows and pause length is indicated in parentheses. A hyphen means that the speaker simply halted in midphrase with no pitch boundary or final lengthening:

> T   Well I flew in I met this guy on the plane↘(.7)
> and he- (.5)
> innerduced me to a couple guys↘ 'n- (.9)
> those guys ended up- (.3)
> you know- (.2)
> being my friends for the whole year they were really nice↘ (.1) 'n-
> (.5) I got to be really good friends with 'em↓

Here the speaker does not necessarily correlate pauses with intonational phrase boundaries; instead, he often pauses in the middle of syntactic and intonational phrases. Nor are syntactic boundaries necessarily associated with pitch boundaries as the speaker frequently rushes from one clause to the next without an intervening pitch boundary. In discourse analyses where it is difficult to identify intonational phrase boundaries, it helps to remember the cluster of phonetic properties of the "ideal" intonational phrase—pitch declination within a phrase and pitch reset at the beginning, as well as final lengthening and changes in voice quality at the end—since syntactic features and pauses are not always reliable.

I turn now to the tones associated with the intonational phrase. In listing the intonation categories in this manner, I am following what Pierrehumbert and Hirschberg (1990) call a "compositional" model of intonational meaning. According to this view, each component, or "tone," adds a small element of meaning to the discourse as a whole.

Pitch Accents and Information Structure

I borrow the term *pitch accent* from Pierrehumbert (1980) to mean the pitch pattern associated with the primary word stress of a lexical item that is salient in the information structure of the discourse. This corresponds in part to what Halliday and Brazil call the "tonic," and what others call the "nucleus." *Information structure* refers to how speakers organize their discourse into message units in terms of given and new information (Halliday, 1967b). If we assume that participants in a speech event construct a mental representation of the discourse as it progresses (Chafe, 1980, 1994; Clark, 1992; Pierrehumbert & Hirschberg, 1990), then at any given point, the pitch accents of the current utterance indicate how the lexical items with which they are associated are to be integrated with what is already in that mental representation: what is to be added as new information, what is withheld, what should be inferred from context, what is contrastive, and so on. As I noted earlier, function words need not be associated with pitch accents unless they play a special role in the information structure of the discourse.

Chafe (1994) provides a psycholinguistic account of the interplay between pitch accents and information structure invoking principles of cognitive psychology. In his view, high-pitched items, with more acoustic energy behind them, are physically easier for listeners to hear. Thus, humans can interact with maximum cognitive efficiency if the items most worthy of attention are articulated with the most energy—the highest pitch. On the other hand, items that a speaker assumes to be already active in a listener's consciousness may be articulated with less energy and lower pitch so that listeners need expend little cognitive effort to process them. With this theory, Chafe, in the American West Coast functionalist tradition, provides an iconic link between the grammar of intonational meaning and real-world motivations.

For Pierrehumbert and Hirschberg (1990), six possible configurations of high and low tones, including both individual and contour tones, are recognized as pitch accents. Each of the six has a unique form as well as a distinctive meaning in the information structure of the discourse. There is no restriction on the number of pitch accents per intonational phrase. Their inventory includes three versions of high pitch accent—H*, L+H*, and H*+L—and three versions of low pitch accent—L*, L*+H, and H+L*. To generalize, any pitch accent in this system involving H* is associated with new lexical items to be added into the mental representation of the discourse; any pitch accent involving L* is associated with items not to be added as new, either because they are to be inferred from the context, or because they are for some reason "extrapropositional" (pp. 292–4) as in vocatives, discourse markers, canonical questions, and certain conventional utterances.

In practice, it is quite a subtle matter to distinguish all of the six configurations of pitch accents with certainty in the analysis of rapid natural discourse. Pierrehumbert's model was originally developed for speech synthesis research and therefore tends to rely on constructed examples of consistently clear, slow speech with exaggerated intonation. Once outside of the laboratory, however, such speech data are rarely available; instead, one is likely to confront a good deal of variation in tempo, volume, and pitch range. An additional problem is that, since pitch is mainly manifest in vowels and sonorant consonants, much of Pierrehumbert's work uses texts constructed to avoid voiceless segments. For example, the word *millionaire* is shown in three contexts by Pierrehumbert and Hirschberg (1990, pp. 275–6) to illustrate the difference between the H*, L+H*, and L*+H pitch accents. This example consists exclusively of vowels, glides, and the sonorant consonants /m/, /l/, /n/, and /r/, which produce a clear, continuous pitch contour. In natural speech, however, the prevalence of voiceless consonants that do not register in the computer analysis of pitch causes breaks in the intonation contour. In one of my own analyses of a series of pitch accents, I tried in vain to obtain a computer pitch reading for the word *fact* uttered in fast speech. The combination of the short vowel and the voiceless consonants /f/, /k/, and /t/ resulted in too little melody for the computer to register its pitch.

One important and comprehensive attempt to stabilize the transcription of Pierrehumbert's system is the ToBI labeling system.[3] Using an adaptation of Pierrehumbert's model, a group of researchers in phonetics has developed a set of training materials that includes examples of each type of tone in the context of a sentence, computerized pitch diagrams for each sentence, and sets of practice exercises for learners (see Beckman & Ayers, 1994, and web sites at Ohio State University). The ToBI system uses four of Pierrehumbert's original six pitch accents; H*, L*, L+H*, and L*+H. Although this body of research does not discuss the interpretation of these tones, I have found that these four pitch accents correspond most closely in their interpretation to what Ladd (1980), Chafe (1994), Halliday (1967b), Werth (1984), Ward and Hirschberg (1985), and others have consistently included in their discussions of information structure and intonation. It is these that I will discuss below and continue to draw on most frequently in this volume.

H* Pitch Accent and New Information: (CÁPITAL LÉTTERS)

There is a fundamental association between high pitch and new information in English. In a textbook for international students learning English, Gilbert (1984, pp. 41–2) uses the following simple dialogue to illustrate the relationship between high pitch and new information, which she calls the "sentence focus." Capital letters indicate the words with H* pitch accents, which at each turn introduce a new idea into the dialogue:

A   I LOST my HAT.
B   What KIND of hat?
A   It was a RAIN hat.
B   What COLOR rain hat?
A   It was WHITE. White with STRIPES.
B   There was a white hat with stripes in the CAR.
A   WHICH car?
B   The one I SOLD!

Each new high-pitched item corresponds to what others have referred to as the *information focus* or simply the *focus* of the phrase (Chomsky, 1971; Halliday, 1967b, Jackendoff, 1972; Levelt, 1989; Rochemont & Cullicover, 1990; Selkirk, 1984). Rochemont and Cullicover describe focus as "the point of information in the sentence that is deemed most valuable or relevant from the speaker's point of view" (p. 18), and that is not "context construable" (p. 20). Halliday writes: " Information focus relates each information unit to the preceding discourse by assigning to it a structure whose elements may be labeled 'given' and 'new'" (p. 176). In the previous dialogue, the focus changes from utterance to utterance as what was formerly new is assumed by the current speaker to be incorporated into the other's mental representation of the discourse as given.

As the term *focus* implies, it is a commonly held assumption that for every phrase *one single* item is more important to the discourse than any other. According to Chafe's (1994) "one-new-idea hypothesis," an intonation contour coincides psychologically with a thought group in which there is a single new idea. His argument is based on the cognitive efficiency of planning and processing information when the idea units are of a manageable size. Chomsky (1971), Cruttendon (1997), Ladd (1980, 1996), Selkirk (1984), and many others have argued that there is one focus per intonational phrase—that is, a single, prominent, "nuclear" pitch accent—which tends to be located at or near the end of the intonation contour.

However, I have found that many intonational phrases have more than one pitch accent and that the last pitch accent does not always have a special status. I argue, therefore, for a system in which an intonational phrase can, in principle, have any number of pitch accents. Both Halliday (1967a) and Brazil (1985) make a concession to this view: their models allow for either one or two points of focus per intonational phrase. Cruttendon (1997), who generally favors a single focus per phrase, is also forced to admit having encountered certain utterances that contain several new ideas, none of which stands out as nuclear. He discusses the following two "out-of-the-blue" utterances in which more than one item is presented as new:

> It's NOT quite the RIGHT shade of BLUE. (p. 43)
>
> Her FACE USED to be much FÁTTER. (p. 44)

He notes that these are likely to be uttered with a descending series of pitch accents and therefore do not conform to a theory of one single nuclear pitch per intonational phrase. Despite this finding, at the conclusion of this discussion Cruttendon writes, "Some analysts indeed think that problems of this sort argue for abandoning the whole notion of nucleus and just settling for a series of pitch accents; this is an extreme view and one which does not take into account the very large number of cases where the nucleus assignment is straightforward" (p. 44). Rather than extreme, the view he critiques (my own) may simply be more explanatory than a single-focus view; we will see numerous examples throughout this volume of utterances in natural discourse that display a multi-pitch-accent pattern. Particularly prevalent in the academic lecture genre are long utterances in which a series of new ideas is presented, as is evident in the following excerpt from a statistics lecture (Corpus 1-B):

> THIS <u>PARTÍCULAR</u> _{PLOT} DEPÍCTS DÁTA↗
> from the RESÚLTS of a STÚDY↘
> on HÝBRIDIZÁTION of TWO different- (.3) CLÓSELY-_{RELATED}
> SPÉCIES of DUCKS((.4)
> the MÁLLARD and the <u>PÍNTAIL</u>↗ . . .

Within this series of four intonational phrases, several new notions are introduced into the discourse. In a single-focus system, the claim would be that the last high-pitched word of each phrase had a special significance, which does not seem to fit the facts. For the current model this poses no problem; there is simply a series of pitch accents within the context of the lecture topic, each one contributing its bit of meaning to the whole. Although in some cases one pitch accent happens to dominate the phrase, counterexamples such as this one are better explained by placing no limit on the possible number of pitch accents.[4]

L+H* Pitch Accent and Contrast (<u>UNDERLINED CÁPITAL LÉTTERS</u>)

The terms *narrow, contrastive,* or *marked* focus have traditionally referred to a steeply rising pitch pattern associated with contrasts in discourse (Chomsky, 1971; Halliday, 1967b; Ladd, 1980; and others). This is consistent with Pierrehumbert and Hirschberg's explanation that the L+H* pitch accent can be associated with a contrast between alternative items on a scale, or ordered set. For instance, we can use L+H* pitch accent in a contrast between two days of the week, as *Monday* versus *Friday,* out of the complete set of seven. Sets need not be ordered for their members to be contrasted, however; if a set has only two members, a contrast of opposites results (as in *night* and *day*). Often sets are created temporarily for a particular discourse context. A pair of domestic partners debating which of three Saturday plans to choose may spontaneously develop a set whose members include cleaning out the garage, going to the ballgame, or taking the dog to the vet. In this case, any of these alternatives could be treated as contrastive to the other two and uttered with L+H* pitch accent. The H* portion of the pitch accent associates with the stressed syllable of whichever lexical item carries the semantic salience of the contrast. In the example of Saturday activities, the first item would be accented on the final syllable of *garáge,* the second on the stressed component of the compound *bállgame,* and the third on the word *vét.* In many cases, the noun is semantically salient, but in principle, any part of speech can be used contrastively, as in *up* or *down* (adverbs), *one* or *mány* (quantifiers), *red* or *dead* (adjectives), *táke it* or *léave it* (verbs). Even a prefix can be singled out as a contrastive element with its own L+H* pitch accent, as in the following constructed example from Wennerstrom (1993):

Around this place, it's hard to tell sanity from <u>IN</u>sanity (p. 311).

As I argued in 1993, any morpheme that has a distinct semantic reality for a speaker in the context of the discourse can be singled out for contrast and thus associated with the L+H* pitch accent.

L* Pitch Accent and Accessible Information: (SÚBSCRIPTED CÁPITAL LÉTTERS)

The association between low pitch and information believed by a speaker to already be accessible in the discourse has been noted by Brazil (1985), Chafe (1970, 1994), Halliday (1967b, 1994), Ladd (1980, 1984), Wennerstrom (1997), Werth (1984), and many others. Chafe (1994) considers low pitch to be the speaker's signal that an associated item should already be active in consciousness and requires minimal cognitive effort for its interpretation. In particular, two low-pitched phenomena have been discussed in the literature in terms of intonational meaning: L* pitch accent (Pierrehumbert & Hirschberg, 1990) and deaccent (Ladd, 1980). I argue that deaccent is one important use of L*.

Pierrehumbert and Hirschberg describe L* pitch accents as associating with those items that a speaker "intends to be salient but not to form part of what [that speaker] is predicating in the utterance" (p. 291). They list several situations in which this might be the case. First, the item may be part of a yes/no question in which the speaker is not predicating anything about the utterance but hoping that someone else will do so as a response. The following example of this (from Corpus 2) appeared in the beginning of the chapter and was shown in figure 2.3.

M   Did you COMMÚNICÀTE in um $_{NEWÁRI}$ all the time↑

It is as if the speaker is reserving judgment as to whether the idea of speaking Newari should be added to the information structure of the discourse until the response is received. L* may even convey incredulity with respect to some proposition if the speaker thinks that what is predicated is incorrect.

L* may also associate with material that is "extrapropositional, such as greetings, vocatives, and so-called cue phrases" (Pierrehumbert & Hirschberg, 1990, p. 293). Apparently, what Pierrehumbert and Hirschberg call "cue phrases" are what Schiffrin (1987) calls "discourse markers," which are typically associated with L* pitch accents in a number of contexts. For example, in the following utterance (from Corpus 2), the speaker associates L* pitch accent with the discourse marker *you know*:

T   Those guys ÉNDED up- (.3) $_{YOU KNOW}$- (.2) being my FRIENDS for
the WHOLE YEAR . . .

As Pierrehumbert and Hirschberg explain, such cue phrases convey structural information about the discourse rather than adding to the propositional content. The intonation of discourse markers is discussed further in chapter 5.

Another important use of L* in Pierrehumbert and Hirschberg's model is that it is associated with items that the speaker thinks are, or should be, already mutually believed (p. 292) and therefore need not be added into the discourse as new. We saw this phenomenon earlier in the example (from Corpus 1-C) about the bicycle in the U.S. and China, reprinted here:

D   . . . for the BÍCYCLE in (.) in the U.S. versus the BíCYCLE in
CHÍNA.

In this utterance, the word *bicycle* is first introduced with H* pitch accent,
but in the second intonational phrase, it has L* pitch accent because it is
already assumed to be in the hearers' consciousness.

It is this last function of the L* pitch accent that I claim coincides
with deaccent, whose meaning has been discussed at length by Ladd
(1980). He provides the following examples (p. 52) to illustrate the association between deaccent and accessible information (deaccent is indicated with subscripts):

1. A Has John read Slaughterhouse-Five?
    B No, John doesn't <u>READ</u> BOOKS.
2. Harry wants a VW, but his wife would prefer an <u>AMÉRICAN</u> CAR.

"In each of these examples," says Ladd, "the deaccented noun has somehow been referred to or alluded to earlier in the discourse" (p. 52). He
also points out that deaccent is not restricted to sentence-final position.
This is illustrated by a comparison between the following two examples
(p. 55):

1. A What's the matter?
    B There's nothing to make FRENCH TOAST out of.
2. A Why don't you make some French TOAST?
    B There's nothing to make FRENCH TOAST OUT of.

In the latter case, *French Toast* has already been introduced into the discourse and is therefore deaccented, in spite of the fact that it comes not
after but before the accented word *out*. Ladd's position is that "the
deaccenting of a syllable can best be understood as a *relative weakening of
its hierarchical rhythmic position*" (p. 56). This is important in explaining
why deaccented items may not always have low pitch in absolute terms;
deaccent interacts with the underlying rhythmic structure of an utterance,
which affects the associated word's position relative to its neighboring
constituents. Thus, in some cases a deaccented word may actually be
higher in pitch than another located elsewhere in the same utterance.

In sum, there is a consistent association between low pitch and a set
of meanings in discourse: lack of predication of an item due to its accessibility, questionability, or extrapropositionality. In the current model of
intonational meaning, this will be treated as an L* pitch accent morpheme, a deliberate lowering of pitch to send a meaningful signal about
the discourse role of the item with which it is associated.[5]

L*+H Pitch Accents and a Question of Relevance (<u>UNDERLINED SÚBSCRIPTED CÁPITALS</u>)

The L*+H pitch accent, though less frequent in occurrence than the other pitch accents, plays an important role in some contexts. This pitch accent can be compared to the L+H* because both are contour pitch accents that slope upward from low to high and both involve set membership. The differences, however, lie in the alignment of the starred component of the pitch accent with the stressed syllable of the associated lexical item and in the meaning of the L* and H* tones. According to Pierrehumbert and Hirschberg, the L*+H is a version of the L* pitch accent. The stressed syllable of the word with which it is associated is low in the speaker's pitch range. It's interpretation involves two elements: first, an L*+H item is being withheld from the information structure of the discourse because the speaker is uncertain whether it is appropriate or should count (Ward & Hirschberg, 1985). In addition, this pitch accent usually invokes membership in a set—one member is being weighed as an alternative to others. Ward and Hirschberg (p. 766) provide an example of this (transcription symbols mine):

A   Is she taking any medication?
B   <u>VÍTAMINS</u>↗

Here the word *vitamins* is offered as one alternative among other possible remedies. The speaker may be uncertain if vitamins count as medication. Figure 2.10 is constructed to illustrate the *vitamins* example wherein the L*+ H pitch accent is followed by a low-rising pitch boundary.

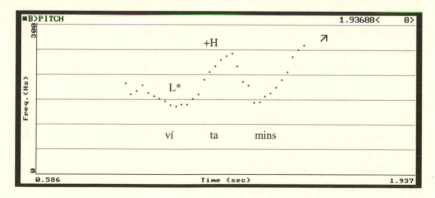

Figure 2.10   When followed by a low-rising boundary, a L*+H pitch accent has a rise-fall-rise shape.

Pitch Boundaries and the Organization of Constituents

A second important discourse function of intonation is to indicate inter-dependencies among intonational phrases. This is achieved at the final boundaries, which indicate whether an intonational phrase depends upon the subsequent one for its interpretation. Because the final syllables of intonational phrases are lengthened, pitch boundaries are perceivable by their shape. An important feature of Pierrehumbert and Hirschberg's (1990) model is that it interprets the intonational meaning of pitch boundaries separately from that of the pitch accents. Boundary meaning is described in terms of speaker intention about the relationship between utterances. In general, a high tone at a boundary indicates the speaker's intention for the hearer to interpret what comes after the tone with respect to what has come before; a low tone at a boundary indicates no intended dependency on the subsequent utterance. Pierrehumbert and Hirschberg write that the "choice of boundary tone conveys whether the current intonational phrase is 'forward-looking' or not—that is, whether it is to be interpreted with respect to some succeeding phrase or whether the direction of interpretation is unspecified" (p. 305). As an example, they claim that we are likely to interpret the following three utterances (from p. 306) as part of one larger constituent because of the high boundary tones (H%) at the ends of the first two (I borrow temporarily the H and L symbols from the ToBI labeling system):

> George likes cake L-H%
>
> He adores pie L-H%
>
> He'll eat anything that's sweet and calorific L-L%

As is evident from the tonal symbols of this example, Pierrehumbert and Hirschberg recognize two levels of hierarchy for pitch boundaries: the level of the "intermediate phrase," which can end with a high or low "phrase accent" (the symbols used are H- and L-), and the level of the "sentence," which contains one or more intermediate phrases and can end with a high or low "boundary tone" (the symbols used are H% and L%). This means that every sentence ends with two tones, a phrase accent from the final intermediate phrase and a boundary tone, which gives rise to four possible contoured pitch boundaries: H-H%, L-H%, H-L%, and L-L%.

Although in principle I accept the pitch accent-boundary tone distinction, I have found it difficult to maintain in transcribing natural speech. One problem is that the grammatical distinction between the intermediate phrase and the sentence is not always supported. Consider the following example, taken from a conversation (Corpus 2) about biking to work (again, ToBI transcription symbols are used, Beckman & Ayers, 1994):

    C But like the first six months I was ridi::::ng H-L%(2.1) to work at 7:20 in the morning. L-L% (.1)

    M Oh god! L-L%

In this example, an H-L% boundary (in my system, the plateau [→]) occurs in the middle of the turn on *riding*. According to Pierrehumbert and Hirschberg, this boundary is possible only at a sentence completion; yet in this context it does not coincide with the end of a sentence. It is also common in fast speech to find short, syntactically complete clauses strung together with no intervening phrase accent or pause. C rushes through the syntactic phrase boundary at *months* without a perceivable pitch boundary, though we might expect this to be the site of Pierrehumbert and Hirschberg's intermediate phrase boundary. Nor is pause length a reliable indicator of boundary location; after the H-L% (plateau) boundary comes a long pause of 2.1 seconds; after *months* there is no perceivable pause, and after the final L-L% (my low [↓]) on *morning*, M appropriately takes the floor after a tiny .1-second pause.

    With syntactic criteria and pause unreliable, one might turn to phonological form to distinguish phrase accents from boundary tones. However, this is not satisfactory either because in many environments an H- phrase accent sounds like an H-H% or L-H% combination, and an L-phrase accent sounds like an LL%. Therefore, for the purposes of this volume, I have made certain adaptations of Pierrehumbert and Hirschberg's model: first, I use the general term *pitch boundary* (or just *boundary*) to encompass both the phrase accent and the boundary tone. This yields four possible combinations for which I use arrow symbols as follows:

H-H%	↑	high-rising pitch boundary
L-H%	↗	low-rising pitch boundary
H-L%	→	plateau pitch boundary
L-L%	↓	low pitch boundary

In addition, I include a boundary not discussed by Pierrehumbert and Hirschberg:

    ↘   partially falling pitch boundary

I have frequently found the partial fall used as a phrase connector in discourse. The boundary begins at the final pitch accent of the intonational phrase and slopes downward slightly from there. It is distinct from the low boundary (↓) in that it does not fall all the way to the speaker's baseline. The partially falling boundary signals a close connection between one intonational phrase and the subsequent one, usually within the same turn. The following example (Corpus 3) comes from K, who uses partially falling boundaries in an explanation of her reluctance to use hormone replacement therapy during menopause. K does not appear to expect backchannels because her pauses are very short:

> K   I didn't want to MESS ABÓUT↘(.1)
>   with SÓMETHING that was ⱼᵤₛₜ a NÁTURAL PRÓCESS↘(.3)
>   unless there was a RÉALLY GOOD RÉASON for DÓING it.↓

Another point in this example is that it consists of a series of intonational phrases, ending with a final low pitch boundary (↓). The result of this combination of pitch boundaries is the development of a large umbrella constituent, consisting of several interdependent intonational phrases working together. It is a common role for the low boundary to bring a long sequence of closely related phrases to a close, and this is frequently a site of turn shift. It would be too simplistic, however, to say that certain boundaries always lead (or do not lead) to particular responses such as backchannels or turn shifts. In saying that a high tone at the end of an intonational constituent is "forward-looking" for its interpretation, Pierrehumbert and Hirschberg emphasize that the next constituent may come either from the same speaker or another. It is safe to conclude that pitch boundaries are a resource in turn-taking but not that particular boundaries always lead to specific interactional patterns.

Key and Attitudinal Stance

Key is described as a three-way pitch range choice (high, mid, or low) at the beginning of every intonational phrase, showing a speaker's attitude or stance in each new utterance with respect to the previous one (Brazil, 1985; Brazil, Coulthard, & Johns, 1980). According to Brazil, the pitch of the first content word of an utterance (in terms of the current model, the first pitch accent) is the key of that utterance.[6] Likewise, the end of an utterance has a "termination" level, also high, mid, and low. I have not included termination symbols in my coding system to simplify the number of symbols at the ends of intonational phrases as much as possible. However, the initial key symbols can be taken to mean a disjuncture (up or down) with respect to the termination of the prior intonational phrase. Thus, a ↱ symbol means a high onset with respect to a preceding mid or low termination; a ↳ symbol means a low onset with respect to a preceding mid or high termination. I have also avoided coding mid key (→) unless there is a special reason to call attention to it. Readers may assume mid key in the transcripts unless indicated otherwise.

Brazil interprets key in terms of expectation: a high key indicates that the unit with which it associates is "contrastive" with expectation; a mid key indicates that the material is simply "additive," or that nothing unexpected will be presented in the associated unit; a low key indicates that it is "equative," or a foregone conclusion (Brazil, 1985, p. 189). To explain the sense of equative, he notes that low key can be used to rephrase the obvious, as in the following example (p. 248, adapted to the current transcription symbols):

HOST   This is MÁRY.
GUEST   PLEASED to MEET you.
HOST   And this is PÉTER↓ ↳ Mary's HÚSBAND↓

In this example, because Peter and Mary are a married couple, the restatement of Peter as "Mary's husband" is a foregone conclusion and therefore that phrase has a low key.

Key is independent of pitch accents and intonation boundaries. It refers not to the shape of the contour itself but to its relative location in the speaker's range. Thus, two utterances could both begin with the same type of pitch accent, but if one were higher in the speaker's range, it would be described as having a higher key. Here are three examples from Brazil (pp. 73 and 79) to illustrate this:

He GÁMBLED↗   → and LOST a FÓRTUNE↓
He GÁMBLED↗   ↱ and LOST a FÓRTUNE↓
He GÁMBLED↗   ↳ and LOST ↓

In all three cases, the first pitch accent of the second intonational phrase is H*, although the key is respectively mid, high, and low. The first case is a simple clarification of what happened when he gambled, expressed in mid key; the second reveals that his losing is contrary to expectation, expressed in high key; and the third one conveys that his losing is a foregone conclusion, expressed in low key. Thus, the initial pitch accent varies not in its category (it remains H*) but in how high or low it is in the speaker's pitch range.

In conversation, key captures the phenomenon of "tone concord" (also discussed by Schegloff, 1998) by which a speaker indicates his or her stance with respect to the previous speaker's contribution. In order to show agreement or rapport, the speaker can pitch the key of the new utterance to coincide with the termination of the previous utterance (tone concord); on the other hand, to indicate some kind of opposition in stance, the speaker can choose a different key to initiate the new utterance in "concord-breaking," which occurs, according to Brazil, "at moments when there is a discrepancy between the ways the two parties assess the context of interaction" (p. 86). These phenomena are discussed in chapter 7 on the analysis of conversation.

Paratones

Paratones, so named because they correspond to written paragraphs, are the expansion of pitch range at the beginning of a new topic unit and a corresponding compression of pitch range at that unit's end. Whether using the term *paratone* or not, many scholars have discussed the relationship between organization and pitch range (Beckman & Pierrehumbert, 1986; Brown, 1977; Brown, Currie, & Kenworthy, 1980; Brown & Yule, 1983; Couper-Kuhlen, 1986; Fox, 1973; Lehiste, 1975; Pike, 1954; Swerts & Geluykens, 1994; Tench, 1990; Thompson, 1994; Wennerstrom, 1992, 1994, 1998; Yule, 1980). Scholars have also claimed that smaller pitch range shifts associate with smaller organizational units of discourse. Yule (1980) and Couper-Kuhlen (1986) discuss "major" and "minor" paratones, the latter associated with subtopics within the former. Although it remains to be empirically investigated, we can conceive of large pitch range expansions at the onset of major constituents forming the top of an organizational hierarchy, whereas smaller expansions associated with subtopics of discourse are embedded within.[7]

Although the high paratone-new topic correspondence is most dramatic and noticeable, I also suggest that there is a low version of the paratone. This is the use of a contracted pitch range to introduce a non-central topic meant to be taken as an aside from the main topic. Going off on a tangent, providing a quick flashback in a narrative, or uttering an aside in conversation can all be made distinguishable by a decrease in pitch range. Even at the level of the intonational phrase, scholars such as Bing (1985) have documented the fact that parentheticals have their own special low-rising intonation contour (Bing calls this the "Class 0 Contour"). Longer "tangents" have also been recognized as having compressed pitch range (Grosz & Hirschberg, 1992; Kutik, Cooper, & Boyce, 1983; Local, 1992). Both high and low paratones are discussed further in chapter 5.

Conclusion

There is clearly a great deal of interplay between a speaker's intonation and discourse meaning and organization. Indeed, in the remainder of this volume I devote more page space to issues of intonation than to any other aspect of prosody. This chapter has provided an overview of some of the theoretical assumptions about intonation that underlie the discussions in later chapters. I have described a system of intonational meaning in which small meaningful units combine to provide an overall interpretation of intonation in discourse. As we have seen, there are four major categories of intonational meaning. One is the pitch accent, indicating which items in the information structure of the discourse are newly introduced or involve a cohesive relationship with what is already in the context of the interaction. A second category of intonation is the pitch boundary at the end of the intonational phrase, which indicates the interdependencies among utterances or turns. A third type of meaning is conveyed in the choice of key at the beginning of each intonational phrase, displaying a speaker's attitude or reaction toward the prior utterance. Finally, paratones are the pitch range choices associated with organizational units, indicating how the new unit is to be topically integrated with the previous ones.

To end on a cautionary note, I intend the description of intonational meaning in the chapter to be quite general. I have introduced each category of intonation with a brief definition and example to show its basic discourse function. Likewise, I have quickly surveyed some of the main trends in the development of my thinking about intonational meaning. However, this basic model is merely a starting point for discussions in later chapters. In part II, we will see that speakers manipulate intonation in a variety of subtle ways depending on the genre of discourse, the relationships among participants, and the interactional purpose at hand. We will also see many more detailed examples of empirical studies conducted on the numerous roles of intonation in discourse. Finally, we will see how intonation is used in conjunction with other prosodic parameters to convey meaning. On this latter theme, I turn now to theoretical issues surrounding rhythm and other paralinguistic aspects of speech.

3

STRESS, RHYTHM, AND PARALANGUAGE

In the last chapter, I described a system of intonation in which meaningful tone components were associated with text based on the context of the discourse. In this chapter, we will see how that intonation system interacts with other systems of prosody. Fundamental to the association between intonation and text are the stress patterns of words because pitch accents link to stressed syllables. To understand stress, one must also understand the role of rhythm as an organizing force in language. Rhythm provides an underlying hierarchical structure upon which stress is built, while intonation components are associated with the high points of these rhythmic hierarchies. There is even evidence that rhythm is maintained across intonation boundaries and from one speaker to the next. Thus, although the assignment of stress is itself fairly mechanical, rhythm, or the alignment of stressed syllables in time, is an important resource in discourse interaction.

Other variables also interact with the intonation system—the tempo and volume with which an utterance is delivered can have consequences for its interpretation. A paralinguistic variation of pitch can be used to highlight particular constituents, exaggerating their basic intonation patterns. Likewise, changes in voice quality can occur in mimicry or in the use of stereotypical voices to achieve interactional goals. In this chapter I review the theoretical assumptions I make about these prosodic variables, and in later chapters they will be revisited, especially with regard to their role in the analyses of conversations (chapter 7) and narratives (chapter 8).

Stress Is Not Intonation

In the previous chapter I used the term *stress* several times to refer to word stress—that is, the configuration of strong and weak syllables within a word. This terminology may be confusing because in lay terms, "stress" can be used to mean "extra emphasis" as in "He really stressed the word *emergency* in his announcement." However, I will continue to use the term to refer only to the stress of words and compound words. Although both stress and intonation use pitch, volume, and length changes in speech production, they are not the same animal; stress is a phonological characteristic of lexical items and is largely fixed and predictable, whereas intonation, as demonstrated in the last chapter, can be altered depending on the discourse role played by the constituents with which tones are associated. Thus, intonation has the greater potential to influence discourse meaning, whereas stress is more a matter of pronunciation. In an analogy between stress and segmental phonology, the substitution of one segment for another, like the substitution of one stress pattern for another, can result in the word losing its identity. For example, if we were to substitute /æ/ for the first vowel of *rocket*, the result would be a different word, *racket*. The same thing would be true if we moved the stress of the word from the first to the second syllable: *rócket* now becomes *Rockétte* (of New York fame). This is not the situation with intonation. The word *rocket* can be recognized as such regardless of what kind of key, pitch accent, or boundary tone is associated with it.

Nevertheless, stress plays an important role for my purposes because it provides a docking site for pitch accents. If a speaker decides to associate a pitch accent with a lexical item, the pitch accent is usually manifest on the primary stress of that item. In this section basic facts about the stress of words and compounds are explained so that stress will not be confused with intonation. Following that is an overview of the underlying rhythmic structure of spoken language and an explanation of the link between stress and intonation in a text.

Word Stress

In English, words are usually considered to have three levels of stress. Syllables can have primary stress, secondary stress, or they can be unstressed, depending, as we will see later in this chapter, on their rhythmic position. Although English stress rules may look a bit chaotic to an adult learning the language for the first time, English-speaking children do rather well in learning these rules. This is not just a matter of memorizing stress patterns as they acquire vocabulary words. Because principles of rhythm favoring the alternation between strong and weak syllables tend to regularize the system, huge classes of English words follow regular patterns, and stress is largely predictable. One measure of the fact that stress rules become internalized is that native speakers can pronounce multisyllabic nonsense words with a good degree of agreement on the word stress, as in words like *jábberwòcky* and *sùpercàlifràgilìsticèxpiàlidóscious*, both of which have alternating stress patterns.

This is not to say, however, that English stress never varies. Throughout history, English speakers have readily borrowed words from other languages, resulting in a system of overlapping stress rules. The most frequently used words of English tend to be Germanic, following a simple Germanic stress rule: stress the first syllable of the word's root, ignoring affixes. This gives English words a basic trochaic, strong-weak, structure, as in *móther* and *kíndness*, sometimes preceded by a weak prefix, as in *forgíving*. English speakers have also borrowed thousands of words from Latin, which has more complicated, though regular, stress rules. For words of Latin origin, stress depends on the number of syllables in the word, the part of speech (noun, verb, adjective, or adverb), the moraic structure of the syllables themselves (whether they have long or short vowels, and whether or not they end in consonants), and the type of affixes attached to the root (some affixes change the stress of the word whereas other stress-neutral ones do not). Furthermore, it matters *when* a word was borrowed as to how it will be stressed. For example, English has borrowed many words for wine from French, including *cláret* and *merlót*. The word *cláret*, a borrowing from French into late Middle English, has been anglicized with a Germanic stress pattern on the initial syllable, whereas *merlót*, borrowed more recently, retains the French stress on the final syllable.

Compound Stress

Compounds are groups of two or more words from major lexical categories (nouns, verbs, adjectives, adverbs, and prepositions) that together take on a holistic meaning, at least somewhat independent of the meaning of the parts. For example, a green hóuse is a house that happens to be painted green, but the compound *gréenhouse* refers to an entity—a particular type of glass building for growing plants. While the individual lexical components of a compound have their own word stress, the compound as a whole is said to have compound stress, associated with the primary word stress of one of its components. In the compound *psychólogy depártment*, while each component has a stress pattern, the compound as a whole has its main stress on the strongest syllable of *psychólogy*. The stress pattern of the compound usually depends on its part of speech and that of its components. For example, in noun-preposition compounds such as *take off,* stress is on the right when the compound is used as a verb (the plane took óff) but on the left when the compound is used as a noun (brace yourself for the tákeoff). When a pitch accent is associated with a compound, it is usually the most strongly stressed syllable of the compound as a whole that acts as host (although I will show an exception to this later in the chapter).

Compared to intonation, then, stress has a relatively small potential to change meaning in discourse because it does not vary depending on situation; instead, it is a phonological property of the words and compounds themselves. Thus, in discourse analysis, intonation rather than stress has the far greater potential as a meaning-bearing system.

Having made this generalization, I nevertheless call attention to a class of exceptions. Since code switching can be a discourse marker of social affiliation (Myers-Scotton, 1993) word-stress alterations could occur as a result of dialect shift in order to achieve social or stylistic goals. For example, in Appalachian English, words such as *cígar* and *hótel* contrast with Standard American English *cigár* and *hotél* (Wolfram, 1991). Thus, in a situation of language contact, a speaker of either of these dialects might adopt the other's stress patterns among a set of other dialectal features in an attempt to be accepted. On the negative side, one might mimic the stress patterns of another dialect or language to make fun of an individual or to create a stereotype of that group. I resume the topic of voice quality, mimicry, and style in chapter 8.

Rhythm Underlies Spoken Language

A sense of rhythm is a universal human trait. The tendency among cultures of the world to create music, chants, drumming sequences, poetry, and other aesthetic forms based on rhythm has been the impetus for many theorists of phonology to assume rhythm as foundational to stress patterns in speech. As Couper-Kuhlen (1993) observes, "The fact that speech, verse, and music all have hierarchically organized metrical structure implies . . . a common cognitive origin. Not only are the principles of organization surprisingly similar for all three faculties, but they also allow for the same play-off between abstract construct or underlying structure and actual realization" (p. 112). It is perhaps not surprising then to note that scholars as diverse as Halliday (1967a, 1994), of the systemic-functional tradition, and Liberman (1975), in the tradition of metrical and, more broadly, generative, phonology, both introduce their theories by presenting rhythm as the underlying building block in phonology. Moreover, they both invoke chants and poetry as evidence for the alignment of rhythmic beats with speech. The following is an illustration from Halliday (1994, p. 293) of how speech is anchored in rhythm, drawing on an example from a child's verse:

Jámes / Jámes / sáid to his / móther / "Móther," he / sáid said / hé

In this line of poetry by A. A. Milne, the slashes indicate *feet*, the basic language units that coincide with the rhythmic beats of the poem. Although each foot takes approximately an equal amount of time, the number of syllables per foot varies. The energy of the rhythmic beat goes at the beginning of the foot, usually on the stressed syllable of the first content word, resulting in a slightly longer, louder, and sometimes higher-pitched syllable. Thereafter, the air pressure diminishes so that the other syllables in the same foot tend to be shorter and of slightly lower volume and pitch. In this sense, English is trochaic, with the stress at the beginning of the foot rather than, as in some languages, at the end. Unstressed syllables tend to have reduced vowels, pronounced as schwa [ə], a neutral, midcentral vowel sound. They do not add significantly to the foot's total time. For example, in the word *móther*, the first syllable is stressed and carries the beat, whereas the second, unstressed syllable is shorter and its vowel reduced. Thus, it takes roughly the same amount of time to say *mother*, which has two syllables, as to say *James*, which has one. Because rhythmic beats align with the stressed syllables of words, English is often referred to as a "stressed-timed" language (Pike, 1945). This may be contrasted with "syllable-timed" languages, such as French or Turkish, in which syllables are more equal in duration.

So far, we have seen only an example from poetry, but it is generally agreed that the same foundation of rhythm underlies nonpoetic speech. "In natural speech," says Halliday, "the tempo is not as regular as in counting or in children's rhymes. Nevertheless, there is a strong tendency in English for the salient syllables to occur at regular intervals; speakers of English like their feet to be all roughly the same length" (1994, p. 293). In this quotation, the word *roughly* is an important one. Couper-Kuhlen (1993) demonstrates that in actual measurements of beat duration, the intervals between beats are never exact. However, she proposes that a regular rhythm can still be perceived because a series of beats is processed as an "auditory gestalt" (p. 69). Auer, Couper-Kuhlen, and Müller (1999) explain this as follows: "To speak of rhythm . . . necessarily implies an interpretation of the physical data, a constructive process in the course of which these data become part of a holistic scheme, which is then able to incorporate further details from the incoming signal" (p. 23). In this way, local irregularities in rhythm are filtered out in perception. Both Halliday and Couper-Kuhlen also allow for the addition of silent beats as time fillers in natural speech. These are not considered rhythmic irregularities if the speech resumes on the beat. Figure 3.1 illustrates the alignment of rhythmic beats in time with the following utterance from a mathematics lecture (Corpus 1-A):

A We're / áll in / túitively fa / míliar with the i / déa of a de/rívative.

The graph shows the amplitude of the beginning of the text with respect to time, and foot boundaries are marked with slashes. Although the alignment of the beats would not stand up to scrutiny with a precise ruler, the beats appear roughly equal.

Rhythmic Hierarchies

A number of scholars have searched for a hierarchical structure underlying the linear series of beats in spoken language (Couper-Kuhlen, 1993; Halle & Vergnaud, 1987; Goldsmith 1990; Hayes, 1984, 1995; Liberman, 1975; Liberman & Prince, 1977; Nespor & Vogel, 1986, 1989; Selkirk, 1984). Liberman, in his dissertation on metrical phonology, uses tree diagrams to reflect the fact that the alternation between strong and weak

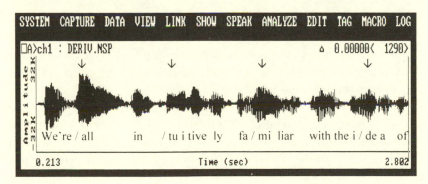

Figure 3.1 The amplitude graph shows a rhythmic series of feet indicated by arrows.

beats is structured hierarchically at the level of the intonational phrase. Along similar lines, Hayes (1995) and other scholars of metrical phonology use a grid notation to represent the hierarchical nature of rhythm in phonology and to illustrate rhythm and stress assignment. For English, Nespor and Vogel (1989) and Selkirk (1984) claim that word stress involves three levels of hierarchy to account for primary stress, secondary stress, and no stress. Thus, a multisyllabic word such as *consérvative*, which has both primary and secondary stress, can be understood as having an underlying rhythmic structure as follows:

Level 3 Primary stress		X		
Level 2 Secondary stress		X		X
Level 1 Syllable	X	X	X	X
	con	sér	va	tìve

The X symbols in the grid represent rhythmic strength, or "weight." Level 1 of the grid shows a small amount of weight for every syllable; level 2 represents secondary stress, wherein slightly more weight is assigned to every other syllable; and level 3 represents primary stress, wherein the most weight is assigned to one main syllable. If we were to continue, a fourth level could be used for compound stress, as in *consérvative báshing*, where both elements of the compound have word-level primary stress, but *consérvative* bears the stress of the compound as a whole, as can be seen in the following grid structure:

Level 4 Compound stress		X				
Level 3 Primary stress		X			X	
Level 2 Secondary stress		X		X	X	
Level 1 Syllable	X	X	X	X	X	X
	con	sér	va	tive	bá	shing

In the unmarked case, the general tendency is for an avoidance of adjacent Xs at higher levels of a grid and, therefore, for an alternation between stronger and weaker syllables.

The grid system also provides a handy formalism to show how word stress interacts with intonation. If a word is to have a pitch accent, that pitch accent will normally dock onto the highest available grid mark in the hierarchy at the level of primary stress or above. Selkirk refers to this as "pitch accent association" (1984, p. 272), which can be represented as follows:

Pitch accent	H*			
Level 3 Primary stress	X			
Level 2 Secondary stress	X		X	
Level 1 Syllable	X	X	X	X
	con	sér	va	tive

Grid notation is to be understood as an abstract representation of the relative metrical strength of the syllables involved. In spoken language, the actual pitch of the syllable might be high in the case of H* pitch accent, low in the case of L* pitch accent, or a sloping contour in the case of L+H* or L*+H pitch accents.

Above the word and compound level, the alignment of pitch accents also tends to be rhythmic. Function words—articles, copulas, auxiliaries, prepositions, pronouns, and so on—are usually unstressed and are timed to fit between the aligned pitch accents. Like the unstressed syllables within words, function words are usually lower in volume and pitch than their stressed neighbors, and their vowels are often reduced to [ə]. On a metrical grid, they can be represented at level 1 or 2 as having little rhythmic weight. Function words are not usually associated with pitch accents, being of little consequence in the information structure of the discourse. Figure 3.2 has a series of pitch accents associated with the primary stresses of the content words of the utterance from figure 3.1. As represented by the alignment between the amplitude peaks in the top of the graph and the pitch peaks in the lower part, there is a regular rhythm. Syllables without primary stress, both in the multisyllabic content words and in the function words *we're, with,* and *the,* contribute little to the timing of the utterance.

However, function words *can* be associated with pitch accents if the speaker considers them salient in the context of the discourse. In such cases, they behave like content words, having full vowels, higher volume, and longer duration. The following exchange (from Corpus 3) contains a pitch accent associated with the function word *was* from K, who has just explained that she experienced symptoms of menopause for eleven years:

A   That was a LONG- (.3) tha- ELÉVEN YEARS _{THOUGH} is a LONG
      TIME↓
K   It WAS a _{LONG TIME}↓ YEAH↓

Here, the copula, *was* has L+H* pitch accent to emphasize the extent of K's agreement with A's remark. There is a contrast in the sense that *was* is the opposite of the negative *was not,* as if K were adamantly conveying, "Don't doubt it for a minute!"

What is noteworthy among all of these examples is the claim that the source of pitch accents lies outside the metrical structure, depending on

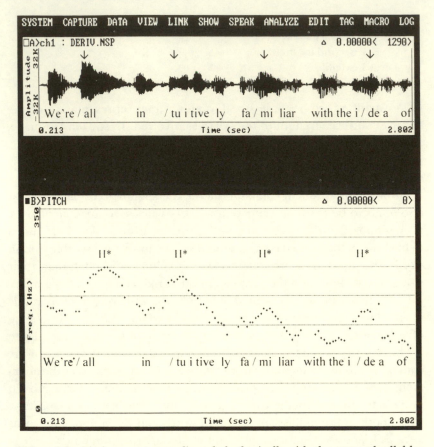

Figure 3.2 Pitch accents are aligned rhythmically with the stressed syllables.

a speaker's intentions and assessments about the discourse. The stress structure represented in the grids stops at the level of compound word stress, and the intonation maps onto these rhythmic peaks.

Rules of Eurhythmy

As we have already seen, an important tendency of rhythmic hierarchies is a preference for a stable alternation within a hierarchy. Hayes (1995) refers to "rules of eurhythmy" as phonological rules that restructure patterns of rhythmic weight so that stress is distributed more evenly and the overall structure will be balanced. He writes:

> Phrasal stress rules typically conspire to achieve a particular rhythmic target. In general terms, the rules tend to create output configurations in which stresses are spaced not too closely and not too far apart. A

grid having these properties is said to be *eurhythmic*; one can also speak of *degrees* of eurhythmy. It has been conjectured . . . that the principles of eurhythmy are invariant across languages, and that they may extend beyond languages into other cognitive domains. (p. 372)

Kaisse (1987, p. 201) uses limericks to illustrate how text aligns with metrical beats in one such rule of eurythmy, "the Rhythm Rule." In the following limerick, the force toward rhythmic alignment overrides what is normally word-final stress in the words *Tennessée, thirtéen,* and *clarinét:*

A Ténnessee drummer named Bette
Played thírteen new tunes in a set
The clárinet player
Was Louie B. Mayer
Who played on a big clarinet

Examples like this occur when two adjacent primary stresses fall within the same phrase: the stress in the first word shifts to keep the rhythmic alignment as balanced as possible, or as Nespor and Vogel (1989) would put it, to avoid "stress clash." If we compare the metrical structure of the word *Tennessée* to that of *Ténnessèe drúmmer,* we can see how the Rhythm Rule balances the timing of the phrase:

		X	X		X		X	
X		X	X		X		X	
X	X	X	X	X	X	X	X	X
Ten	nes	sée	Drúmmer	→	Tén	nes	see	Drú	mmer

Instead of two stressed syllables in a row at level 3, the weight is redistributed more evenly throughout the hierarchy. Further examples include *ábstract árt* preferred over *abstráct árt, fífteen mén* preferred over *fiftéen mén,* and *bámboo cháirs* preferred over *bambóo cháirs.* The clashing stresses need not be on adjacent syllables, as in *Cálifornia Dréaming* preferred over *Califórnia Dréaming:* although a small unstressed syllable, *nia,* separates the primary stresses at level 1, the Rhythm Rule is triggered by the adjacent stresses at level 3.

	X		X		X		X	
X	X		X		X	X		X
X	X	X	X	X	X	X	X	X	X
Càl	i	fór	nia Dréaming	→	Cá	li	fòr	nia Dréaming

In natural speech, rhythmic adjustments of this type are not unusual. They account for the fact that in stretches of syllables with no primary stress, a pitch accent may be associated with a function word or other syllable that would not normally be stressed. In the following example (Corpus 1-C), a portion of which appears in figure 3.3, the speaker adjusts the rhythm on the compound *United States* so that *United* has more stress than *States*.

D   If you're TRÝING to MÁRKET something↘ YOU as a-
SÓMEBODY in the UNÍTED States↘ TRÝING to ₘₐᵣₖₑₜ something in- uh CHÍNA . . .

An idealized version of the middle intonational phrase is represented in the following metrical grid. *United States* is stressed as it would be in its citation form in which *States* has the highest stress of the compound:

```
                                        X
X                              X        X
X           X                  X        X
X     X     X     X     X     X     X     X
sóme bo    dy    in    the   U    ní   ted   States
```

Since the highest grid mark is supposed to be the docking site for a pitch accent, the word *States* would normally have the H* pitch accent. However, this structure would contain a stretch of seven weak syllables in a row, from the second syllable of *somebody* to the last syllable of *United*, with no pitch accent, leaving a rhythmic imbalance in the phrase. As a result, the speaker restructures the stress of the phrase in a trochaic, strong-weak-strong-weak pattern so that the pitch accents are distributed more evenly, as follows:

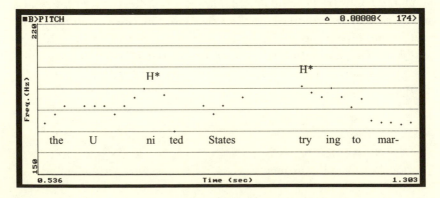

Figure 3.3   Rules of eurythmy apply as the speaker puts the pitch accent on *United* instead of *States*.

```
H*                              H*
                                X
X                               X       X
X           X                   X       X
X    X      X    X    X    X     X    X    X
sóme bo    dy   in   the  U     ní   ted  States
```

Another type of rhythmic adjustment occurs when there are several monosyllabic words in a row with pitch accents. To avoid stress clash in such cases, the duration of the pitch accented syllables must be lengthened or silence added if the rhythmic intervals are to remain regular. This process has been called "beat insertion" by Nespor and Vogel (1989). In the following example (Corpus 2), T has commented that Newari, not Nepali, is the dominant language in Katmandu. He continues (slashes indicate rhythmic beats):

T   ᵧᴋɴᴏᴡ / SOME of the / ÓLD / PÉOPLE / DÓN'T / SPÉAK Ne / PÁLI at / ÁLL

Here are monosyllabic feet in the cases of *old, don't*, and *all* whose duration is lengthened to be roughly equivalent to that of the multisyllabic ones. The added time is represented in the grid below with star symbols:

```
X           X        X          X           X
X           X        X          X           X
X    *      X    X   X    *      X    X    X    X
old         peop le  don't       speak Ne  Pa  li
```

The discussion so far has centered on remedies for stress clash that make speech more rhythmic. However, Uhmann (1996) found many instances in a corpus of German conversation data of stress clash used deliberately in assessment sequences: that is, when a speaker was expressing a strong opinion, stress clash could provide extra emphasis. In such cases, instead of the unmarked alternating pattern, several adjacent syllables could have pitch accents. Even unstressed syllables with vowels reduced to [ə] could occupy a single beat and in principle have a pitch accent. Although Uhmann notes certain differences between the metrical patterns of German and those of English, the phenomenon of expressive stress clash can be found in both languages. In the following example drawn from a conversation in English (Corpus 3), J has just expressed regret at not being able to have more children with the onset of menopause. S voices a vastly different perspective. In the relevant lines, rhythmic beats are indicated with slashes. Accent marks are also added to show where even unstressed syllables have pitch accents, elongated vowels are marked with colons (e:::), and pitch extremes are marked with plus signs (+E:::VER+):

```
1       S   see I'M on the ÓTHER ₑₙ_D↓
2           / FÍVE / KÍDS / Í / CÁN / NÓT/  ⌈+WÁIT+↓
3       ALL                                 ⌊ah ha ha ha!
4           ((extended laughter))
5       S   ⌐ʳI mean it's like- (.2) +PLE:::ASE+ ꜰᴏᴅ↓ I've +DONE+
6           (.5) the DUTY↓
7       ALL ha ha ha ha ((more laughter)) ah ⌈huh huh huh
8       S                                    ⌊+PULLÉASE+↓ (.5)
9           / Í    / ÁM       / (.2)    / +DÓNE+↓/ (.3)
10          I don't wanna +É:::VER+ be +Á:::BLE+ to HAVE children
11          AGÁIN↓ ɪ ᴍᴇᴀɴ I LOVE my KIDS↗ but
12          ↳/ Í   / DÓN'T / WÁNT / Á / NÓ / THÉR
13          / Bə ⌈/ HÁY / BÉE (("baby"))
14      A      ⌊hn hn
```

This excerpt contains a good deal of emphatic material: people in the group are laughing; in several instances S raises her pitch to an extreme and lengthens her vowels. There are also three sequences with deliberate stress clashes as described by Uhmann. In lines 2 and 9, the function words *can* and *am*, respectively, receive full rhythmic beats and H* pitch accents along with surrounding content words. In lines 12–13, even the unstressed syllables of *another* occupy full beats in a string of syllables with equal timing. This sequence is shown in figure 3.4, where the amplitude graph indicates syllable alignment.

Rhythm in Interaction

The importance of rhythm as an organizing force in phonology has further implications for the analysis of interactional discourse. Citing re-

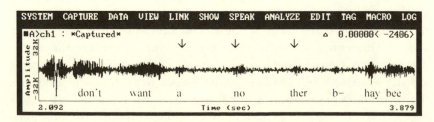

Figure 3.4 A sequence of syllables, some of which would normally be unstressed, are spaced at equal intervals to convey extra emphasis.

search by Allen and Hawkins (1980), Auer et al. (1999) explain that rhythmic speech is easy to process, as hearers' attention is guided from one phonetically prominent point to the next. Because these points tend to hold the most salient information, hearers are able to perceive and process the discourse in regular beat-sized cycles (p. 16). It follows that such fine-tuned sensitivity to underlying rhythmic patterns will influence turn-taking behaviors and may have the potential to explain several interactional phenomena: that participants in discourse take turns with little silence between speakers (Sacks et al., 1974); that one speaker may overlap the speech of another with the same timing (Couper-Kuhlen, 1993, p. 74); that participants usually agree when an "awkward" pause occurs; and that participants are able to synchronize the rhythm of their talk across turn boundaries. As Couper-Kuhlen (1993, p. 74) demonstrates in the following example, this last phenomenon is not unusual (slashes indicate rhythmic beats):

```
H   /Welcome Missis    /
    /Giles, (.02)       /
G   /hello Mister       /
    /Hodge,=
H              =how d'you /
    /do madam.          /
```

In this sequence, rhythm is maintained across three turns. The latch (indicated by the equals sign) between the end of G's turn, and the beginning of H's second turn takes place within a single rhythmic interval.

Awareness of rhythm, however, is not slavish. Auer et al. (1999) document an alternation between rhythmic and arrhythmic sequences in typical conversations, a fact that they attribute to participants' interactional goals. For example, rhythm might be delayed at certain points to dramatize the introduction of "hot news" (p. 203), or a regular rhythm might serve to camouflage the effect of face-threatening material (p. 204). As I discussed earlier, Uhmann (1996) found stress clash used deliberately for extra emphasis. Fiksdal (1990; chapter 7) suggests that disrupted rhythm can be taken as a sign of interspeaker trouble. In adviser/advisee discourse, she highlights what she calls "uncomfortable moments" during which the rhythmic structure of the discourse breaks down and the content also reflects some awkwardness or disagreement. These ideas are revisited in chapter 7 on prosody and the analysis of conversation in which Fiksdal is a guest contributor of a sample analysis.

Thus, rhythm can be considered an organizing force in spoken discourse. Stress patterns within words tend to have a rhythmic base, and pitch accents themselves tend to be rhythmically aligned. I have drawn upon the grid system as a useful way to represent the hierarchical nature of rhythm in language. I believe that this model captures, at least in the abstract, the important concept that rhythmic stability is global. Rhythmic adjustments occur not just from one word to the next but in the context of a hierarchy of rhythmic weight, which, in the unmarked case, tends toward balance throughout a constituent of whatever size. Moreover, research suggests that speech with regular rhythm is optimal for processing. However, from this idealized balance, speakers also have the option to manipulate rhythm for interactional purposes.

Paralanguage: The Color of Everyday Speech

In an intriguing video presentation, Archer (1993) provides various examples of what he calls "vocal paralanguage," to demonstrate that the *way* something is said may vary, although the words remain the same. In a particularly dramatic demonstration of this point, Archer includes footage of Martin Luther King Jr. giving the "I Have a Dream" speech before a cheering crowd of thousands. Simultaneously, a typed text of the words of the speech is superimposed upon the screen. Archer suggests that had King simply distributed printed flyers of his speech, the impact would have been minimal in comparison with his powerful vocal delivery, which not only carries the message over a long distance but conveys the urgency, anxiety, commitment, and all the other emotions that people still associate with the speech decades later.

Paralanguage, then, is the variation of pitch, volume, tempo, and voice quality that a speaker makes for pragmatic, emotional, and stylistic reasons and to meet the requirements of genre. Paralanguage is manifest in every speech act, whether the speaker is shouting cheers at a basketball game, growling for her morning coffee, whispering at a theatre during a play, cooing to a baby, yacking with an old friend on the telephone, lecturing to fifty undergraduates, or mimicking the voice of a domineering policeman. Paralanguage is available to speakers regardless of language background, although the appropriate contexts for certain types of paralanguage may be culturally influenced and quite ritualized. For example, in many cultures, members of audiences are encouraged to scream at particular junctures in a sports event but may be chastised for doing so in a theater production. The resulting variation in voice can be analyzed independently of the grammatical, lexical, phonological, and intonational structure. This is not to say that structural components of language do not vary for generic, pragmatic, and emotional reasons as well (see Biber, 1994, for ample documentation of grammatical variation of language by register). However, the focus of this discussion is on how speech characteristics may vary, regard-less of the other structural aspects of the text.

Some of the best transcription conventions for paralanguage have been developed by conversation analysts, as represented in Jefferson (1984). These rely on single and double parentheses and certain other textual symbols. Single parentheses are used to enclose pause length in seconds. For example, (.3) would be a three-tenths of a second pause. Double parentheses are used to enclose other paralinguistic information, giving the analyst a good deal of flexibility for commentary in the tran-script. For example, ((shouts)) would indicate that a speaker began to shout at a much louder volume; ((mimics deep policeman's voice)) might refer to a change in voice quality in a quoted passage. For the purposes of this volume, I will use the symbols for paralanguage shown in table 3.1, many of which are borrowed from Jefferson (1984).

At this point, it is necessary to say a few more words about pitch, for it has been discussed at length in the previous chapter on intonation but also appears on this list of paralinguistic features. Bolinger (1986) and Chafe (1994) draw an iconic connection between primitive cries of arousal and high pitch as the evolutionary origin of systems of intonation, of which cer-tain aspects have become grammaticalized in the development of human

TABLE 3.1 Symbols for Paralanguage

Phenomenon	*Symbol*
pitch extremely high	⁺screech⁺ or even ⁺⁺screech⁺⁺
pitch extremely low	_fee fi fo fum_
volume	((louder / shouting / crescendo))
quiet speech	°don't let anyone hear us!
voice quality	((shrieks / mimics Groucho Marx voice / clenches jaw))
sound effects	((whistles / makes truck noise / imitates dog barking))
laughter	hh; ha ha; huh; ah hah hah (transcribed to approxi-mate the actual sound)
sounds from elsewhere	((siren goes by / slapping sound))
rhythmic beats	/ beat / beat
tempo speeds up	>>
tempo slows down	<<
elongated syllable	:::
pause in seconds	(x.x)
unmeasured micropause	(.)

languages. In Bolinger's opinion, "we have a mixed [intonation] system, expressive at base but with adaptations that differ from culture to culture" (p. 198). In other words, we would expect a universal tendency for speakers of any language to associate pitch extremes with emotionally charged text, regardless of what system of intonation that language might have developed. Therefore, it is important to make a distinction between the language-specific English intonation system outlined earlier and the more universal paralinguistic pitch variation referred to here. As Shen (1990), who works on Chinese intonation, writes, "Emotional, expressive, or emphatic nuances (anger, irony, astonishment, apprehension, etc.) can be superimposed upon almost any utterance" (p. 9). Ladd (1980) explains shifts in pitch range as the "gradient" aspect of intonation versus the phonemic, "all-or-none" aspect, drawing a useful analogy with expressive lengthening in segmental phonology: the meaning distinction between the words *big* and *bi-i-ig*, he points out, is not phonemic (as would be *big* and *beg*) but rather gradient, for an expressive purpose (p. 113). Similarly, an intonational phrase may have a particular configuration of key, pitch accents, and pitch boundaries, but the pitch of those tones relative to that of other intonational structures of the same type will be a matter of degree, depending on just how emotional, dramatic, or expressive the speaker is, or whether he or she is mimicking the voice of another person. According to Ladd (1996), these attitudinal modifications are not generally confounded by listeners with the basic intonational structure of the utterance. Thus, pitch extremes appear on the list of paralinguistic features in the table to refer to the alteration of pitch range as a whole for stylistic and other reasons. The following example (Corpus 5), shown in figure 3.5, illustrates the use of extremely high pitch for special emphasis on the word *totally*. The superscripted plus symbol (+) is used to indicate the pitch extreme in the transcript.

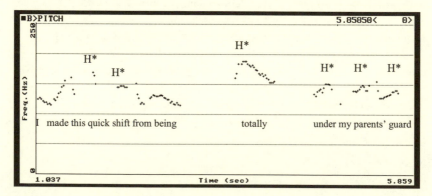

Figure 3.5 Although several words have H* pitch accents, the word *totally* has higher pitch for extra emphasis.

H   I made this QUICK SHIFT from be::ing↘ (.6) +TÓTALLY+
(.5) ÚNDER my PÁRENTS GUARD↗ (.2) to ʙᴇ́ɪɴɢ ᴛᴏ́ᴛᴀʟʟʏ (.2)
NOT ᴜ́ɴᴅᴇʀ ᴛʜᴇɪʀ ɢᴜᴀʀᴅ↓

Although several words in this utterance have H* pitch accents, the
speaker, a man, has chosen to raise the pitch of *totally* to an extreme to
dramatize his experience.

One particularly rich genre for research on paralanguage is the oral
narrative. Wolfson (1982) discusses "performance features" as an important choice for storytellers, who may dramatize their telling with gestures,
mimicry, volume and pitch variation, and other paralinguistic features.
In a discussion of evaluative language in narrative, Labov (1972) includes
quoted speech as an indicator of a speaker's strong attitudinal attachment
to a particular narrative event. Quoted speech is marked by paralinguistic
shifts—the tempo, pitch range, volume, and other aspects of voice quality change during the quoted portion. Bauman (1986) makes a similar
point using data from both narratives and jokes wherein a punch line is
delivered by the storyteller in quoted speech, which involves alterations
in voice quality. These matters are taken up in chapter 8, which covers
the prosody of narratives.

Paralanguage is also an important factor in the development of individual speech styles. In the paralanguage video by Archer, mentioned
earlier, one scene depicts actors delivering a short script in several different styles. Although the text itself does not vary, the message takes on
a range of meanings depending on the paralinguistic features: one rendition conveys a defensive, fearful persona as the actor speaks with a
halting, quiet intensity; another conveys anger as the actor delivers the
lines with clenched teeth; and a third conveys reassurance and love with
a quieter, higher pitched, somewhat cloying voice quality. Such prosodic
qualities are important as individuals create speech styles that reflect different aspects of their identity (Johnstone, 1996).

In cross-cultural communication, Gumperz's (1982) studies of "contextualization cues" also include many aspects of paralanguage. Gumperz
is concerned about how prosodic cues may be misinterpreted cross-
culturally such that speakers from one culture attribute attitudes and emotions to those of another based on variations in volume, pitch, and the like.
A communication problem may stem from the fact that what is part of the
intonation structure of one language or dialect may be perceived as paralinguistic in another. Therefore, it may sound as if a person is deliberately
being snooty, aggressive, or whining when in fact these features are part of
the intonation system of the native language. These issues are taken up in
chapter 9 on the analysis of second-language discourse.

In sum, although paralanguage may not be so neatly systematized as stress, intonation, phonology, and syntax, from a discourse analysis perspective, it is a very rich area for the study of communication and self-expression and can be a basis for mutual understanding that transcends the limitations of the lexicogrammatical and intonational structure of a text.

Conclusion

This chapter began by emphasizing that intonation is not to be confused with stress. A basic stress pattern, including primary stress, secondary stress, no stress, and compound stress, is a phonological property of lexical items and compounds, depending on their history, morphology, and syllable structure. On the other hand, intonation is a system of meaning in discourse, which associates with text by mapping onto the rhythmic stress patterns of the words.

The chapter has also described a system wherein a universal human sense of rhythm forms the foundation of prosody in languages. This simply means that constituents of speech, from the syllable all the way to the discourse level, tend to follow an alternation of strong and weak beats at regular time intervals. This contributes to the predictability of word stress, but the prevalence of rhythmic patterns also extends hierarchically beyond the level of the single word or compound. We have seen examples of rhythmic adjustments, such as the Rhythm Rule, that balance the rhythm of larger constituents at a global level.

Also of relevance for the discourse analyst is the fact that participants in social interaction apparently use this rhythmic foundation as a resource. We have seen that speakers can maintain a rhythmic pattern from one turn to the next in conversation. Thus, rhythm is arguably an important factor in accounting for the ability of participants in conversation to take turns with little overlap or silence. There may also be a strategic value in the distribution of rhythm to achieve other interactional goals. Delayed rhythm may, for example, be a way of creating suspense. Stress clash can be used deliberately to intensify one's utterance. While regular rhythm may be a sign of rapport, a breakdown of rhythm may indicate a discomfort in the conversation.

Finally, I have introduced a number of paralinguistic features, including volume, pitch extremes, voice quality, and pausing. These vary for emotional, stylistic, and pragmatic reasons, to bring out nuances of meaning beyond what the more systematic, structural aspects of the text convey.

II

_____

APPLICATIONS TO
DISCOURSE ANALYSIS

4

INTONATION, MENTAL REPRESENTATION, AND COHERENCE

Coherence distinguishes a text from a random group of words or utterances based on the relationships among the ideas behind it. One aspect of coherence is cohesion, the connections between linguistic elements within the text. It is not unexpected that intonation plays a role in cohesion and, thereby, coherence; it is one of the linguistic resources available to speakers to link elements in the text together so that the discourse as a whole makes sense. In chapter 2, we saw that a pitch boundary at the end of a phrase can anticipate the next constituent to complete its interpretation. We also saw that L* pitch accents can be associated with lexical items that a speaker believes should already be accessible to the hearer, whereas L+H* pitch accents can signal a contrast relationship with items that have come before. These and other pitch morphemes help hearers draw connections between what is uttered and what is already represented in their minds during the interaction.

Consider, for example, a short excerpt (Corpus 1-C) from an academic discussion class on the topic of international marketing. The class has been discussing various factors that might influence a company's decisions in selling a product overseas. D, the professor, now asks how cultural factors might enter into the marketing plan. The other participants are students in the class.

1	D	⇑So what Ó(hh)THER THINGS CAN YOU THINK OF↓ other-
2		(.2) perhaps ÓTHER CÚLTURAL (.3) FÁCTORS THAT (.4)
3		ÍNFLUENCE TÁKING YOUR PRÓDUCT ABRÓAD↓ (1.2)
4	B	C- um→ (.7) COMPETÍTION with ANÓTHER (.4)
5		PRÓDUCT↓ (.5) An EXÍSTING product↓ (.4)
6	D	OK↗=
7	B	=LIKE YOU SAID (.5) a CÚISI ⌈NART- (1.3)
8	D	⌊SURE↓
9	B	is competing with a→(1.8) SMALL SPACE and- (.3)
10		CHÓPPING knife↘ or- (.5) uh some ÓTHER- (.2)
11		Um→(.6)
12	D	Γ_OK↗so you're THÍNKING of COMPETÍTION↗(.2)
13		you're ÁLSO THÍNKING OF SÚBSTITUTE PRÓDUCTS↓
14		(.6)
15	B	SÚBSTITUTE PRÓDUCTS↓ (.2)
16	D	Uh huh↗(.7)
17	K	ΓÁLSO the DISPÓSABLE ÍNCOME of the→(1.)
18		MÁRKET- (.4) you're SÉLLING to↓ (.3)
19	D	OK↗(1.5) ΓCan you THINK of any WAYS that you
20		c'n- (.1) um- (.2) if you're- if you're TRÝING to
21		MÁRKET SÓMETHING↗y- YOU as a- (.5) somebody in
22		the UNÍTED States TRÝING TO MÁRKET SÓMETHING IN (.3) uh→
23		(.1) CHÍNA↓ (.2) HOW would you find OUT about
24		DISPÓSABLE ÍNCOME↓ (.1) WHERE would you go to FIND
25		THAT INFORMÁTION↓ (1.25)
26	K	Uhh→in THAT CASE I'd- (.9) ASSÚME there'd be→(.2)
27		some NÚMBERS from the GÓVERNMENT
28		SÓMEWHERE↓

I will use this excerpt to illustrate a number of points as the chapter unfolds, but, initially, I focus on the words *disposable income*, introduced in line 17 by K, a student. As shown in figure 4.1, the term is uttered with H* pitch accent, as is appropriate for a new idea: it is an additional factor that might affect marketing decisions. D accepts the idea into the discussion and asks how marketers might learn what a particular country's disposable income is. In her repetition of the term *disposable income* in line 24, the pitch is low, shown in figure 4.2, because the notion is established at this point and therefore accessible to K as well as to the rest of the class. The sequence is germane to the topic of coherence for two reasons: first, D's L* pitch accent on *disposable income* reinforces the cohesive link between the first and second mention of the term. Second, the connection takes place across speakers, as it is K who introduces the term with H* pitch accent and D who repeats it with L* pitch accent. These facts illustrate the dynamic nature of discourse and mental repre-

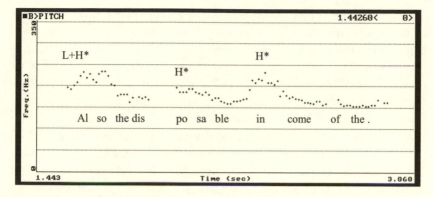

Figure 4.1   K, a student, introduces the new idea of *disposable income* with a H* pitch accent.

sentation: what is new in line 17 becomes accessible thereafter as the participants readjust their mental models to incorporate each new idea in a coherent manner. Furthermore, the process is collaborative, for D's low pitch indicates that she has added K's idea to her own mental representation of the discourse and assumes that others in the class have done the same.

This chapter continues to explore the contribution of intonation to the cohesion of a text and, therefore, indirectly, to its coherence, the central claim being that intonation can provide more information than can the lexicogrammatical structure alone. I will begin with a discussion of mental representation in spoken discourse, drawing from Brown (1995), Clark (1992), and Sperber and Wilson (1995), all of whom emphasize the collaborative nature of comprehension, as well as the fact that

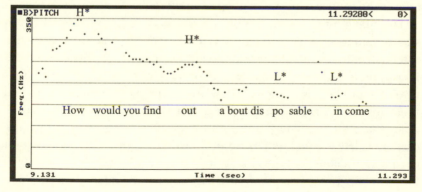

Figure 4.2   D, the professor, repeats the term *disposable income* with a L* pitch accent because it is already accessible.

understanding is always a relative notion. I also assume, following Bartlett (1932) and many others, that long-term memory is organized schematically; that is, that related ideas are stored and retrieved in associated clusters. From this perspective, I will consider the notion of cohesion as treated by Halliday and Hasan (1976) and show how the lexicogrammatical structure combines with other sources of input to create a mental representation of discourse. In addition, I argue that, because low pitch is an indicator of what a speaker assumes to be accessible to hearers, low-pitched material provides a window into the cultural knowledge interlocutors take for granted. This has implications for studies of cross-cultural communication because, as Clark (1992) maintains, shared knowledge is based on community membership; hence, I claim that certain facts about one's social affiliation are revealed through choice of intonation. At the end of this chapter, I explore this claim in a sample analysis of a statistics lecture wherein intonation provides information about cultural assumptions shared within a classroom community. By assessing the pitch of certain lexically cohesive items, I suggest that the professor's assumptions about what is common knowledge and what students need to learn are illuminated.

Mental Representation and Discourse

As people communicate, each builds a mental representation of the discourse as it progresses. This is a short-term memory system, constructed for the purpose of the current communication, which interacts with other cognitive systems, such as perception and long-term memory (Brown, 1995; Clark, 1992; Kintsch, 1988; Levelt, 1989; Sperber & Wilson, 1995; Tomlin, 1997; Werth, 1984).[1] Turn by turn, participants interpret each new utterance in the context of the mental representation that they have constructed so far, taking into account the prior text, previous knowledge schemata stored in long-term memory, the social relationships among participants, listener feedback, relevant information in the immediate physical environment, and inferences derived from all of these factors. New contributions involve a speaker's assessment of how others are likely to have constructed their mental representations and what common knowledge they may already share. In face-to-face interactions, speakers are guided in this process by evidence from listeners' responses showing that they either accept each new installment of the talk or need more clarification (Brown, 1995; Clark, 1992). To a great extent, such assessments also depend on common community membership (Clark, 1992). If I am describing this book to my mother, I will make different assumptions about how she will construct her mental representation of my description from those I would make if I were describing it to a linguist. Even if I were not personally acquainted with the linguist, I would assume certain specialized background knowledge common within the community of linguists. With my mother, I would assume less background knowledge and be more likely to rely on examples and general explanations in my description.

However, despite our best efforts at collaboration, comprehension is not an all-or-nothing state of affairs that either succeeds or fails. Speakers and listeners have independent and not necessarily identical goals (Brown, 1995). For example, we can easily imagine a speaker who deliberately presents complex ideas to addressees who have little knowledge of them in order to impress them. Cowed by this arrogance, listeners may give feedback that indicates understanding to avoid appearing ignorant, when in fact they have attained only partial understanding. Moreover, success of communication is itself a relative notion. Consider the academic lecture described at the beginning of the chapter. At the end of the hour, the students will have differing degrees of understanding of the material on international marketing, depending on previous background knowledge of the topic, level of interest and attention to the lecture, anticipation of upcoming exams, and the like. In this circumstance, it would hardly be fair to say that the professor "failed to communicate" if students had different levels of understanding. A model of mental representation needs to account for those students who got the gist of it, understood the first part but not the end, or critiqued it as nonsense. All have constructed a mental representation that resembles the professor's to some degree but is unlikely ever to be identical.

The lecture situation also illustrates the inadequacy of communication models that assume only one speaker-listener pair. A discourse situation may involve one or more direct addressees; other participants who are present, though not directly addressed by the speaker; and possible overhearers, whose presence may influence a speaker's utterance design (Clark 1992; Goffman, 1981). Clark uses the example of two politicians addressing each other directly in a broadcast discussion, well aware of the public audience who will overhear their debate. Although not speaking directly to the public audience, they nevertheless design their utterances very cunningly to affect this group of overhearers. In the lecture excerpt at the beginning of this chapter, the technicians running the video camera as part of the data collection process also provide an example of overhearers whose knowledge of social conventions will probably lead them to exclude themselves from the discussion.

We are now in a position to define a coherent discourse from a listener's perspective as one for which a mental representation can be constructed that is as adequate as possible or necessary for the goals and circumstances at hand. Thus, coherence is a relative notion, because what is adequate for one set of circumstances may be less so for others. In the following sections I will discuss three important sources of input to the mental representation of discourse:

1. Linguistic input
2. Previous knowledge
3. Perception of the physical environment

Expanding what has traditionally been considered "the text" in such discussions, I will consider intonation to be as integral to the linguistic input as the lexicogrammatical structure. The intonation of a text interacts with the other sources of input, facilitating the integration of new input into the mental representations of participants in a coherent manner. In some cases, intonation contributes more precise information about the relationships among elements in the discourse than would otherwise be available through lexicogrammatical structure alone.

Linguistic Input

A useful place to begin a discussion of coherence and linguistic input is with Halliday and Hasan's (1976) taxonomy of cohesion. They define cohesion as follows: "Cohesion is a semantic relation between an element in the text and some other element that is crucial to the interpretation of it. This other element is also to be found in the text; but its location in the text is in no way determined by the grammatical structure" (p. 9). Halliday and Hasan's notion of "element" in their definition is a lexicogrammatical one: they identify five categories that contribute to the cohesion of a text in consistent ways, described briefly here:

1. *Reference* includes items in a text which, "instead of being interpreted semantically in their own right . . . make reference to something else for their interpretation" (p. 31). The category includes personal and demonstrative pronouns, definite determiners, and certain adverbs.
2. *Substitution* is a small class of words such as <u>one</u> and <u>do</u>, which can stand in place of semantically richer lexical items.
3. *Lexical cohesion* refers to full lexical items that are to be interpreted as semantically connected with other items, through repetition, synonymy, antonymy, sub- or superordinacy, and collocation.

4. *Ellipsis* is considered simply "substitution by zero" (p. 143); the cohesive constituent is omitted.
5. *Conjunction* involves words such as <u>and,</u> <u>but</u>, and <u>however</u> that link constituents of text together while describing the relationships between them.

I suggest that while these five categories all refer to cohesive ties in text, the nature of the cohesive tie involved can be understood more precisely when one takes the intonation into account.

Anaphor-Antecedent Relationships

The first three of Halliday and Hasan's categories involve anaphor-antecedent and other reiterative relationships among the lexical items in the text. That is, all represent a sense of "givenness" in the discourse. In terms of the current model, this means that the associated intonation is potentially the L* pitch accent. Indeed, as Halliday and Hasan themselves remark, "anaphoric items in English are phonologically non-prominent. . . . [I]n other words, they are 'reduced'" (p. 271).[2] Chafe (1994) expresses this relationship in terms of cognitive load: A given item is assumed by a speaker to be active in consciousness, and thus accessible to other participants, requiring that little intonational effort be expended during its articulation. To illustrate this, I draw two examples of substitution from Halliday and Hasan:

1. Do you remember that thunderstorm we had last time we were here? That was a terrifying $_{\text{ONE}}$ (p. 94).
2. Is he going to pass the exam? I hope $_{\text{SO}}$ (p. 138).

In the second sentences of each of these two examples, the words *one* and *so*, printed in subscripts to show their L* pitch accents, substitute for the constituents in the first sentences, *thunderstorm* and *he is going to pass the exam*, respectively.

   It is interesting to note that Halliday and Hasan's fourth category of cohesion, ellipsis, is also, in a curious way, anaphoric. It is the omission of a constituent whose referent is accessible, as in the following example wherein the word *verses* is ellipted at the end of the second sentence:

Would you like to hear another verse? I know TWELVE MORE Ø (p. 143).

If this category is regarded iconically, it is as if, in Chafe's (1994) terms, the item's interpretation is so obviously retrievable by a hearer as not to even bear articulation. If ellipted material is added back into a text, it is usually associated with L* pitch accent. In the previous example, we can reinsert the word *verses* with the following result:

Would you like to hear another verse? I know TWELVE MORE _{VÉRSES.}

In this sense, ellipted items can be regarded as deaccented out of existence, which is consistent with the current claim that speakers associate low pitch with items judged to be accessible in the mental representations of listeners.

However, low pitch (or no pitch) is not the only possible intonation to associate with cohesive items. In one project, I searched in vain to find statistical evidence that reiterated items were lower pitched on average than their antecedents in a description task conducted by ten native speakers of English (see Wennerstrom, 1994). Due to a surprisingly high number of H* pitch accents associated with repeated items, I was not in fact able to make this claim. The association of H* pitch accent with an anaphor may indicate that in the speaker's judgment, the antecedent is no longer accessible in the hearer's mental representation, or that for some other reason the item needs to be reinstated into the foreground of the discourse. For example, in the lecture at the beginning of the chapter, D, the professor, offers B, a student, the term *substitute products* to help express his idea about competing products that might affect one's marketing strategy. B immediately repeats the term with H* pitch accent:

D ⌐ OK↗ so you're THÍNKING of COMPETÍTION↗ (.2) you're
ÁLSO THÍNKING OF SÚBSTITUTE PRÓDUCTS↓ (.6)
B SÚBSTITUTE PRÓDUCTS↓ (.2)
D Uh huh↗ (.7)

Even though the term *substitute products* is surely accessible in D's mental representation of the discourse, B associates it with H* pitch accent. He seems to be "trying out" the term as a representation of his own idea to be added to the discourse.

There are a variety of other reasons for speakers to re-foreground referents with H* pitch accents. Nootebaum and Terken (1982) propose that an intervening referent introduced between the first and second mention of an item leads to H* pitch accent on the second mention. Terken and Hirschberg (1994) and Werth (1984) claim that the surface grammatical position of the reiterated item is important. Werth, who uses Halliday's (1985) system of functional grammar, suggests that a repeated noun phrase in thematic position (roughly, subject position) has a higher likelihood of H* pitch accent than when it is in the rheme (predicate position). Related to this issue is Fox's (1987) study of anaphora, in which she considers the circumstances under which a pronoun may be substituted for a full noun phrase. She concludes that it depends on how deeply embedded within the episodic structure of the discourse the reference is from its original antecedent. Although Fox does not discuss intonation, her question is related to mine because it hinges on the speaker's judgment about the accessibility of referents in the hearer's mental representation of the discourse. Presumably a full noun phrase is used when an item is judged to be less accessible and would be more likely to have H* pitch accent than would a pronoun.

Another possibility for items in Halliday and Hasan's first three categories of cohesion is that they may be used contrastively. The L+H* contrastive pitch accent may then become a crucial factor in recognizing the relationship between anaphor and antecedent. The following dramatic example of this is adapted from Gilbert (1984):

1. If Harry finds out about our secret plot, HE'LL KILL US!
2. If Harry finds out about our secret plot, HE'LL KILL US! (pp. 41–42)

In both sentences, the pronouns *he* and *us* are cohesive in Halliday and Hasan's first category, reference. *He* refers to *Harry* and *us* is cohesively linked with *our*, which refers to the speaker and one or more addressees. The intonation associated with the pronouns differs between the two sentences: in the first, they have L* pitch accents, meaning "accessible in the discourse," their respective referents being part of the linguistic input from the previous clause. Apparently "we" are plotting something that would make Harry mad enough to kill us. In the second rendition, the pronouns have L+H* pitch accents, allowing a contrastive interpretation: we are plotting to kill Harry, but instead Harry might kill us first to save himself.

A final possibility is that a reiterated item may be associated with L*+H pitch accent when its relevance to the discourse is being questioned. The following is an example of an exact repetition of a lexical item with L*+H pitch accent in the marketing class (Corpus 1-C). At the beginning of the class, D, the professor has asked students to picture a French company trying to market a bicycle in the United States. The students are asked to consider what an American customer might need a bicycle for. As they contribute suggestions, D repeats their answers in what Halliday and Hasan call "same-word reiteration" (p. 288), a subcategory of lexical cohesion. Here is the excerpt:

1   D   ... WHAT does the CÚSTOMER (.3) NEED A BÍCYCLE
2   FOR IN THE UNÍTED STATES↓ (.4)

3	K	TRANSPORTÁTION↑ (.3)
4	D	⌈TRANSPORTÁTION↗ (.3)
5	R	⌊RECREÁTION↑
6	B	LÉISURE→ (.4)
7	D	LÉISURE→=
8	J	=FÁSHION↗ (1.0)
9	D	FÁSHION↑ hn hn hn=
10	J	=WELL→=
11	D	⌈MAYBE↗
12	J	=⌊you'd want to get a FRENCH BÍCYCLE because it's
13		from FRANCE↓ (.5) YOU KNOW, we have this- (.4)
14		THING IN OUR HEAD that says that=
15	D	=OK↗ so STÁTUS↓ . . .

In lines 4 and 7, D's repetitions have H* pitch accents, affirming that the students' contributions should be added to the information structure being created.[3] However, when J offers the word *fashion* in line 8, D repeats the item with L*+H pitch accent as, shown in figure 4.3. This intonation, followed by a brief chuckle, indicates that she questions the relevance of J's contribution. Picking up on this cue, J explains that Americans might buy French bicycles because they generally admire French culture, an idea that D finally accepts in line 15. Meanwhile, the students whose ideas were repeated with H* pitch accents did not recognize a need to elaborate. The important point is that although Halliday and Hasan's taxonomy can classify many cohesive relationships, intonation can often provide more information about the exact nature of the cohesive tie, adding to the coherence of the discourse.

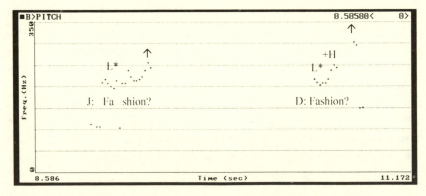

Figure 4.3 D, the professor, repeats J's contribution with a skeptical L*+H pitch accent.

Conjunction

Halliday and Hasan's last category of cohesion is conjunction, lexical items such as *and, but, therefore,* and *next,* which perform the function of linking constituents of text together while at the same time indicating the semantic connection between those constituents. For example, *next* indicates the addition of a new installment in a sequence, whereas *therefore* indicates a cause-effect relationship. I will refer to such items as *lexical conjunctions* so as not to confuse them with what I will argue are intonational forms of conjunction. A certain similarity may be observed between the patterning of lexical conjunctions and that of pitch boundaries and key. Both lexical conjunctions and these intonational morphemes tend to be located at the periphery of constituents, pitch boundaries at the end, and key at the beginning, of intonational phrases. Both categories also tend to be preceded or followed by pauses. Finally, both provide hearers with information about the nature of the relationship between the constituents with which they associate. Although lexical conjunctions and pitch phenomena often occur in tandem, in some cases the prosody provides crucial information for the interpretation of a lexical conjunction and may even act in lieu of it.

For an illustration of these points, I return to the excerpt of classroom discourse from the beginning of this chapter. Here the discussion centers on why Japanese customers might be reluctant to buy a Western product when competing substitutes are already an established part of their own culture:

```
1     B   LIKE YOU SAID (.5) a CÚISI      ⌈NART- (1.3)
2     D                                   ⌊SURE↓
3     B   is competing with a→(1.8) SMALL SPACE and- (.3)
4         CHÓPPING knife↘ or- (.5) uh some ÓTHER- (.2)
5         um→(.6)
6     D   ⌈°OK↗ so you're THÍNKING of COMPETÍTION↗ . . .
```

In this collaboration between D and B, a contrast is made in lines 1–4 between a Cuisinart brand of food processor, on one hand, and a list of two alternatives—a small space and chopping knife, or some other substitute product—on the other. The point of the contrast, raised earlier in this class, is that it may be difficult for a Western company to market a large product such as a Cuisinart food processor in a country like Japan where kitchen space is at a premium and a chopping knife or some other small gadget may be preferred. The lexical conjunctions *and* and *or* are both used in the contrast construction, but, as is shown in the diagram in figure 4.4, they have a different scope: *or* is the higher level conjunction in the organizational structure because it links the two alternatives

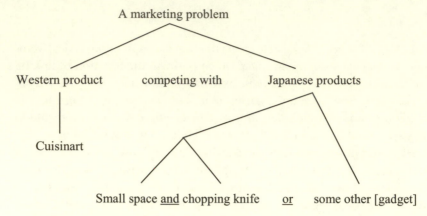

Figure 4.4   This contrast contains embedded hierarchical structure.

that together compete with the Cuisinart. *And* works at a lower level in that it links the two noun phrases within the first alternative—*small space* and *chopping knife*. The prosody tells us the scope of the lexical conjunctions: the conjunction *or* is preceded by a partially falling pitch boundary (↘) after the word *knife*, indicating that there are two separate, though interrelated, intonational phrases. In contrast, *and* is in the same intonational phrase as the two noun phrases it connects, with neither pause nor pitch boundary preceding it, an indication that it is embedded within, rather than peripheral to, its thought group.

The classroom excerpt also contains an example of prosody indicating the relationship between two sequential constituents in the absence of a lexical conjunction. In the following segment, K suggests, in lines 1–2, that the disposable income in a country where a foreign company wishes to sell a product will affect the marketing strategy:

1	K	↱ALSO the DISPÓSABLE ÍNCOME of the→ (1.)
2		MÁRKET- (.4) you're SÉLLING to↓ (.3)
3	D	OK↗ (1.5) ↱Can you THINK of any WAYS that you
4		c'n- (.1) um- (.2) if you're- if you're TRÝING to
5		MÁRKET ꜱᴏ́ᴍᴇᴛʜɪɴɢ↗ y- YOU as a- (.5) somebody in
6		the UNÍTED States ᴛʀÝɪɴɢ ᴛᴏ ᴍᴀ́ʀᴋᴇᴛ ꜱᴏ́ᴍᴇᴛʜɪɴɢ ɪɴ (.3) uh→
7		(.1) CHÍNA↓ (.2) How would you find OUT about
8		ᴅɪꜱᴘᴏ́ꜱᴀʙʟᴇ ɪ́ɴᴄᴏᴍᴇ↓

In line 3, D reacts to K's suggestion, saying "OK," with a low rising pitch boundary. This pitch boundary indicates that the constituent should be followed up by another one for its interpretation. D waits 1.5 seconds for K to elaborate and then continues with a high key, "↱ How would you find out about disposable income," meaning that her stance in the new constituent is in some way at odds with what has come before. In a sense, the low-rising pitch boundary and high key can be said to take the place of the lexical conjunction *but*. It is as if the professor reacts to K's contribution by saying, "I will accept your idea, *but* I also want you to probe it further." Again, this is an example of how intonation can provide more information about cohesion than can the lexicogrammatical structure alone.

To summarize, in the construction and processing of linguistic input, prosody plays an important role. Speakers associate particular intonational morphemes with the lexicogrammatical structure of the text to indicate how they expect that structure to fit into the mental representation that they assume listeners have constructed during the interaction: is a cohesive item already accessible? Is it contrastive? Or does the speaker have some other intention that requires a "re-foregrounding" or a questioning of the item? The pitch accent will provide information about these intentions. In addition, pitch boundaries, key, and pauses provide information about how lexical conjunctions are used to organize constituents: is the link within the intonational phrase or at a higher level? In short, prosody adds an important element of cohesion to a text to help listeners derive a coherent interpretation. In chapter 5, we will also see examples of how this works at higher levels as speakers organize their topics.

Previous Knowledge Schemata

Halliday and Hasan make it clear that cohesion is only a part of what contributes to coherence. "Cohesive ties, especially those with the immediately preceding text, are only one source for the information that the reader or listener requires. Both situational and more remote textual information are necessary components" (p. 303). In other words, the lexicogrammatical structure is only one source of input to a coherent mental representation of discourse. In addition to what is actually verbalized, the background knowledge of the participants is important is well. To explain the interaction between text and world knowledge, schema theory (Bartlett, 1932) can be invoked. According to Rubin (1995), a schema is an abstract, idealized representation of a commonly experienced situation. By drawing on schemata in both the production and the interpretation of discourse, speakers can omit many mundane details of a description, tale, or explanation, while verbalizing only that of special relevance to the current circumstances. Carrell (1982) emphasizes the cultural influence on how we store information and interpret text. She notes that people from the same backgrounds, communities, or cultures are likely to have stored similar knowledge schemata and may thereby be able to make associations and inferences with little need for explicitly cohesive language. Carrell offers the following picnic example:

> The picnic was ruined. No one remembered to bring a corkscrew (p. 484).

According to Carrell, those who are able to interpret this text as coherent do so because they have a familiar schema for wine and corkscrews associated with picnics. The interpretation is made by parsing the utterances, retrieving the relevant schema from long-term memory into the current mental representation, and drawing the picnics-need-corkscrews connection. Carrell calls attention to the lack of overt lexicogrammatical cohesion in this picnic sequence. Without the underlying schematic association, she points out, there is no obvious collocation between the words *picnic* and *corkscrew*.

L*Pitch Accent and Previous Knowledge

I now turn to the interaction of intonation with the retrieval of previous knowledge schemata. My favorite illustration of this point comes from Ladd (1980, p. 65):

> A   How did your operation go?
> B   Don't talk to me about it. I'd like to STRÁNGLE THE BÚTCHER

Because there is no obvious cohesive link between the actual words *operation* and *butcher* in this exchange, a coherent interpretation can be attained only through stored schemata about operations and butcher shops. The L* pitch accent on *butcher* in B's utterance conveys the meaning that butcher should be accessible in the discourse and that A should search his mental representation for the interpretation.[4] If A is sufficiently tuned in to his culture's fears of surgery and negative images of brutish butchers, he will succeed in finding a link between a cleaver-wielding meat chopper and a heavy-handed surgeon. Ladd points out that if B's utterance had H* pitch accent on *butcher*, it would be difficult to parse coherently:

> A   How did your operation go?
> B   Don't talk to me about it. I'd like to STRÁNGLE the BÚTCHER.

With no L* pitch accent to indicate accessibility, A is likely to try to add *butcher* to his mental representation as a new referent, imagining an actual rather than a metaphoric butcher.

Sperber and Wilson (1995, p. 211) also discuss the importance of intonation as it interacts with schemata in the determination of what is relevant in the discourse. One of their examples is quite interesting:

1. Sorry I'm late. My CAR BROKE DOWN.
2. Sorry I'm late. My CAR was BÓOBY-trapped (p. 211).

Here the intonation differs on the constituent referring to the cause of the car trouble: *broke down* has L* pitch accent; *booby-trapped* has H* pitch accent. In the first sentence, Sperber and Wilson claim that a listener will make an "anticipatory hypothesis" upon hearing the apology, followed by the H* pitch accent on the word *car*, that something must have gone wrong with the speaker's car. One schema likely to be invoked involving "cars causing a delay" would be that of a car breaking down, a familiar headache in modern culture. The L* pitch accent on *broke down* is consistent with the hypothesis: nothing out of the ordinary has occurred beyond normal car trouble. As Sperber and Wilson point out, one could even say, "Sorry I'm late. My damned car!" (p. 212) in the same context and listeners would still be likely to infer that car trouble had been the reason for the delay through a similar schema-based inference. In contrast, the H* pitch accent on *booby-trapped* in the second sentence indicates the speaker's assumption that this is very unlikely to be in an average person's schema about things that go wrong with cars and must therefore be added to the mental representation as a new item.

A potential implication of the association between L* pitch accents and accessible items is that they can provide insight into what members of a culture consider common knowledge. In Sperber and Wilson's car example, notice how humor could be derived in a community where there had recently been a rash of terrorist car bombs. Suppose the second sentence were uttered with L* pitch accent on *booby-trapped* as follows:

Sorry I'm late. My CAR was BÓOBY-TRAPPED.

Here the implication would be that car booby-traps have become so commonplace that they belong among the schemata of the routine, modern driving experience. Thus, by looking at the low-pitched lexical items in a text, a discourse analyst could potentially discover something about the composition of the speakers' stored schemata. This is the focus of the sample analysis of this chapter in which the intonation of a lecture excerpt is analyzed to estimate the professor's assumptions about the students' prior knowledge.

L+H* Pitch Accent and Previous Knowledge

Another possible relationship between schema and text is that a lexical item may contrast with what is already assumed to be in a schema invoked by previous discourse. In this case, the speaker is likely to utter the contrasting item with L+H* pitch accent. In fact, the antonym for the contrasting word need not have actually been uttered, if it is assumed to be retrievable within the mental representation. This is illustrated by an excerpt from a conversation about Nepal (Corpus 2) in which the speaker, T, is expressing the opinion that it is difficult for a Westerner to be close friends with very traditional Nepali people:

```
1        T    It's HARD TOO↘ I MEAN they were- I KNEW a lot of
2             people who were RÉALLY TRADÍTIONAL but- (.2) it's
3             HARD to ÁCTUALLY RÉALLY be their FRIEND↘
4                 ⎡Y'KNOW    ⎤ =
5        M    ⎣YEAH↓    ⎦(.3)
6        T    =⎡You CAN'T RÉALLY have THAT much⎤ =
7        M     ⎣Well THAT'S what I was
8             having a HARD TIME IMÁGINING↓    ⎦
9        T    =in CÓMMON↓ (.2) You can TALK TO THEM and- (.5)
10            MÁYBE at a- (.1) FEAST OR SÓMETHING KIND OF KNOW
11            THEM↗ (.1) but- (.5) as FAR as their DÁILY- (1.6) you
12            KNOW↗ (.2) you j- you CAN'T END up RÉALLY being
13            their FRIEND↓.
```

In this segment, T associates L+H* pitch accents with several items to develop a contrast between being someone's close friend and being their acquaintance at a more superficial level, or merely "knowing" them, as he puts it in lines 1 and 10. Although, out of context, the lexical item *know* does not obviously contrast with being someone's friend, T relies on certain ideas of friendship assumed to be within the schemata of his listeners to make this contrast work. In lines 1–3 he uses contrastive pitch accents on *knew*, *hard*, and *friend*, creating a juxtaposition between "knowing" traditional Nepali people, which was common for him, and "actually really" being their friend, which was "hard." At this point, he has invoked a culturally based schema about friendship wherein one can differentiate between levels of closeness: to call someone a true friend goes beyond simply knowing him or her. He then continues to use L+H* pitch accents on lexical items whose antonyms are in the schema rather than the text. In his last turn, *talk, feast,* and *know,* on one hand, are contrasted with *daily* and *friend,* on the other. The implication is that the kind of talking that goes on at a formal public event such as a feast is more superficial than what goes on when one is privy to a person's daily activities, as would characterize a more serious friendship.

To summarize, many details of talk may be omitted among community members who share similar schemata. As participants build and adjust their mental representations of a discourse in progress, they rely in part on intonation to indicate how, when, and from what source to retrieve or invoke schemata. Whereas H* pitch accents direct listeners' attention to material that must be added to their mental representation, L* pitch accents associate with those details assumed by the speaker to be accessible in the mental representation of listeners through memory schemata. Finally, L+H* pitch accents associate with items whose ties to the mental representation are in contrast to what is already accessible via the schema, even if a direct antonym has not been verbalized in the text itself.

Perception of the Physical Environment

I now turn to the third source of input to one's mental representation of discourse, perception, which involves nonlinguistic material visible, audible, or otherwise perceivable in the physical environment of an interaction. Clark (1992) refers to the environment of the discourse as that which is "physically copresent" with the discourse participants. He points out that, regardless of one's ability to understand language or one's membership in a community that shares cultural knowledge schemata, that which is physically perceivable is potentially available to all. Intonation plays a role, along with deictic language, pointing gestures, and direction of gaze, in bringing certain features in the immediate environment to the foreground of attention, while other features remain in the background.

More specifically, pitch accents can be associated with lexical items whose referents are perceivable in the surrounding environment to either foreground them (H*), contrast them (L+H*), indicate that they are already believed to be present in the mental representation of the discourse (L*), or to question their relevance (L*+H). For example, in the utterance "Look out the WÍNDOW," the H* pitch accent on *window* indicates that listeners are to direct their attention to a window that may previously have been part of the background, along with the floor, the ceiling, the light fixtures, and the house plants. L+H* pitch accent could be used to contrast the window with some other portal—"Not the <u>DOOR</u>, the <u>WÍNDOW</u>!" L* pitch accent would show that the speaker assumed the window was already accessible within the foreground in listeners' minds—"The _{WÍNDOW} is BOARDED ÚP!" (It is clear which window is being referred to; we can all see it!) And finally, L*+H pitch accent could be used when a speaker was uncertain whether the window was relevant to the context at hand—We're trapped in a locked warehouse—"The _{WÍNDOW} might _{WORK}↗."

Also of interest is the intonation of deictic pronouns, such as *this, that, I,* or *you.* On one hand, it is not uncommon for these to be treated as function words: if they are not salient in the information structure of the discourse, they have no particular pitch accents and derive their pitch from surrounding tones.[5] On the other hand, deictic pronouns may also have pitch accents if they are singled out to participate in the information structure. If two entities are to be contrasted, the L+H* pitch accent may be associated with the items involved. If I say, "Not <u>THAT</u> one, but <u>THAT</u> one," it is clear that the two uses of *that* have two different referents. The L+H* pitch accent indicates that, within the set of plausible distal referents for the pronoun, a contrast is being made between two of them: one is being selected over the other. The marketing class offers another example: the pronoun *you* is routinely used without any particular pitch accent during much of the interaction among the professor and the students. Cues to the identification of the referent of *you* are provided by who is speaking, the physical location of the people in the room, eye contact, gesture, body stance, and cultural knowledge about who may address whom in American classrooms. However, in the following excerpt (Corpus 1-C), D, the professor, singles out a particular student who has been waiting for a turn to express his opinion while she has been busy with others:

D   Um, JIM, <u>YOU</u> had SÓMETHING that you were gonna
mention↓ (.6).
J   I- (.2) you CAN'T- (.2) uh I was thinking↘ you CAN'T e- export
GUNS to JAPÁN↓

D uses a L+H* pitch accent on *you* to indicate that J is being called on *in contrast to* some other student. D's utterance is shown in figure 4.5.

To summarize, what is perceivable in the physical environment is potentially accessible to participants in discourse to add to their mental representations. A speaker's intonation is one means of indicating which items are especially salient in the current communication at a particular

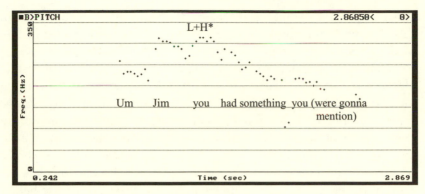

Figure 4.5 The word *you* has a L+H* pitch accent in order to single out a particular person.

point, as distinct from others in the background. These facts are part of a more general argument that prosody contributes directly to the cohesive structure of a text and is therefore part of what makes it coherent.

Unresolved Issues

For discourse analysts interested in matters of cohesion, coherence, and communication, I submit that many unanswered questions remain about the role of prosody. Traditional topics in cohesion research, such as contrast, synonymy, and deixis, can be revisited with an eye for the interaction of intonation with other variables. Other questions stem from the fact that the relationship between intonation and information structure provides clues about how the participants in discourse have organized their mental representations. Items signaled as cohesive through intonation can reveal a speaker's assumptions about a common schema shared among participants. Thus, the addition of prosodic analyses to prior work could potentially provide a better understanding of the thought processes behind speech, the structure of schemata, and the relationship between community membership and discourse. Although a prosodic analysis should never be the only one done, I recommend that where research may have previously excluded prosody, such analyses might offer new insights. I present several unresolved questions here.

What Is the Relationship Between Reference and Intonation?

Although there is undoubtedly a correspondence between low pitch and cohesive, or "given," information, it remains an unresolved question as to when speakers re-foreground referents already introduced. Earlier in this chapter, I said that there were a variety of reasons proposed in various studies for speakers to reiterate referents with H* pitch accents (Nootebaum & Terken, 1982; Terken & Hirschberg, 1994; Wennerstrom, 1994; Werth, 1984). Related to these studies are Fox's (1987) work on anaphora and Prince's (1981) taxonomy of information structure. Prince rejects the binary dichotomy between given and new information in favor of a classification system that distinguishes "new" from "brand new" and "given" from "inferable," along with other subcategories. If choice of pitch accent reflects a speaker's judgment about how accessible a referent is in the discourse, and if choice of anaphor also reflects beliefs about accessibility, research on anaphora and pitch accents could be mutually informative in developing a better understanding of reference in general.

What Is the Relationship Between Intonation and Contrast?

Contrast, clearly marked by intonation, is an interesting object of study. Werth (1984) describes contrasts in terms of set theory: in the set of twelve months of the year, a speaker can make a contrast between two alternative months—May versus June, for example. A binary contrast, in this framework, is simply a contrast between members of a set of two. As Halliday and Hasan (1976) point out, certain binary contrasts between polar opposites are inherent in the English language, such as light and dark, on and off, large and small, and so on. However, in naturally occurring speech, I have found that contrasts do not always break down so neatly, as speakers have a habit of establishing their own sets and membership criteria. They may redefine the parameters of the inherent sets mentioned above—Was it pitch dark or just dim? Was it on or just sort of flickering?—or, more interestingly, they may create unique sets for the purpose of the discourse at hand—Did you remember the photos? No, but at least I remembered the milk! Here, a set of "things I was supposed to pick up on the way home from work" has two members, photos and milk. Out of context, photos and milk would not likely be classified as a set of polar opposites, yet the contrast is coherent in this situation.

Because contrasting items are associated with L+H* pitch accents, it is possible to identify from intonation how speakers construct such sets. Discourse analyses of how people construct contrasts could in turn lead to possible conclusions about lexical storage, schema theory, and rhetorical organization. A brief example of this appears in the sample analysis for this chapter, which contains spontaneously constructed contrasts in a lecture.

How Does Intonation Reflect Community Membership
in Cross-Cultural Interactions?

In the course of communication, speakers constantly make decisions
about what is or is not accessible in others' mental representations of
the discourse in progress. Some of these judgments are derived from
an assessment of what knowledge schemata a listener is likely to have
retrieved from long-term memory, based on a sense of common community membership (Clark, 1992). In cross-cultural communication
among people from diverse speech communities, assessments of common knowledge may be more difficult to make. In such interactions,
which often involve an unequal power distribution, it would be interesting to analyze how members of one community are able (or unable)
to establish common ground with those of another, as in the following
types of interactions:

- interethnic discourse
- child-adult discourse
- doctor-patient discourse
- employer-employee discourse
- teacher-student discourse

Because intonational choices reveal participants' assumptions about
which ideas are accessible to others by virtue of commonly held schemata—L* can indicate accessibility of an item while L+H* can indicate
the accessibility of a contrasting item—an analysis of intonation could
potentially offer a new methodological tool in the study of cross-cultural
communication.

How Do Children Use Intonation as They Develop
Schematic Organization?

In the process of primary language development, as children begin to
combine words into syntax, an interesting question is how they distrib-
ute pitch accents in their utterances and what that reflects about their
mental representation of the discourse. For example, one of my own
extraordinarily precocious children is on record at about two years of age
as having uttered "MY ₜᵤᵣₙ" with L+H* pitch accent on *my* and L* pitch
accent on *turn*. From this, one might hypothesize that the child had a
schema for taking turns, including the knowledge that if someone else
was having a turn, it would soon be time for hers. She assumed that *turns*
were already a salient feature of the situation and did not feel the need
to introduce them with H* pitch accent. My suggestion is that a longitu-

dinal analysis of intonation in child discourse could reveal facts about the development of knowledge schemata. A similar methodology could be used to investigate the development of a child's sense of community membership and of others' points of view. At what stage does a child's distribution of pitch accents begin to reflect assumptions about how others are likely to have structured their mental representations of discourse? Does intonation reveal judgments about others' memory schemata? These are open questions.

How Does the Intonation of Classroom Discourse Reflect
the Building of New Schemata in the Learning Process?

By looking at the information structure of classroom discourse and the associated intonation, one could determine which items were considered new, contrastive, accessible, and so on. This in turn could lead to a better understanding of the collaboration among the students and the teacher in developing and restructuring knowledge schemata. If we return to the notion that community membership is a basis for speakers' assumptions about knowledge schemata held in common with others, an intonation analysis could potentially show what information a teacher believed to be "in the schema." A social implication of such an analysis might be to pinpoint the sorts of assumptions teachers make about the knowledge schemata of students, and from there to identify areas where members of marginalized discourse communities might need academic support. In the sample analysis that follows, I investigate an academic lecture to illustrate how such a project might be undertaken.

Sample Analysis: What Can Pitch Accents Tell Us about Learning?

This is an intonation analysis of an excerpt from a lecture on statistics, drawn from Corpus 1-B. I chose this particular monologue because I believe that it shows how intonation interacts with lexical items to help students develop new knowledge schemata. The purpose of the analysis was simply to find examples in support of the claim that the pitch accents and the lexical items with which they associated reflected the professor's assumptions about the mental representations of the lecture discourse that students in the class were likely to have constructed and about the knowledge schemata they had stored in long-term memory. Specifically, by looking at the pitch of individual words, I hoped to determine which notions the lecturer introduced as new (with H* pitch accents) and which were assumed accessible by virtue of their connection to previous knowledge schemata already invoked. The latter would be associated with either L* pitch accents if considered already accessible, or L+H* pitch accents if considered to have an association with an accessible but contrasting item.

The statistics lecture was particularly well suited for this purpose because it was given as part of a project to create videotapes of "typical American classes" for international students. The lecturer, a native speaker of English from Chicago, had been asked to give an introductory lecture in statistics to a small audience of four native speakers of English with whom she was unfamiliar. She was told only that the students had had at least some college education but had no previous knowledge of the topic. Thus, the lecture was not part of a course in progress within which members had built a body of knowledge over time; instead, the lecturer was guessing at the background knowledge of the students, based on general cultural assumptions about what the average college student in the United States might be expected to know and on whatever immediate comprehension feedback she received from the students as the lecture progressed. These facts were an advantage in the analysis phase because, as researcher, rather than guessing at the information given in previous classes, I could assume a perspective similar to that of the class members toward what was being taught.

The lecture excerpt was chosen from a point where the professor had just finished her introduction to the topic, the statistical concept of correlation. Her organization plan was to explain four examples of different studies involving correlation. At the beginning of the lecture, she had passed out a sheet with four graphs showing the correlation patterns for the four different studies. The same graphs were also drawn on the blackboard. The excerpt, the "Ducks Text," began her discussion of the first of the four graphs, involving duck species reproduction, to illustrate the concept of correlation. Briefly, the "ducks" research involved the crossbreeding of the mallard and the pintail, two closely related species of duck. The offspring were coded for appearance and behavioral characteristics. For the purpose of the statistics lecture, the study provided an example of positive correlation: the more a duck's appearance resembled that of the pintail species, the more its behavior was also similar to that of the pintail, and vice versa for the mallard. There were no student questions during the excerpt.

The text was transcribed (from Corpus 1-B) and the intonation categorized based on the system described in chapter 2, as follows:

DUCKS TEXT

1   ⇑Let's BEGÍN I think the BEST _{WAY}↘ (.2) _{TO BEGÍN}↗ (.3)
2   is by LÓOKING at- (.4) some EXÁMPLES↓. (.6) So
3   REFÉR _{FIRST OF ALL}↗ to→ (.5) the ÚPPER
4   RÍGHTHAND _{PLOT ON YOUR HÁNDOUT.}↓ (1.4) This
5   PARTÍCULAR PLOT depicts DÁTA↗ from the
6   RESÚLTS of a STÚDY on HYBRIDIZÁTION of TWO
7   _{DÍFFERENT} (.2) CLÓSELY _{RELÁTED} SPÉCIES of DUCKS↗
8   (.3) the MÁLLARD and the PÍNTAIL↗ (.7) and the
9   QUÉSTION that was being ADDRÉSSED by this
10   PARTÍCULAR _{STÚDY}↗ (.5) was whether→ (.6)
11   CROSS_{BREEDS}↗ (.4) ⇓so (.2) DUCKS that had→ (.4) a-
12   ONE MÁLLARD _{PÁRENT} and ONE PÍNTAIL _{PÁRENT}↗ (.5)
13   ⇑ if you LOOK at _{THEM}↗ (.1.4) and→ (.1) you NÓTICE
14   that a PARTÍCULAR duck LOOKS more like the
15   PÍNTAIL _{PÁRENTÚ THAN IT DOES LIKE} (.2) th- the MÁLLARD
16   _{PÁRENT}↗ (.5) is it ÁLSO _{TRUE} that its BEHÁVIORAL
17   _{CHARACT-} BEHÁVIORAL _{CHARACTERÍSTICS} (.3) WILL BE MORE
18   _{LIKE THE PÍNTAIL}↓ (.5)
19   ⇑So what we HAVE _{HERE} is we have a SCALE↗
20   (.6) where→ (.6) the→ APPÉARANCE of the _{DUCK}↗ (.5)
21   is _{RÁTED ON A SCALE} from→ ZÉRO ÁCTUALLY all the way
22   up to TWÉNTY ⇓(we only OBSÉRVE _{VÁLUES} between
23   _{FOUR AND SIXTÉEN})↗ (.5) ⇑ AND we've ÁLSO got (.5)
24   OBSERVÁTIONS on the BEHÁVIOR of _{DUCKS}↘ (.7) _{SCALED IN}
25   _{THE SAME} WAY↗ (.8) SMÁLLER _{VÁLUES} CORRESPÓND
26   to _{BÉING MORE LIKE} a- (.4) like a MÁLLARD↗ (.2)
27   LÁRGER _{VÁLUES CORRESPÓND TO BÉING MORE LIKE A}
28   PÍNTAIL↗ (.5) and we have THIS- (.5) PARTÍCULAR
29   SCÁTTER _{PLOT}↓.

My analysis focused on what the professor's intonation revealed regarding her cultural assumptions about her audience and the opportunities available for students to reorganize their knowledge schemata and create knew knowledge.

The Professor's Assumptions

After introducing the general topic and orienting students to the handout, the lecturer introduced a number of new ideas in lines 4–11 having to do with the structure of the first plot she was describing. She had no reason to assume that the students had heard of this experiment before, so she used H* pitch accent, appropriately, to introduce these notions, which were all meant to be added to the mental representation of the

discourse that students were building. The following is a list of newly introduced words with H* pitch accents associated with the first plot:

- plot
- data
- results
- study
- hybridization
- two
- closely (related)
- species
- ducks
- mallard
- question
- addressed
- crossbreeds

From these words, one may surmise that a genetics schema would be invoked by students. The question was, what did the professor assume to
be in that schema? One clue was her use of L* pitch accent on the word
parent four times between lines 12 and 16. The first two uses are shown in
figure 4.6. This intonation is noteworthy because although the word had
not been introduced into the discourse previously, the professor evidently
judged it accessible to students. Therefore, she must have also assumed
that the following facts were part of students' general knowledge, although none was actually verbalized in the lecture:

- Breeding leads to offspring
- Animals who have offspring are parents

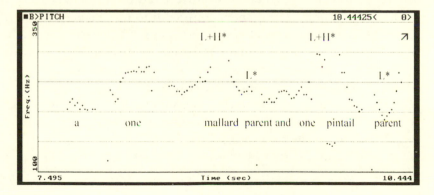

Figure 4.6 *Mallard* and *pintail* are contrasted with L+H* pitch accents while
two instances of *parent* have L* pitch accents.

- All offspring have parents
- Offspring have characteristics of their parents

In sum, the L* pitch accent on the initial introduction of the lexical item *parents* provided a clue about how the lecturer imagined her students' mental representations of the lecture: by virtue of common membership in a community having a general academic background, students were assumed to have access to a basic schema about breeding and genetics.

Restructuring Students' Knowledge

Next, I searched for an example of how contrasting information contributed to student knowledge. In three instances in the lecture excerpt, *mallard* and *pintail*, the two species of duck involved in the study, were contrasted:

1. TWO DÍFFERENT (.2) CLÓSELY RELÁTED SPÉCIES of DUCKS↗ (.3) the MÁLLARD and the PÍNTAIL↗
2. DUCKS that had a- ONE MÁLLARD PÁRENT and ONE PÍNTAIL PÁRENT↗
3. and→ (.1) you NÓTICE that a PARTÍCULAR duck LOOKS more like the PÍNTAIL PÁRENT↗ THAN IT DOES LIKE the- the MÁLLARD PÁRENT↗

In each case, the L+H* pitch accent was associated with at least one member of the contrasting pair. The second case appeared in figure 4.6. There was no reason to suppose that the students (not being ornithologists) had previously stored a schema involving these species of ducks or given any particular thought to how much variety there might be among duck species. Upon hearing them contrasted in this lecture, however, those for whom the information was new (I myself had never heard of a pintail) could construct a mental representation that included mallards and pintails as distinct species that could nevertheless interbreed. Those who considered these ideas important enough could store them in long-term memory and be able to retrieve this more enriched schema about species of ducks later, the next time the topic rolled around in conversation, (or on the exam, for that matter!)

A similar contrast was made between how a duck looked and how it behaved:

⇑ if you LOOK at THEM↗ (.1.4) and→ (.1) you NÓTICE that a PARTÍCULAR duck LOOKS more like the PÍNTAIL PÁRENT↗

THAN IT DOES LIKE the- the MÁLLARD ₚₐᵣₑₙₜ↗ (.5) is it ÁLSO ₜᵣᵤₑ
that its BEHÁVIORAL ₒₕₐᵣₐ꜀ₜ⁻ BEHÁVIORAL ₒₕₐᵣₐ꜀ₜₑᵣíₛₜᵢ꜀ₛ
(.1) WILL BE MORE LIKE THE PÍNTAIL↓

Again, students may have had no previous schema to tell them that appearance and behavior were factors worth comparing in a study of genetics. However, the professor's L+H* pitch accent on the words *looks* and *behavioral* indicated that these characteristics were being contrasted. The contrast was reinforced when the professor described how the data were graphed:

[W]e have a SCALE↗ (.6) where→ (.6) the→ APPÉARANCE of the
ᴅᵤ꜀ₖ↗ (.5) is ᵣₐₜₑᴅ ₒₙ ₐ ₛ꜀ₐₗₑ from→ ZÉRO ÁCTUALLY all the way up
to TWÉNTY ⇓we only OBSÉRVE ᵥₐₗᵤₑₛ between ꜰₒᵤᵣ ₐₙᴅ ₛᵢₓₜéₑₙ↗ (.5)
⇑ AND we've ÁLSO got (.5) ₒᵦₛₑᵣᵥáₜᵢₒₙₛ on the BEHÁVIOR of ᴅᵤ꜀ₖₛ↘

Here, *appearance* and *behavior* had L+H* pitch accents. Again, the knowledge that these variables were measured and compared could enrich a previous schema about animal breeding and genetics and be stored in long-term memory.

As these few examples suggest, part of the learning process in this lecture involved the classification of scientific notions. It is my claim that by analyzing this professor's intonation—what was presented as new, accessible, and contrastive—we have gained some insight into what she evidently assumed the students already knew and what they still needed to learn about. The intonation of contrasts also offered students the opportunity to juxtapose certain notions that they may not have previously realized were related. As it happens, this excerpt did not contain any student questions or comments, but a future analysis might also look at how such interactions confirmed or refuted the teacher's assumptions. Such an analysis applied to problematic educational settings could perhaps yield a better understanding of areas where a teacher assumed too much or two little common knowledge.

Chapter Conclusion

The purpose of this chapter has been to show that intonation plays an important role in coherence. I have introduced the notion of a mental representation that each participant builds during a discourse of the information structure of the text, that is, what is being introduced as new, and what is "cohesive," or related in some way to previous text. As participants in discourse build and readjust their mental representations of the interaction in progress, each makes judgments about how others are likely to have constructed theirs. The intonation of an utterance reveals a speaker's assumptions about what information is accessible in others' mental representations of the discourse and how the utterance is to be integrated within that representation.

I have discussed three sources of input to the mental representation. The first is the linguistic input, for which Halliday and Hasan (1976) have provided a thorough classification system of possible cohesive relationships. I have also suggested that intonation, being linguistic, should be taken into account as part of the interpretation of cohesive relationships. There are many examples in the chapter of contexts wherein pitch accents are associated with cohesive lexical items to provide crucial information about their interpretation beyond what is available from the lexico-grammatical structure alone: L* pitch accents signal that an antecedent is believed to already be accessible in the mental representation, or that for other reasons it is not to be added; L+H* signals that the cohesive relationship involves a contrast with a previously mentioned item; H* can be associated with a cohesive item to be reemphasized or brought back to the foreground; and L*+H can indicate that the relevance of a cohesive item to the information structure is being questioned. Pitch boundaries may supply information about cohesion much as conjunctions do, by indicating the level and type of interdependency among constituents.

The second source of input to mental representation is previous knowledge, which is stored in memory in associated clusters, or schemata, as a result of one's life experiences. When two people are members of a common community, each can assume that the other has certain similar memories and ways of organizing memory schemata. Therefore, not every detail needs to be provided for a discourse to be coherent; the linguistic input triggers the retrieval of associated knowledge, which, when relevant, can be integrated into the mental representation of the discourse. To show how intonation interacts with schemata, I have given examples in which L* or L+H* pitch accents are associated with lexical items that have no antecedent in the lexicogrammatical structure of the text itself. They can be interpreted only by virtue of some schema that the speaker evidently believes to be available to listeners. I have suggested that this view of pitch accents provides an interesting window into a speaker's assumptions about others' mental organization and could possibly provide a new methodological tool in the study of communication.

The third source of input to mental representation of a discourse is what is perceivable in the physical environment. The deictic language used in reference to entities in the speakers' immediate surroundings can be made specific through its intonation, much as it can with cohesive language: pitch accents can function to foreground particular items, to contrast them, or to indicate that they are assumed to be in the foreground already.

Finally, I used the sample analysis of this chapter to begin to explore the claim that intonation can lead to insights about speaker assumptions in cross-cultural communication. The cultures "crossed" in this case were those of an expert lecturer in statistics and a group of novice students. Concerning science and statistics, these two groups had in common the general knowledge of an academic community. By analyzing the professor's intonation, I could derive some of her assumptions about the students' knowledge and discover potential opportunities for learning.

5

PROSODY AS A
DISCOURSE MARKER

The questions addressed in this chapter, as in the last, pertain to discourse coherence. However, this time, instead of looking at how prosody associates with information structure, I turn to questions of how prosody contributes to the organization of a text as a whole. In addition to the pitch accent, this chapter is concerned with the role of prosodic boundaries at higher levels—shifts in initial and final pitch range and pauses—in the segmentation of the discourse. Prosodic boundaries of this kind, or paratones, can be said to perform a function similar to that of lexical discourse markers, such as *you know, anyway, so,* and *oh,* for they bracket constituents of the text into organizational units.

Schiffrin (1987), who analyzed discourse markers in a large corpus of conversation, defines them as "sequentially dependent elements which bracket units of talk" (p. 31). According to Schiffrin, "sequentially dependent" means that the occurrence of a marker depends on the sequence of events at the level of the discourse, rather than at the local level of the clause. "Bracket" means that discourse markers tend to occur at the periphery of other "units of talk." Schiffrin is deliberately flexible about how a unit is defined, pointing out that discourse markers may associate with several different types of constituents. The unit may be syntactic—the phrase or clause; semantic—the proposition; or phonological—the intonational phrase. In Schiffrin's research, "element" refers to lexical elements, but as I will argue, there is no reason to rule out prosodic elements as discourse markers as well. Henceforth, I will refer to the traditional discourse markers as "lexical" to distinguish them from prosodic elements that function in a similar manner.

The central argument of this chapter is that studies of discourse organization are only to be enhanced by the inclusion of prosodic variables. I will discuss two main topics: first, the consistent association between lexical discourse markers and certain prosodic features calls for analysis of both so that the functions of discourse markers can be better understood; and second, prosodic features themselves can function as discourse markers. On the second point, Schiffrin's definition of discourse marker is flexible enough to accommodate prosodic phenomena, which are phonological, rather than lexical, elements of a text. Certain prosodic features are sequentially dependent on discourse level organization and can bracket units of spoken discourse by associating with text at the periphery of utterances, turns, topics, and so on.

The chapter begins with the association between lexical discourse markers and certain pitch phenomena. Following is a review of research on the paratone, the pitch range shift associated with topic units, with an eye for its "marker-like" behavior in discourse. Then, I include a discussion of the elusive nature of topic structure and its effect on methodology in this type of research. Finally, I list several unresolved issues involving prosody and discourse organization. The sample analysis for this chapter is contributed by Kathleen Ferrara, who is interested in how the intonational forms of *anyway* can distinguish its adverbial uses from its function as a discourse marker.

Prosody and Lexical Discourse Markers

In many situations discourse markers are associated with L* pitch accents, to the extent that they have little ideational value and therefore do not contribute to the information structure of the discourse. Instead, they tend to have organizational and interactional functions. Pierrehumbert and Hirschberg (1990) refer to them as "cue phrases" (p. 293) among several other types of extrapropositional elements likely to be associated with L* pitch accents. The following utterance from a conversation about the languages spoken in Nepal (from Corpus 2) contains three discourse markers, two instances of *you know* and one of *like*, associated with L* pitch accents (in subscripted capital letters):

T   ... some of the VÍLLAGES $_{Y'}$ $_{KNOW}$ around the VÁLLEY ↘ $_{Y'}$ $_{KNOW}$
    <u>OUTSÍDE</u> $_{OF}$ $_{KATMANDÚ}$ are- (.3) maybe $_{LIKE}$ <u>99%</u> NEWÁRI↓.

Here, T uses the marker *you know* twice at the periphery of adverbial units describing the location of certain villages in Nepal and *like* prior to the number of Newari speakers in those areas. Schiffrin claims that *you know* has an interactional function as an appeal for the hearers' attention. Similarly, Underhill (1988) suggests that *like* can function as a marker of focus, serving as a kind of springboard to call listeners' attention to upcoming accented material. Thus, the L* pitch accent is appropriate for these interactional discourse markers, which in both cases are extrapropositional.

It is also an option, however, for lexical discourse markers to have other types of pitch accents if a speaker intends them to participate in the information structure of the discourse. As Schiffrin points out, the markers *oh* and *well* are likely to interact with the ideational structure (in my terms, the information structure). Hence, we find cases like the following wherein two instances of the marker *oh* have H* pitch accents. The conversation (from Corpus 2) centers on T having consumed a contaminated beverage in Nepal:

```
1    T    so I DRANK a LOT THAT DAY and it
2         ⎡just about       ⎤
3    M    ⎣OH GOD↓⎦ (.8)
4    T    OH maybe TWO or THREE weeks LÁTER it was the
5         TRÍPLE WHÁMMY↘ YOU KNOW↘ (1.1) WORMS→ 'n =
6    M    = RRRÉALLY?↑ (.2)
7    T    YEAH AMÉOBAS→ . . . .
```

Here, *oh* is associated twice with H* pitch accents in lines 3 and 4. Both uses correspond to Schiffrin's finding that *oh* is important in the management of information where speakers shift their stance with respect to the flow of ideas. This shift can include an affective aspect, as in line 3, where M begins to have an emotional reaction to T's story, or it can have more to do with the integration of new information into the story, as in line 4, where the speaker conducts a brief memory search prior to contributing information about the time of a later attack of parasites.[1]

This example is consistent with the findings of Local (1996), who investigated the phonetic features that accompanied various uses of the discourse marker *oh* in a large corpus of conversation. Local describes *oh* as a marker occurring at "news-informing" completion points (p. 182, citing Heritage, 1984). The most typical case in Local's data was for *oh* to be rhythmically prominent and rather long in duration, with initial glottal closure, diphthongization, creaky voice, and a falling pitch boundary (low ↓ in the current system). However, this cluster of phonetic features was found to vary in context depending on whether *oh* was free-standing or followed by additional components, offered in response to a question versus a statement, or uttered in surprise (pp. 206–207). The two uses of *oh* in my example coincide with Local's category of "oh-tokens with additional components in the same turn" (p. 206). The first use of *oh* ("Oh God!") matches what he calls an "assessment formulation" in which the speaker is evaluating received news. Although my example does not encode the level of phonetic detail of Local's study, the intonation is in line with his findings for this category: *oh* is rhythmically prominent, having H* pitch accent, and the expression *oh god* as a whole has a falling intonation—a low pitch boundary.

The same correspondence between H* pitch accent and ideational value can serve to distinguish adverbs from lexical discourse markers. Schiffrin distinguishes deictic *now*, the adverb of time, from *now*, the discourse marker of continuation, in that the former has "tonic stress and high pitch" (p. 231), whereas the latter often lacks these prosodic features. An identical finding comes from Hirschberg and Litman (1987), who analyzed the same two functions of *now* in data from a radio call-in show. This makes sense in light of the current model of intonational meaning: when *now* is a deictic adverb, the speaker is adding a new idea, "present time," into the information structure of the discourse; therefore, it is associated with H* pitch accent, or perhaps L+H* pitch accent if contrastive. As a discourse marker, however, *now* is more likely to have L* pitch accent. Being organizational rather than ideational, it is not to be added to the information structure of the discourse. A similar study that distinguishes the intonation of an adverbial from that of a discourse marker in the case of *anyway* comes from Ferrara (1997), a version of which appears in the chapter sample analysis.

Besides pitch accents, other aspects of intonation consistently coincide with subcategories of interpretation for lexical discourse markers. Consider, for example, Schiffrin's statement about the pitch boundaries of the marker *you know* in utterance-final position:

> Rising intonation conventionally signals that a speaker has not yet completed an information unit, e.g., it is used with interrogatives (incomplete propositions). As we saw earlier, rising *y'know* solicits hearers' recognition of a particular piece of information; thus, the completion of an information unit framed by *y'know?* depends on the hearer displaying knowledge of that information rather than the speaker him/herself retrieving the needed information. Falling intonation, on the other hand, conventionally indicates that a speaker has completed an information unit.
>
> My data suggest that this intonational difference reflects a pragmatic difference in speaker certainty about hearer knowledge, i.e., the

degree to which a speaker assumes his/her hearer is mutually account-
able to information. (p. 291)

In terms of the current model of intonation, whose inventory of pitch
boundaries includes more than Schiffrin's binary rising or falling options,
"rising intonation" could refer to either a high-rising ↑ or low-rising ↗
pitch boundary. Both boundaries anticipate a subsequent constituent for
their interpretation, but the high-rising boundary is especially common
in the solicitation of backchannels. Thus, it makes sense for this latter
boundary to accompany *you know* in utterance-final position when speakers are seeking hearers' confirmation that they are following the thread.
Schiffrin's "falling intonation" could be a partially falling ↘ or a low ↓
boundary. The former occurs in line 5 of the previous example, "you
know↘ (.) worms." The resulting interpretation is that T intends to continue and desires the others' attention toward what he is about to say,
but he is not asking for a confirmation of their understanding at that
point.

To summarize so far, I have hypothesized that the relationship between intonation and lexical discourse markers is consistent with the
informational contribution of a particular discourse marker. Because
many discourse markers perform organizational and interactional functions in text, they are extraneous to the propositional content and likely
to have L* pitch accents. This does not exclude the association of lexical
discourse markers with H* or L+H* pitch accents in cases where the
marker does play a role in the information structure of the discourse. In
addition, I have shown cases in which pitch accents and pitch boundaries
differentiate functions of a single lexical discourse marker. As studies of
the relationship between prosody and lexical discourse markers are fairly
sparse, the issue merits a more detailed look in future analyses.

The Paratone as a Discourse Marker

Putting lexical discourse markers aside for the moment, I will focus on
the relationships between prosody itself and organizational structure. As
introduced in chapter 2, the paratone, a term coined by Fox (1973),[2] is
the prosodic equivalent of a written paragraph, whereby speakers manipulate pitch, volume, tempo, and pause at transition points between topical constituents to indicate the relationships among those topics. I will
discuss both high and low versions of paratones and consider the possibility of embedded paratones. Finally, I will raise the question of methodology in studies of prosody and topic.

High Paratones (⇑)

Brown and Yule (1983) define the paratone as follows:

> The "speech paragraph," or paratone, like the orthographic paragraph,
> is identified by its boundary markers. . . . At the beginning of a paratone,
> the speaker typically uses an introductory expression to announce what
> he specifically intends to talk about. This introductory expression is
> made phonologically prominent and the whole of the first clause or
> sentence in a paratone may be uttered with raised pitch. The end of a
> paratone . . . can be marked by very low pitch, loss of amplitude, and a
> lengthy pause. (p. 101)

They support this view with examples of pitch and pause patterns of natural speech from a conversational monologue. It is not inappropriate to
call the paratone as previously described a "discourse marker"; it certainly
falls within the domain of Schiffrin's definition—it is an element of text
(prosodic in this case) that brackets the talk into units at the discourse
level. Indeed, we will even see examples in which the "introductory expression" of Brown and Yule's definition need not occur. The prosodic
marker alone is enough to signal the topic shift.

The association between intonation and topic structure has been noted
by numerous other researchers (Brazil, 1985; Brazil, Coulthard, & Johns,
1980; Brown, 1977; Brown et al., 1980; Couper-Kuhlen, 1986; Cruttendon,
1997; Crystal, 1969; Kutik et al., 1983; Lehiste, 1975, 1980; Menn & Boyce,
1982; Swerts & Geluykens, 1994; Tench, 1990; Wennerstrom, 1992, 1994,
1997, 1998; Yule, 1980). Pierrehumbert and Hirschberg (1990) briefly note
the phenomenon, suggesting that there is an expansion of the speaker's
pitch range to signal the beginning of a new topic, whereas the degree of
final lowering at the end of an utterance reflects its finality in the discourse
organization (p. 279). Other prosodic features may also be involved with
topic shift. According to Lehiste (1980), final lengthening and laryngeali-
zation (creaky voice) occur at the ends of topic units. In a conversational
monologue, Brown et al. (1980) identified a "topic pause" that ranged from
1.0 to 1.8 seconds (p. 68). Likewise, in data from public speaking, Stenstrom
(1986) found that long unfilled pauses characteristized topic transitions.
Volume may also be a feature, as Brown and Yule's (1983) definition describes a loss of amplitude at the end of a topic unit, but there is less empirical evidence for this in the literature. In 1994, for example, I found a statistically significant difference in pitch in paragraph-initial position in oral
readings but no corresponding difference in amplitude (p. 412).

To illustrate the high paratone, I will consider an example from
Corpus 1-B of a topic transition within a statistics lecture on correlation.

The lecture is organized around four examples of data sets graphed on a blackboard. The following text illustrates the major topic transition between the first and second graph. It is clearly marked lexically, "Let's skip for right now onto the next plot" in line 11:

1   . . . What can we see? When you make a plot of two
2   variables, what you want to do is stand back away
3   from your plot and look at its basic shape. When I
4   look at this plot, I see a cloud of points that is
5   basically oval in shape with the oval pointing from
6   lower left to upper right. That means to me that ducks
7   that had a higher plumage rating tended also to have
8   a higher behavioral rating. Ducks that had a lower
9   plumage rating tended also to have a lower
10   behavioral rating. (2.1)
11   ⇑Let's skip for right now onto the next plot, the
12   plot that's labeled demographics on your handout.
13   And this particular plot depicts data, ah, from various
14   countries. We have on the horizontal axis, the
15   percentage, the percentage of economically active
16   women in each of these countries, and on the vertical
17   axis, we have the crude birth rate. . . .

Figure 5.1 shows the transition from the final utterance of the first paragraph to the initial utterance of the second one. From the figure, we can see that the pitch range of the speaker (a woman) is expanded at the topic change: the pitch maximum in the final utterance of the first topic is 398 Hz and the pitch maximum of the initial utterance of the second is 434 Hz. This difference occurs even though the utterance prior to the

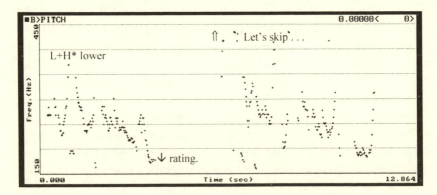

Figure 5.1   The lecturer associates a high paratone (⇑) with the shift to the new topic.

topic shift contains a contrast on the word *lower*, with L+H* pitch accent. Because we would expect the speaker to exploit a wide pitch range to make a contrast anyway, it is all the more noteworthy that a 36 Hz pitch increase marks the onset of the new topic. The figure also shows the timing of the transition: while the whole figure represents 12.1 seconds of speech, the pause between topics lasts a full 2.1 seconds.

It is also possible to have a high paratone in the absence of a lexical marker of the topic transition, as confirmed in my study of paratones (Wennerstrom, 1992). Ten speakers were asked to read aloud two similar versions of a text in which the paragraphing, as indicated by the indentation, differed. Texts were constructed so that a single test sentence could make sense in either paragraph-initial or paragraph-final position. The following is one of the text pairs used in the study with the test sentence printed in italics (it was not highlighted in any way for the subjects in the study):

Version 1:

Heavy rains and high winds will continue in the Seattle area today and throughout most of the week. Expect temperatures in the mid- to upper 50's. *These unseasonable conditions are due to a tropical storm in the Pacific.*

Version 2:

Heavy rains and high winds will continue in the Seattle area today and throughout most of the week. Expect temperatures in the mid- to upper 50's.
   These unseasonable conditions are due to a tropical storm in the Pacific. This is the same storm which caused flooding in coastal areas of northern California late Sunday night.

To compare the two versions, I measured the pitch maximum, the pitch mean, and the preceding pause length for the test sentence for each speaker. The result was a statistically significant difference in both the pause length preceding, and the pitch mean during, the test sentence, averaged across all speakers. In other words, when speakers were given an orthographic signal of topic shift, even in the absence of any lexical transition markers, they manipulated their prosodic patterns accordingly to include a paratone.

These findings on the high paratone are consistent with Givón's (1983) research on linguistic features and topic structure. His numerous cross-linguistic studies indicate that when anaphors are used at major topic junctures, they are likely to be stressed. In my terms, this presumably means that they have H* or L+H* pitch accent and the effect of a high paratone. In contrast, Givón finds that when a topic is in progress, anaphors are more likely to be unstressed or to have L* or no pitch accent and no paratone effect. Givón articulates these findings as a general principle of iconicity in the American West Coast functionalist tradition: "The more disruptive, surprising, discontinuous or hard to process a topic is, the more *coding material* must be assigned to it" (p. 18). This explanation of the interaction between cognition and topic is compatible with Chafe's (1994) opinion regarding intonation: verbalizations with high pitch are more easily processed in the face of a heavy cognitive load. Hence, at topic boundaries, where a high demand is placed on processing resources due to the introduction of new referents, settings, times, and so on, it would hardly be surprising to find a high paratone, as well as more explicit grammatical forms.

Low Paratones (⇓)

Although the high version of the paratone at a topic shift is most noticeable and dramatic, there is also evidence for what I call the low paratone, defined as a compressed pitch range associated with the onset of constituents that are subordinate to, or tangential to, the main topic. One characteristic use of the low paratone is in association with parentheticals. Bing (1985) identifies the "Class O Contour" (for "Outside Class"), which can associate with parenthetical material such as vocatives, epithets, certain tag questions, expletives, and sentence adverbials. In semantic terms, the contour contains material that "does not seem to contribute to the truth value of the sentence" (p. 21). Bing describes this contour as having a low onset and an optional rising pitch boundary at the end.

A similar contour was identified in a phonetic study (Kutik et al., 1983), in which subjects read a series of constructed sentences containing parentheticals. In these readings, each parenthetical constituent was found to occupy its own intonational phrase, with a lower-pitched declination contour, distinct from that of the main clause. That is, the parenthetical clause was not only lower in pitch but its baseline declined at a different rate from that of the main clause. After the parenthetical, the pitch rose sharply as speakers returned to the main clause.

In another study of parentheticals, Local (1992) investigated "self-interrupting" talk in naturally occurring dialogues. Again, speakers lowered their pitch for asides and then resumed the main thread of talk at a higher point in their pitch ranges. Local also found a further prosodic distinction: the rate of speech increased during these inserted segments of talk. Meanwhile, interlocutors appeared to be sensitive to speakers' intention to insert parenthetical segments—they generally did not attempt to take the floor during the self-interrupting talk, indicating that they did not confuse the associated cues with those of turn relinquishment. Finally, similar results were found by Grosz and Hirschberg (1992), who asked subjects to perform a labeling task in a corpus of three news stories. Passages labeled by subjects as parentheticals correlated with lower pitch range, rapid tempo, and an additional prosodic variable, lower volume.

Beyond the single intonational phrase, there is evidence that low paratones can extend to several phrases, as long as the material is subordinate to the main organization of the text. The following illustration, drawn from an oral narrative, demonstrates an organizational shift of gears treated prosodically as a low paratone. The speaker (an adult American man) is a graduate student in a discourse analysis class, where participants have been asked to tell personal narratives about their lives as part of an assignment. He is sitting in a small group with a tape recorder in front of him. As he begins his story, he stops after the initial utterance to make some adjustments to the tape recorder. After this "aside," he returns to his narrative. Part of the sequence (from Corpus 5) is printed here:

```
1    F   My PÁRENTSSS↘ (.3) I don't KNOW↓ My- I
2        think- (.2) the MISTÁKE MY PARENTS MADE was
3        that- (.8) they THOUGHT I wasss (.2) TOO
4        GOOD of a KID↓ (1.2)
5        ⇓That thing's SHÓOTING way UP there↓
6        SÓRRY↓ (.2) I don't know if it's LOUD ENOUGH
7        OR NOT↓ (1.3) Umm (1.8)
8        ⇑They THOUGHT I was TOO GOOD of a KID.
```

Figure 5.2 shows the pitch (in the lower part) and the volume (in the upper part) for this speaker during these transitions. As can be seen in the figure, the pitch range and volume drop as he perceives a problem with the tape recorder. These prosodic cues distinguish the little stretch of speech in lines 5–7 as separate from his main topic, the narrative about his parents. As he returns to his narrative, his pitch and volume rise again in a high paratone. The shift is not only one of topic but also one of deixis (from the past world of the story into the present world of the classroom and back again) and of genre (from the assigned storytelling task to the conversation about the tape recorder and back). He also uses a lexicogrammatical strategy to mark the act of reentry into the story world, repeating the phrase he left off with, "They thought I was too good of a kid."

In sum, the low paratone can be described as a lowering of pitch at the onset of tangential or subordinate constituents of variable size—as small as a single intonational phrase, as in Bing's Class O contours, or

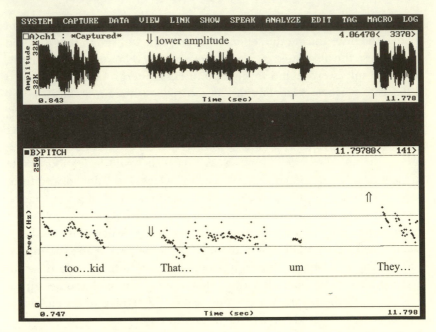

Figure 5.2 As the speaker checks the tape recorder, his pitch and amplitude decrease in a low paratone (⇓).

larger. It may also be associated with an increase in tempo and a decrease in volume.

The Embedding of Paratones

Brown et al. (1980), Couper-Kuhlen (1986), and Yule (1980) all make a distinction between "major" and "minor" paratones in reference to their level of embedding in the organizational structure of the discourse. Tench (1990) also envisions a prosodic hierarchy with two levels above the intonational phrase: the "intonation group" for Tench, like the minor paratone, consists of one or more intonational phrases that coincide with a subtopic in the discourse, while the "phonological paragraph," like the major paratone, is composed of one or more intonation groups. Similarly, Brazil (1985) and Brazil et al. (1980) recognize a hierarchical level above the intonational phrase, the "pitch sequence," "a stretch of speech which ends with low termination and has no occurrences of low termination within it" (1985, p. 182). As I read Brazil, the pitch sequence coincides with the "minor," rather than the "major," paratone: his examples of pitch sequences correspond to turn exchanges or grammatical sentences consisting of more than one clause, rather than to major paragraph-level units. Whatever the terminology, the concept of embedded paratones is consistent with the view that spoken discourse is organized hierarchically and that prosodic cues mark the levels of the hierarchy.

A study by Couper-Kuhlen (1996) will illustrate a paratone distinction at a very minor level of embedding. In her project she investigated a difference in the use of the discourse marker *because* in a series of natural dialogues. The first function of *because* was as a direct statement of the cause of a prior utterance, as in the following examples (p. 403):

1. I feel the difference, because we haven't got the heat on.
2. I wasn't that concerned about the time, because I'm not a fast runner.

In these examples, the *because* clause tells the reason for the first clause. The second meaning of *because* was of a more subordinate nature—to augment or justify prior material, as in the following example (p. 403):

She [a cat] doesn't know she's seventeen and a half, because she still chases the squirrels.

In this case the *because* clause provides the reason why the speaker knows the first clause to be true—the cat *must not know* how old she is and the speaker knows this *because* of the cat's "youthful" behavior of chasing squirrels. Couper-Kuhlen's prosodic analysis focused on the reset of declination—the natural downward drift of pitch during an intonational phrase, which restarts at the onset of each new one. The finding was that for the "direct cause" meaning of *because*, speakers began the clause with a full reset of declination, whereas, in the indirect case, their pitch remained at a more neutral level—a partial reset of declination. This finding comes as no surprise: the higher pitched onset of a *because* clause represents a return to a higher level of organization. It might be fair to consider this a minor paratone at quite a deep level of embedding (within a grammatical sentence). The more neutral pitch, on the other hand, corresponds to a continuation of the same train of thought without changing the organizational level.

In view of the complexity of topic structure, however, a word of caution about embedded paratones may be in order. Beckman and Pierrehumbert (1986) rightly point out just how complicated the organizational substructure within a topic unit may be:

[T]he stretch of discourse from one pitch range expansion to the next is not necessarily a constituent in the discourse structure. . . . This is the case because the pitch range can be expanded to initiate a subtopic

> when the larger topic marked by a previous expansion is not yet complete. The stretch from a pitch range expansion to the matched application of final lowering is a constituent. But it may be a very extended one, containing a great deal of internal structure. (p. 304)

Thus, while there is clearly a pitch-range-topic relationship, involving a nesting of constituents, we are not in a position to claim an exact one-to-one correspondence between relative pitch range, or pause length, and level of topical embedding. In the following discussion, I continue to argue for a high and low paratone distinction, leaving the precise mechanics of paratone embedding an open question.

Methodology in Studies of Topic Structure and Prosody

At this point I review in detail three studies of paratones, all dealing with natural discourse data, by Menn and Boyce (1982), Swerts and Geluykens (1994), and Wennerstrom (1998). I have chosen these particular studies because they represent a range of methodological decisions in the face of this largely uncharted territory of discourse analysis. Moreover, each study uses different types of discourse data. Menn and Boyce analyzed parent-child conversations; Swerts and Geluykens looked at instructional monologues; and I used lecture discourse of Chinese speakers of English as a second language.

Menn and Boyce (1982)

This research analyzed 1700 clauses from parent-child interactions with two- to five-year-old children. The researchers identified twelve possible discoursal relations that could occur between two sequential clauses and compared the pitch maximum, or "clause-peak pitch," of the first clause to that of the second for each pair. To normalize the measurement of pitch maximum across speakers (the children, of course, had very high pitch ranges), absolute F_0 (pitch) values were converted to z scores (that is, the standard deviation of the average pitch maximum for each speaker was used as a unit for comparison). The researchers were interested in determining whether any consistent increases or decreases in pitch coincided with particular discoursal relationships between clauses.

For the purpose of this discussion of paratones, the most interesting finding was that, of all the categories of discoursal relations, the greatest difference in pitch maximum between first and second clauses was at topic change, and this was statistically significant. Menn and Boyce (p. 346)[3] provide the following two examples of a topic change, which can be either cross-speaker or same-speaker:

1   MOTHER   I like peppermint tea.
      CHILD   Could you please stand right over there?
2   MOTHER   I don't think that's the right thing.
      MOTHER   Let's—let's do something else.

In other words, the category represents a shift from one topic to a completely different one. There were 55 such examples in their data, which, on average, were associated with a large increase in pitch. This provides clear support for a high paratone effect associated with topic shift, even in conversation.

Another interesting finding was in the category that Menn and Boyce refer to as "consonant utterance pairs," for which the second utterance elaborated cooperatively upon the first. Here are examples (p. 348):

1   MOTHER   These are like the little ones I have at home.
      CHILD   Like the baby food.
2   MOTHER   Pretty big bag.
      CHILD   For all those heavy things.

In this category, where there were 289 utterance pairs, the pitch maximum from one clause to the next was very similar. This is consistent with the idea that when the flow of the discourse continues without topical disruption, there is no prosodic disruption either.

A final finding of relevance to my paratone discussion was that "aspect change" from the first clause to the second correlated with a slight increase in pitch. Aspect changes involved "a shift in approach or focus" within the same topic (p. 346). Menn and Boyce equate this category to Ochs Keenan and Schiefflin's (1976) "incorporating discourse topic" category. Here are two examples (p. 347), the first occurring as a question, and the second as a statement:

1   MOTHER   This is a store.
      MOTHER   Do you want to play the man who owns the store?
2   MOTHER   Lots of times people drive cars.
      MOTHER   We drove a car to get here.

In the data there were 121 aspect changes in statement form and 105 in question form. In the question category there was a statistically significant increase in pitch maximum across clauses, but this increase was smaller than for complete topic changes. This finding is quite important because it indicates that at an intermediate level of topical embedding, between a full-fledged topic shift and a same-topic continuation, an intermediate level coincided with a moderate increase in pitch maximum— what others have called a "minor paratone." Other findings of this study had more to do with turn-taking than topic: both short answers and back-channels were found to have lower pitch with respect to the previous utterance.

Swerts and Geluykens (1994)

These authors report the results of both a production and a perception study of the relationship between topic and the prosodic variables of pitch and duration. I review only the production study.[4] The data, in Dutch, consisted of spontaneously produced, step-by-step instructions from one speaker to another explaining how to assemble a set of cardboard shapes into a picture of a house. Each step in the instructions was taken as a coherent topic unit. There were eleven speakers in the study, three of whom were selected for analysis due to the fluency of their monologues. Three measurements of pitch were taken. First, the pitch boundaries of each clause were coded as "low" or "nonlow." In terms of my model of intonation, the former reflected low pitch boundaries (↓) for which the pitch fell all the way to the bottom of the speaker's range, and the latter, nonlow, reflected all other pitch boundaries. For this measure, nonlow pitch boundaries were more likely to occur in the middle of a topic, whereas the low pitch boundaries were more likely to occur at the end.

The second measure of pitch was a comparison between the pitch maximum of the noun phrases (NPs) that introduced new topics versus other NPs. In addition, the position of each NP in the clause was noted, whether in first position or elsewhere. Here the significant finding was that for two of the speakers in the study, topic-introducing NPs were higher in pitch than other NPs, regardless of their position in the clause. In other words, it was the association with a new topic rather than place-ment in first position in a clause that led to an NP having a higher pitch. To connect this to previous discussions of pitch accents and information structure, although both types of NPs had H* pitch accents, an aware-ness of a higher-order organizational structure of the discourse led speak-ers to place the topic-initial H* pitch accents even higher in their range than other H* pitch accents. This supports the claim that paratone struc-ture is independent of pitch accent structure.

A third measure of pitch was a global average taken for each clause of the entire topic constituent. The hypothesis in this part of the experiment was that throughout each topic unit, there would be a clause-by-clause decrease in pitch. Although this measure did not lead to a statistically significant result, it provides an interesting methodology for future studies to assess whether levels of embedded structure exist within a topic unit.

Finally, Swerts and Geluykens measured pauses of .1 second and above in three environments: between topics, after the introduction of a new topic, and elsewhere. Much as expected, they found that, on average, pauses were longer between topics than within and that, for two of the three speakers, the pauses after introductions to new topics were also longer than elsewhere within a topic unit.

This research presents highly conclusive evidence of the relationship between prosody and topic. Although one might wish for a greater number of subjects, the study represents a solid methodology that others can replicate.

Wennerstrom (1998)

This study, involving second-language speakers of English, provides indirect evidence for the paratone as part of the English language. Twenty native speakers of Mandarin Chinese participated in the study, ranging in level of English language proficiency from intermediate to advanced.[5] All were graduate students at a major U.S. university, enrolled in a required English course, for which their final exam required them to give a short lecture in English in their field of study. The purpose of the exam was to determine whether each student was comprehensible enough to assume teaching responsibilities at the university. Three raters scored each exam on a scale of 0–3 in each of four categories; the relevant score for my discussion was a measure of English language production. The exams were taped and transcribed so that for each subject there was a speech sample and an English language score. Several measures of intonation from the speech samples were used as independent variables in a multiple regression analysis. The English language score was the dependent variable. The research question was whether there would be a statistical relationship between the intonation and the English score; in other words, did those who used more native-like intonation score better on the English test?

Among several intonation measurements, a paratone value was calculated as follows: for each lecture, the first ten major topic transitions were identified based on a common-sense judgment about the lecture organization and on the presence of lexical transition markers, such as "Now, let's move on to an example." The pitch range of the final utterance of one topic was compared to that of the initial utterance of the next topic for each transition. To control for pitch-range variation, ranges were converted to a percentage value. The statistically significant result was that the greater a subject's average pitch increase, the higher the English score. It would seem, then, that part of the acquisition of the English language involves the acquisition of this prosodic marker of topic shift.

To synthesize, all three of these studies show that pitch change is associated with topic shift in English and a closely related language, Dutch. From Menn and Boyce, we secure additional support for an intermediate level of topical embedding with a corresponding moderate pitch-range increase. From Swerts and Geluykens, we also find a pause-length correlate of topic shift and evidence for a distinction between the H* pitch accent and the high paratone onset. From my study, we add the possibility that the high paratone can be acquired by nonnative speakers of English and that it may influence raters' perceptions of comprehensibility of lectures. However, all three studies involved a struggle to obtain a clear-cut determination of topic, and I turn now to this problem.

The Problem of Topic

Authors who have worked on prosody and discourse organization tend to acknowledge the difficulty of discussing the notion of topic in a systematic way, without reference to prosody. Swerts and Geluykens (1994) describe "the danger of circularity":

> Since topic structure often cannot be identified unambiguously, especially in uncontrolled spontaneous speech materials, it is tempting to use prosodic criteria for determining the discourse structure. Such an approach ultimately leads to circularity, since it begs the question of the role of prosody in demarcating topic structure. (p. 23)

In their experiment, they attempted to solve this problem by confining their investigation to a particular, narrowly defined genre of discourse: giving step-by-step instructions. Presumably each step in the process was easy enough to distinguish from the previous one by common sense and could be considered a topic constituent in the analysis. In Wennerstrom (1998), I also wrestled with the problem of circularity in identifying topic constituents. Using the lecture genre was somewhat helpful—formal lectures tend to be deliberately organized into topics and subtopics, which are overtly marked with Chaudron and Richard's (1986) "macro-markers" (such as "Let's skip for right now onto the next plot").

In more spontaneous genres such as conversation, the delineation of topic may be all the thornier. As Schegloff (1990) documents, conversants often engage in "topic shading" (p. 51), the gradual shifting of the topic over a series of turns. A research methodology requiring an exact point of topic transition is challenged by such factors.

Swerts (1997) addressed the problem of topic by averaging the judgments of a large number of subjects (38), who were asked to divide transcripts of Dutch monologues into topic units. Subjects were divided into two groups: those who could hear the spoken version of the monologue and those who could not. By averaging all of the judgments, Swerts obtained a boundary strength measure for each constituent of text, depending on the extent to which the subjects agreed on the juncture. Swerts found statistical evidence that those who heard the spoken monologue were more unified in their judgments of topic division than those who only saw the printed version. Acoustical analysis of the monologues showed that pause, pitch reset after the juncture, and low pitch boundary before the juncture—in my terms, the features of the paratone—were all correlated with subjects' judgments. When subjects disagreed on the exact location of a topic juncture, they did tend to agree on a "transition region," no doubt related to Schegloff's (1990) idea of topic shading.

Instead of looking at topic organization "from the top down" and then measuring prosodic features at topic shifts, Menn and Boyce (1982) took the opposite approach in their study of conversation. They developed a typology of various clause-to-clause relationships and then measured prosodic features at each clause boundary. To expand on this approach, a more complex model, rhetorical structure theory (Mann & Matthiessen, 1991; Mann & Thompson, 1989, 1992) could be employed. The model encompasses topical embedding at the local level by distinguishing a "nucleus" and "satellite" relationship between two constituents, and at the global level by allowing for a building-block arrangement of each clausal interaction into a branching structure. After a rhetorical analysis of a text along these lines, an independent prosodic analysis could be done at each level of embedding to determine the paratone structure.

Another approach to developing an independent determination of topic structure would be to consider the internal lexicogrammatical features of a text that coincide with topic. Scholars such as Fox (1987), Givón (1983), Hinds (1977), Tomlin (1987), Van Dijk (1982), Wolfson (1982) and others have found consistent relationships between certain grammatical features—such as NP structure, focus constructions, clefting, and word order—and topic structure. Fox's work, for example, shows that the choice between pronouns and full NPs depends not on the sheer distance between anaphor and antecedent but rather on the level of organizational embedding. In her data, full NPs were more frequent at transitions to higher organizational levels, whereas pronouns were more likely to be

embedded within topic constituents. Again, one could search for correlations between such features and prosodic variables at topical junctures.

To sum up this long discussion of methodology and topic, I believe
that prosodic studies would benefit from a more fully defined model of
discourse organization. This is particularly the case in casual speech,
where there is less overt agreement about what a "well-organized" topic
unit is supposed to look like. I have recommended existing models of
rhetorical embedding (such as Mann & Thompson's, 1989) as a good
starting place for investigations of prosody and topic. I have also suggested
that previous work on the grammatical features of topic be integrated with
prosodic studies. In the long run, I believe that just as the study of topic
can enhance research on prosody, the study of prosody has the potential
to add a triangulation to research on discourse organization. If we can
recognize consistent correlations between prosody and rhetorical structure and combine this knowledge with established relationships between
lexicogrammatical features and topic structure, then we are closer to a
more robust definition of topic.

Unresolved Issues

There is still much research to be done on the subject of prosody's role as
a discourse marker in the organizational structure of discourse. If we regard prosodic features as internal elements of text, it becomes evident that
a marriage of lexicogrammatical and prosodic treatments of text organization would benefit all. I also encourage the inclusion of a variety of genres
for analysis. There has been a tendency in paratone research to steer toward genres of discourse such as the giving of lectures and directions, which
can be parsed most safely into clearly defined topic units. However, a
broader generic scope might lead to more universal findings about the
nature of prosody with respect to discourse structure. Finally, I suggest a
need for the expansion of research on prosody and discourse organization
into a wider variety of languages and dialects. The following are a number
of unresolved questions that focus mainly on the integration of prosody
with what is already known about discourse organization.

What Can the Study of Prosody Add to Our Knowledge of Lexical Discourse Markers?

Studies such as Schiffrin's (1987) could be replicated to determine
whether distinctive prosodic features consistently coincided with certain
functions of discourse markers. Schiffrin mentions some intonational

characteristics of the discourse markers in her study, but that is not her main focus. Research such as Local (1996) notwithstanding, studies of the prosody of discourse markers has been sporadic, and much remains to be discovered through the investigation of other data corpora, in other dialects and genres. The sample analysis for this chapter, by Ferrara, provides a model of how to design exactly this type of project. A similar methodology could be applied to discover the prosody of other discourse markers. The pitch accents of discourse markers in particular contexts, their intonation boundary shapes, their relative location in the speaker's pitch range, their duration, and the length of pauses surrounding them are all matters of potential interest.

What Is the Relationship Between Prosody and Rhetorical Structure?

As discussed in a previous section on problems of topic, researchers often rely on a common-sense justification for the division of text into organizational or "topical" constituents. A more rigorous approach would consist of hierarchically analyzing a spoken text into organizational units and then looking for consistent prosodic features at each level of organization. A well-designed rhetorical model for this purpose is Mann and Thompson's (1989) rhetorical structure theory, which incorporates a complex vision of topic not as a monolithic structure, but as a set of hierarchically embedded components. One could measure the variation in pause length, pitch range, or volume between constituents at various rhetorical junctures. Such a study could provide more information about degrees of paratone structure corresponding to hierarchical levels of organization.

How Does Prosody Interact with Grammatical Correlates of Topic?

Previous research on the behavior of anaphors with respect to topic shift has shown a tendency for more explicit grammatical forms to coincide with the initiation of new topics whereas pronominal forms occur mid-topic (Fox, 1987; Givón, 1983). This claim could be tested for spoken discourse by searching for correlations between prosodic structure and the distribution of anaphors. One could consider whether high paratones would coincide with the onsets of constituents containing full NPs versus those with pronominals. (This is not to be confused with a study of the pitch accents of anaphors, another interesting piece of research in its own right.) The findings of such a study could be combined with those from the previous question to achieve a triangulation effect: studies of rhetorical structure, studies of grammatical correlates of topic, and studies of paratones could all potentially reinforce each other.

It would also be interesting to study topic shift in languages such as Korean that have overt lexicogrammatical markers of topic. Do lexical markers substitute for or coincide with prosodic parameters of topic in such languages?[6] In languages wherein topic is encoded in the grammar, some problems of circularity encountered in the identification of topic in the English and Dutch data could possibly be avoided.

What Is the Relationship Between Paratone and Key?

Paratone, the pitch range choice associated with topic, and key, the pitch range choice associated with attitude or stance, have been treated separately in the literature on prosody. I have also presented them as separate phenomena in this volume. However, I suspect that they are both part of one larger phenomenon, that of pitch range shift as an indicator of general discontinuity—of topic, attitude, and perhaps other categories. As Yule (1980), Couper-Kuhlen (1986), and others have pointed out, minor paratones may be embedded within major ones. At some point such subdivisions come down to the pitch range choice a speaker makes at the level of each intonational phrase: the choice of key. Although this issue may boil down to one of terminology, the actual work of demonstrating that the concepts are compatible remains to be done.

What Is the Relationship Between Prosody and Discourse Organization in Other Discourse Genres?

To say the least, the interaction between organizational structure and prosody is likely to show variation from genre to genre. As Swerts and Geluyken's (1994) study demonstrates, certain genres of discourse lend themselves more to organizational division than do others. In their study, the genre of "giving instructions" was sufficiently restricted to confine the identification of "topic" to a single instruction out of a set. I have found the lecture genre to afford the easiest access to clear rhetorical divisions. For some genres, however, terms such as "topic structure" and "topic shift" may not be appropriate at all. Even so, a consistent relationship between prosody and certain structural components of the genre might still exist. For instance, Bauman (1986) found that in the genre of humorous anecdotes, the punch line was often delivered in quoted speech, accompanied by marked prosodic shifts. Likewise, in the genre of the oral narrative, Labov (1972) noted that evaluative components were frequently associated with marked phonological features, among which might well be prosodic features. Tench (1991) found distinctive intonational features in several genres including newscasts and public and private prayers.

More examples are needed of research identifying structural features of prosody that characterize particular genres of speech.

Sample Analysis

At this point I turn to this chapter's sample analysis, by Kathleen Ferrara, in which the intonation of a rarely studied lexical discourse marker, *anyway*, is investigated. The analysis is drawn from a larger study (Ferrara, 1997) in which the sociolinguistic distribution and historical development of the marker are discussed in greater detail. In its present form, this study succeeds in identifying three unique intonational forms of *anyway*, each of which corresponds to a distinctive meaning. Ferrara hypothesizes that these distinct subtypes of *anyway* have developed through a historical process of grammaticalization. More generally, the study demonstrates that an analysis of discourse markers is potentially richer when prosody is included. Furthermore, it provides a model for how other lexical discourse markers might be researched.

Intonation in Discourse Markers—The Case of *Anyway**

Schiffrin's work (1987) on discourse markers constitutes a powerful foundation for comprehending the structure and social handling of language. After examining the function of discourse markers such as *well, now, y'know, but, then,* Schiffrin concludes that they work to subordinate and coordinate various levels of a spoken or written text, as well as to express interactional alignments and convey social meanings. If discourse markers follow the course of other aspects of language—and why not?—we can expect them to follow the course of grammaticalization hypothesized for many other aspects of language (Hopper & Traugott, 1993) in that they appear to have evolved from lexical items.

This analysis uses evidence from intonation, along with syntactic position and semantic information, to investigate this evolution and to differentiate three different subtypes of *anyway*. Two are adverbial and one is a discourse marker. I suggest that the discourse marker has evolved from the other two. The discourse marker *anyway* is a topic shifting and resumption signal (see Ferrara, 1997; Polanyi & Scha, 1983; Prince, 1982).

---

*This section was contributed by Kathleen Ferrara.

This analysis explores the fact that *anyway* has other, although not unrelated, meanings (chiefly adverbial) in addition to being a discourse marker. As Stein (1985, p. 299) observed, this fact "is also true of other discourse markers of Modern English such as expressions like *well*, which has quite a range of syntactic functions besides acting as a discourse marker." An investigation into the polysemy of discourse markers may yield valuable insight into the development of these "mystery particles," as Longacre (1976) termed them. A study of intonation contours is central in providing evidence of these distinctions.

There has been a tendency in the literature to treat discourse markers as separate from other aspects of language, as somehow special or rare. One might suspect that they are not. Just as Schwenter and Traugott (1994) and Hopper and Traugott (1993) observe, discourse markers may actually reflect cases of grammaticalization (GR). They see GR as involving functional change, with ripping to initial position and addition of intonational cues. This hypothesis of addition of intonation cues needs to be investigated.

Accordingly, this study provides a quantitative and qualitative analysis of the linguistic variation of the form, explores its grammatical history, and illustrates the value of studies of intonation for understanding discourse principles of organization.

Data

The principal source of data was 167 tape-recorded oral narratives that contained 150 tokens of *anyway*. These were part of a larger corpus of natural, elicited spoken narratives gathered in sociolinguistic interviews in Texas from 1992 to 1994 from people of all ages, educational levels, and ethnicities (chiefly Anglo, African American, and Hispanic). Narratives were replete with the token *anyway*, occurring as often as 2.5 times per narrative. The interviews were conducted by trained student fieldworkers, who interviewed friends, relatives, and neighbors in familiar surroundings. As shown in table 5.1 more than a third of these narratives (36%) contained the relevant tokens. In all, 60 speakers produced 150 tokens of spoken *anyway* or its variants.

TABLE 5.1 Tokens in the Texas Narrative Corpus

	N	(%)
Spoken narratives not containing *anyway*	107	(64)
Spoken narratives containing *anyway*	60	(36)
Total number of narratives	167	(100)

Method of Analysis

Oral speech samples were used to identify form and function differences and quantify types of *anyway* by percentages. Not only was the target utterance in focus but both preceding and succeeding utterances were used to provide the context for determining meaning. These contextual clues were used in tandem with analysis of linguistic features such as syntactic position, semantic and pragmatic information, and intonation contours. For the study of intonation contours, two pitch tracking computer software programs were used on a subset of male informants in the corpus (to be described).

The Study

The purpose of the study was to establish the discourse marker *anyway* as independent of two lexical uses of *anyway* by defining and illustrating three subtypes of *anyway* that are not interchangeable: two adverbs and one discourse marker. I term the two adverb types *Anyway*₁ and *Anyway*₂. Only the third subtype, labeled *Anyway*₃, is a discourse marker. It alone is a sentence-initial adverbial conjunct that functions to connect utterances or levels of discourse. The other two subtypes retain semantic content and occur mainly in sentence-medial or sentence-final position. Likewise, the intonation study shows that these types of *anyway* differ in acoustic as well as in syntactic and semantic properties. In (1), both definitions and short examples are given to show the existence of three subtypes. Following that, intonation contours are discussed.

The first subtype, *Anyway*₁, carries the meaning "besides." I label it ADDITIVE *Anyway*. The second subtype, *Anyway*₂, carries the meaning of "nonetheless." It is termed DISMISSIVE *Anyway*. Halliday and Hasan (1976) discuss this form. The third type, the discourse marker, is labeled *Anyway*₃, or RESUMPTIVE *Anyway*. It reconnects utterances to chunks of discourse. It provides macro-level organizational continuity.

(1) Types of *Anyway*

a. ADDITIVE *Anyway*₁ (semantically equivalent to *besides*)
   We didn't rent the apartment because it was too expensive. It was in a bad location *anyway*. (*besides; *nonetheless*)
b. DISMISSIVE *Anyway*₂ (semantically equivalent to *nonetheless*)
   It was ugly but he wanted to buy the dog *anyway*. (*nonetheless; *besides*)
c. RESUMPTIVE *Anyway*₃ (a discourse marker that reconnects utterances to chunks of discourse)
   He drove to the dealership. He'd always wanted a Jag. I think I heard a noise. *Anyway*, he decided to buy one. (discourse marker)

Linguistic Subtypes of *Anyway*

In this section the three linguistic subtypes of *anyway* are explicated. The examples from Texas speakers in (2) illustrate typical uses of *Anyway*₁ with the meaning of "besides."

(2) Examples of ADDITIVE *Anyway*₁ (can be replaced with *besides*)

a. JUAN   One of them ended up breaking my pole so I had to buy a new one. It wasn't made for big fish. We didn't think there was big fish in there *anyway*, just you know average size.

b. PHIL   You basically have to point out to ocean and paddle as fast as you can towards the oncoming waves which we couldn't see very well *anyway* because it's deep water (.5) and the waves don't start to rise up until they're pretty close and it's too late to escape.

c. JOE   And there was an industrial building which had the lights on all night so (2.0) illumination was there, I mean, to a degree I could see. I had 20/20 vision then *anyway*. So, all of a sudden I saw this guy trying to get in the window!

d. OMAR   (after car ploughs through his apartment) We're not gonna move back. No uh we didn't like the place (laugh). It was full of cockroaches *anyway*.

Although it is possible for *Anyway*₁ to occur clause medially, *Anyway*₁ typically is syntactically positioned at the end of a clause, and the clause that precedes it is sketched out in (3). The structure in this representation shows that the clause containing *Anyway*₁ is presented as not necessary to the argument. In utterances with *Anyway*₁, typically the speaker gives a conclusion and one reason to justify it, then adds the clause containing *Anyway*₁ as an extra reason. The speaker pretends not to utilize the argument containing *Anyway*₁ but does evoke it.

Ducrot (1980) has described the meaning in French of *d'ailleurs* with a similar profile and the schema in (3) is similar to that of Ducrot.

(3) TYPICAL SENTENCE PATTERN WITH *ANYWAY*₁

Conclusion	Argument given to justify conclusion	Reason presented as not necessary to the argumentation (speaker pretends not to utilize the reason but does invoke it)	*Anyway*₁ *besides* **nonetheless*

In (4) examples from the corpus of the second subtype of *anyway* are shown. *Anyway₂*, DISMISSIVE *Anyway,* usually co-occurs with a negative observation followed by *but* and a positive or neutral evaluation. Rather than meaning "besides," it is equivalent to "nonetheless."

(4) DISMISSIVE *Anyway₂* (can be replaced with *nonetheless*)

a. PAT   Me and another guy did not qualify but we (1.5) got to go along
           on the trip *anyway* because we had been in the semifinals.

b. VICKIE It would have been a special moment *anyway* but it was re-
           ally special for me because I had lost my first baby.

c. JAMES   We saw this car mhm parked right outside with brights on
           (.) just like shining right (xxx) on our house. And we got
           (.) we got all scared and (1.5) you know, and we (xxx) going
           to call the cops. And we say, "No, don't call the cops." And
           like five minutes later the cops came *anyway* because ((laugh))
           one lady who lives down the street called the cops on us.

d. BILL   (describing a robbery at the grocery store where he worked)
           But the kicker was that Robert Davidson had gotten out of
           out of prison about three days before this (.) and he had
           come to Food Town applying for a jo:b (.) and they didn't
           need any help and so I guess he figures, "Well since they
           won't hire me I guess I'll just take their money *anyway.*"

The typical structure showing a (usually) negative observation followed by *but* and a positive or neutral evaluation is given in (5)

(5) TYPICAL SENTENCE PATTERN WITH *ANYWAY₂*

Negative observation	but	Positive or neutral	*anyway₂*
		evaluation	*nonetheless*
			*besides

The preceding two subtypes of *anyway* are adverbial. Examples of the
third subtype, the adverbial conjunct or discourse marker, are given in
(6). Notice that the discourse marker *Anyway₃* is always sentence-initial.
This is RESUMPTIVE *Anyway₃*. As a discourse marker, it subtly signals a
resumption of the trend of thought of the narrator.

(6) Narrative Extracts containing DISCOURSE MARKER *Anyway₃*

a. ANNIE   And um ((laugh)) and I don't know how if you buy blanks
           or what but somehow we worked it out so that you can make
           a gunshot noise but we didn't actually shoot anything. *Any-
           way,* so we sent my brother up there.

b. BRAD   Well, I drove him back home even though we weren't that
           far. I felt bad. John would do anything and we needed to

be careful. (2.0) *Anyway* I took him home and we went in-
side his house and his mom saw him and said, "John what
happened?" And he knew if he told her the truth that he'd
be in trouble ...

C. WALTER   Yeah I had a- my grandmother, my dad's mother, Mary Inez
Dromgoole, was very she had this thing about germs. She
was very clean and you couldn't drink out of other people's
bottles or you couldn't put something in your mouth and
bite it and give it to somebody else to eat. (2.0) *Anyway* back
in the 50s it was black and white t.v.

Consider in detail the usage in example 6b. In this segment from a
narrative, Brad says in the time sequenced portion of the narrative, "I
drove him back home." He then gives some orientation, background
information (his feelings, relative position, a character's temperament),
pauses, and then resumes with the preterite, "I took him home." He signals his resumption of the storyline with *Anyway*₃. By using *Anyway*₃ Brad
is able to signal that the event portion of his narrative is being resumed.
It is too simplistic to say that *Anyway*₃ gives cohesion to the preceding
sentence only, because there are examples that span much more of the
text. I claim that *Anyway*₃ connects more than two sentences; it connects
two levels of representation, and the resumptions can span large passages
of intervening text in personal narrative.

This syntactic markedness of preposing a former adverb is one device employed in English to indicate discourse markers of organization.
Although there is some uncertainty about how English utilizes specialized grammatical items to demarcate discourse segments or chunks, there
is evidence that English utilizes a specialized syntax of preposing or clause
adjunction of otherwise ordinary lexical items (frequently former adverbs)
to provide macro-level organizational cues (cf. Dry's [1983] explication
of *now*, as in "Now Esau was a hairy man.")

Intonational Differences

In addition to word position difference and functional differences, there
are intonational differences between the three subtypes of *anyway*. This
concertizing of clues is fully unsurprising. What is surprising is that to date
few studies of discourse fully use information contained in intonation.
This section attempts to provide a model for how this can be done in
discourse.

In a number of samples collected, the same speaker used two subtypes of *anyway* within the same narrative. Adverbial uses of *Anyway*₂

alongside *Anyway₃*, the discourse marker, clearly underscore the need for a general understanding of the role of *anyway* in discourse. How do listeners know the difference? We have already seen that syntactic position is one cue because the discourse marker always comes in initial position and is a sentence adjunct, bleached of the semantic sense of the two adverbs, but there are additional cues of an acoustic nature. I claim that the three types of *anyway* carry different intonational patterns. These pitch contours can be heard by ear and, as shown in the next section, they can be determined by computer pitch extraction programs. By using different types of *anyway* from the same speaker, we can be sure of a base of comparison. Cross-subject measurements are also valuable in illustrating differences.

INTONATION STUDY The intonation study subjected natural tape-recorded language samples from principally adult male speakers to two different pitch extraction programs, Phonology Lab in a Box (PLIB) and Signalyze™.[7] The early results of using the Signalyze program, a Macintosh application, provided evidence that separate contours for each of the three subtypes were clearly visible. Next the tape-recorded speech samples were input to a more sophisticated program, the PLIB. This PLIB uses an IBM PC to digitize, edit, and replay speech and calculate and display fundamental frequency (F_o) and amplitude. The program was written especially to deal with long stretches of discourse.

I compared usage of each subtype by five separate men and incidentally looked at F_o of three women.[8] It was also possible to take advantage of five sets of the same speakers using two different subtypes of *anyway* in the same context to extract fundamental frequencies for each subtype. This was useful in having a point of comparison not only across speakers but within speaker discourse. The intonation contours evident in these pitch extractions also held up across speakers. (For the acoustic analysis, men's voices were preferred because the range of pitch variation among men is less than that for women.)

Three distinct contours were visible. *Anyway₁* shows a flat or level intonation contour with the value for two men maintained at a steady level of 85 Hz. There was an average fluctuation of 11 Hz between high and low points, not significant. This pattern may be represented by L* L in the Pierrehumbert notation (Beckman & Pierrehumbert 1986).[9]

Anyway₂ shows a quite different pitch contour. A gentle rise is followed by a gentle slope down. The average drop in value was 29 Hz. The peak value for men averaged 119 Hz and the average low was 93 Hz. A typical contour was 129–101 Hz. We can represent the pattern as H* L.[10]

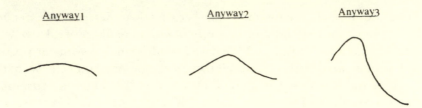

Figure 5.3   Three versions of *anyway*.

However, the pitch contour for *Anyway₃* is very distinct from that of the other two types. Men demonstrated a sharp rising peak up to 181 Hz, followed by a low with an average drop of 57 Hz. A typical contour for *Anyway₃*, the discourse marker, followed the pattern 153–181–123. We can represent this as L + H* L (H% or L%).[11] The three distinct intonation patterns for *Anyway1, 2*, and *3* are represented by the contours in figure 5.3. As these sketches show, the discourse marker, *Anyway₃*, has the most dramatic and attention-getting contour. Sample pitch tracking is shown in figures 5.4–8. The figures illustrate contours for the three types of *anyway*, a comparison of *Anyway₁* and *Anyway₃* by the same speaker, and a sample contour by a female speaker for *Anyway₃*.

Intonation provides one strong clue to the perhaps unconscious signaling in discourse about how to perceive organization. McLemore (1991) reports that phrase-final low tones are used in discourse to segment. That is clearly what *Anyway₃* is achieving. It functions as a discourse marker that alerts listeners to segment out the previous short interchange in favor of the macro-level organizational schema. It is the push-pop marker that Polanyi and Scha (1983) discuss.

Frequency Differences in Three Subtypes of *Anyway*

In addition to intonation differences and syntactic and pragmatic differences, there are large differences in the frequency of use of the adverbial and discourse markers. As table 5.2 shows, the discourse marker, *Anyway₃*, was far more frequent than the adverbial uses *Anyway₁* and *Anyway₂*. The adverbs accounted for only 11% of all tokens. However, *Anyway₃*, the discourse marker and its variables, accounted for 89% of the cases of *anyway*. Thus, the discourse marker is frequent enough in tape-recorded narratives to bear a more fine-grained analysis. This finding of increased frequency for the more grammatical type versus the content types of *anyway* is consistent with notions of GR proposed by Hopper and Traugott (1993).

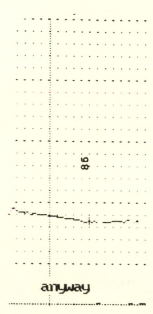

Figure 5.4 Sample pitch contour for *Anyway*₁ by a male speaker.

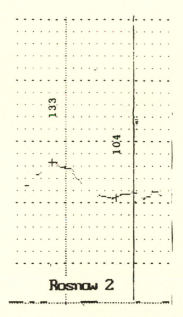

Figure 5.5 Sample pitch contour for *Anyway*₂ by a male speaker.

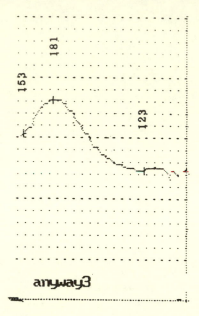

Figure 5.6   Sample pitch contour for *Anyway*₃ by a male speaker.

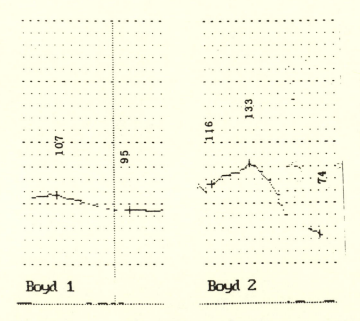

Figure 5.7   Sample comparison of pitch contours for *Anyway*₁ and *Anyway*₂ by a male speaker.

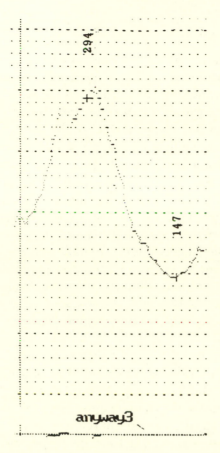

Figure 5.8   Sample pitch contour for *Anyway₃* by a female speaker.

<small>TABLE</small> 5.2 Distribution of Three Subtypes of *Anyway* in Tape-Recorded Narratives

Part of Speech	Subtype	N	(%)
	*Anyway*₁ Additive	6	(4)
Adverbs			
	*Anyway*₂ Dismissive	11	(7)
Discourse marker	*Anyway*₃ Resumptive	133	(89)
Total		150	(100)

127

Summary and Discussion

The discourse marker *Anyway₃* is a frequent token in narrative, occurring in a third (33%) of the tape-recorded narratives in the Texas corpus. Each speaker in the corpus who uses *anyway* uses, on average, 2.5 tokens per narrative. The discourse marker *anyway* (type 3) is far more common than either of the other two adverbial types of *anyway* (types 1 and 2). The discourse marker accounts for 89% of all tokens of *anyway. Anyway₃* is used to manage discourse and give clues to the listener about how to organize the talk. It is used more frequently by a speaker to resume his or her own thread of discourse (74%) than to regain control of talk from the co-participant "listener" (26%). That is, it is speaker-triggered more often than "listener"-triggered. However, it arises in interaction and is ultimately driven by interactional needs. It functions as a signal to listeners of how to interpret segments or chunks of discourse. It interweaves levels of discourse, showing the difference between orientation and event elements, for example. Thus, we can conclude that a major function of *Anyway₃* is digression management in interaction. Primarily it serves as self-digression management (74%).

Another important finding is that if indeed the discourse marker under study here evolved from adverbs, the characterization of *anyway* supports Hopper and Traugott's (1993) theory of GR. The historical development of discourse markers appears to follow the principle of economy, specifically the economy of reusing extant forms for new purposes (Hopper and Traugott, 1993, p. 65). Hopper and Traugott say that "to date there is no evidence that grammatical items arise full-fledged, that is, can be innovated without a prior lexical history in a remote (or less remote) past" (p. 128). My claim is that the discourse marker *Anyway₃*, as a development out of adverbial use, has arisen as a signaling device *in interaction* that the previous short segment is to be treated by the listener as a digression, in other words, to meet a pragmatic need. (Compare Sankoff and Laberge's [1984] discussion of Tok Pisin future marker *bai* arising from *baimbai*.)

A second issue that the findings here bear upon is the strong hypothesis of unidirectionality of GR. The suggested development that *anyway* follows is a typical path of development, a cline of decategorialization. According to Hopper and Traugott (1993), clines are "paths along which certain grammatical properties cluster around constructions with family resemblances" (p. 105). As seen in (7) typically the starting point is a full category such as a noun or verb, and the tendency is for the lexical item to become more grammatical. Thus, the theory of unidirectionality hypothesizes that diachronically all minor categories have their origins in major categories such as noun or verbs. Hopper and Traugott (1993, p. 104) illustrate a change happening in a cline of categoriality:

(7) CHANGE IN A CLINE OF CATEGORIALITY

Major category	>	Intermediate degree	>	Minor category
(noun or verb)		(adj/adv)		(prep, conj, aux, pro, demonstrative, "closed" categories)

Evidence of a cline of categoriality may be seen in the grammaticalization of the modern discourse marker *anyway*. A lexical item, a noun, *way* (meaning "manner") and commonly associated adjective *any* came to be used as an adverb *anyway*. (Cf. An example of the noun from the corpus: "I couldn't get any more scared. I mean there just wasn't *any way*.") The lexical item *anyway*, found clause medially or finally and serving as an adverb, then came to serve a needed discourse function and became syntactically fixed as the clause-initial discourse marker *anyway*. To do this involved bleaching and the taking on of a different intonation pattern. A further indication of GR is the noted increased frequency of the discourse marker shown here (89% discourse marker vs. 11% adverbs in the corpus). Hopper and Traugott (1993, p. 103) see increased frequency as an indication of GR.

The study of how forms are distributed in discourse is indispensable in the understanding of a powerful process such as GR. As Chafe (1988, cited in Hopper & Traugott, 1993, p. 173) writes, "[W]e cannot overlook the role of intonation as a morphosyntactic phenomenon." Accordingly, the study of intonation in discourse is an important next step. This study has attempted to illustrate how analyses of intonation can help elucidate features of discourse such as discourse markers.

I claimed that intonation has played a role in the development of the discourse marker *anyway* from previous adverbs. The intonation differences are recognizable and measurable. The ultimate theory of language will almost certainly depend on a full understanding of discourse and discourse management techniques and the role of intonation. The study of the topic shifting and resumption signal *anyway* is merely a beginning.

Chapter Conclusion

The focus of this chapter has been on the interaction of prosody with the large-scale organization of discourse. I began by pointing out predictable correspondences between lexical discourse markers and certain prosodic patterns. First, the pitch accents associated with lexical discourse markers tend to support the function of those markers in the discourse: many markers, organizational and interactional rather than ideational in function, have L* pitch accents. In Pierrehumbert and Hirschberg's terms, they are "extrapropositional." However, if certain discourse markers do contribute to the information structure of the discourse, speakers have the option of associating them with other pitch accents. I have also suggested that for lexical discourse markers that have more than one function, intonational patterns can often disambiguate these functions.

In reviewing the literature on the paratone, I have argued that this cluster of prosodic features—altered pitch range, pause, and possibly volume—functions as a discourse marker to bracket the text into hierarchical units of topical organization. When a speaker changes to a new topic, there is likely to be a high paratone at its onset, whereas the end of the topic is low in the pitch range. In contrast, a low paratone is initiated lower in the speaker's pitch range, at a lower volume, and in some cases at a faster tempo, and is associated with subordinations, parentheticals, and digressions—that is, material not meant to be part of the main topic. Paratones may be a matter of degree, reflecting nested structures of discourse organization. I have cautioned, however, that it would be beneficial to develop a better understanding of "topic structure" in embarking on future studies. Several unresolved issues have been presented, involving the general problem of the interaction between prosody and discourse organization. By turning to existing models of topic structure and looking for associated prosodic patterns, one could achieve a better understanding of the role of prosody as a discourse marker. In addition, studies could examine the correspondence between prosody and other linguistic features shown to correlate with organizational structure, such as lexical discourse markers, anaphora, and topic markers in other languages. Research is also needed on prosody and organizational structure in different genres of discourse, different dialects, and different languages. Finally, Ferrara's sample analysis of the intonation of *anyway* has left us with a good example of how a prosodic analysis can enhance previous discourse analyses whose focus has traditionally been lexicogrammatical.

6

INTONATION AND SPEECH ACT THEORY

The focus of this chapter is the relationship between intonational meaning and the pragmatics of spoken language within the broad framework of speech act theory. One central question is how intonation contributes to the "illocutionary force" of an utterance—that is, how does the intonation help to convey the speaker's intention in producing it. I will examine cases wherein intonation can be the key factor in distinguishing one speech act from another, even if the lexicogrammatical structure remains constant. For example, intonation plays a role when what is grammatically a statement is uttered with a question intonation, as in "We're out of chocolate syrup?" which in my family sounds more like an accusation directed at the person whose job it is to do the shopping than a statement of fact.

After a brief historical overview of the development of speech act theory, I will review writings on the contribution of intonation to the structure and interpretation of speech acts. Such work reveals both a direct and an indirect interaction between intonation and illocutionary force: intonation contributes a direct meaning component to the illocutionary force of an utterance, as do grammar and the lexicon. There may even be "intonational idioms," certain contours whose very shapes convey conventional meanings. However, the illocutionary force conveyed by intonation can also be interpreted indirectly via pragmatic principles in con-

131

text. A speech act can be indirect with respect to its intonation just as it can be indirect with respect to its lexicogrammatical structure. Afterward, I will consider the more general issue of how intonation should be integrated into a speech act theory framework—is intonational meaning properly considered semantic or pragmatic? Finally, I discuss several unresolved issues concerning speech acts and intonation. A sample analysis contributed by Philip Gaines provides a pertinent example of how an intonation component can add a new dimension to our understanding of speech acts in courtroom proceedings. Using data from the O. J. Simpson trial, he argues that lawyers can manipulate the intonation of tag questions to achieve a particular illocutionary force.

Historical Overview

In discussions of speech act theory, three philosophers have made the most substantial contribution: Austin, Searle, and Grice. Writing in the 1940s to the 1970s, these three were entering a philosophical debate already in progress between the earlier logical positivists, such as Ayer and Russell, and the pragmatists, such as Peirce, Strawson, and Wittgenstein in his later writings. The positivists wanted to reduce language to a mathematical system of logic. Any utterance could be parsed into atomistic components and its "truth value" verified based on a one-to-one mapping between those components and a real-world state of affairs. A distinction was maintained between confirmable facts, at the core of a linguistic model, and any emotional, expressive, or moral overtones, considered extraneous to meaning. The pragmatist philosophers, however, rejected the notion of absolute truth and argued that linguistic meaning resided instead in the consequence of an utterance in the real world. Strawson (1952) attacked the adequacy of truth value as a measure of interpretation on the grounds that an utterance could be *neither* true *nor* false if the presuppositions behind it were false. One can see the pragmatists' influence in later works of discourse analysis in that, in simplest terms, they recognized that a philosophy of language is not fully explanatory if it ignores the role of context. Continuing in this vein, Austin, Searle, and Grice elaborated the pragmatist philosophy further into speech act theory.

John L. Austin

In a series of lectures delivered at Harvard University and subsequently published in *How to Do Things with Words* (1962), Austin put forth his theory of Speech Acts, commonplace today in the vocabulary of most discourse analysts. His method involved a discussion of "performatives," utterances that by their very content, change some state of affairs in reality. Among the more obvious of these are utterances that contain "performative verbs," such as *dub* in "I dub thee knight," or *pronounce* in "I pronounce you husband and wife." Such utterances, he pointed out, were neither true nor false. Austin observed that there were dozens of other performative verbs—to order, to warn, to promise, and so on—the utterance of which constituted an act ("speech act") on the part of the speaker: an order, a warning, a promise. He demonstrated that such speech acts did not necessarily depend on the lexicogrammatical form of the utterance for their success; although an utterance might overtly lack a performative verb, the act of ordering, warning, or promising could still be accomplished. "After all," explained Austin,

> it would be a very typical performative utterance to say "I order you to shut the door." This satisfies all the criteria. It is performing the act of ordering you to shut the door, and it is not true or false. But in the appropriate circumstances surely we could perform exactly the same act by simply saying "Shut the door," in the imperative. Or again, suppose that somebody sticks up a notice "This bull is dangerous," or simply "Dangerous bull," or simply "Bull." Does this necessarily differ from sticking up a notice, appropriately signed, saying "You are hereby warned that this bull is dangerous"? It seems that the simple notice "Bull" can do just the same job as the more elaborate formula. (1970, p. 243)

What the speaker (or sign writer in the case of the warning about the bull) intends to communicate—the illocutionary force—is freed from an exact linguistic form: the locution. Instead, illocutionary force may be achieved indirectly, taking the context into account.

John R. Searle

Another philosopher associated with speech act theory is Searle, whose early interest lay in classifying similar speech acts into categories and establishing specific criteria for determining whether one could "count" a speech act as having been accomplished. Searle (1969) recognized five broad types of speech acts, whose purposes are summarized by Martinich (1984, p. 60):

Representatives:	To say how something is.
Directives:	To get the hearer to do something.
Commissives:	To impose an obligation on the speaker.
Expressives:	To express some attitude.
Declarations:	To create a fact [similar to Austin's performatives].

Since we cannot necessarily rely on linguistic form to recognize a speech act, how can we interpret a speaker's intention? Searle (1975) hypothesized the following:

> In indirect speech acts the speaker communicates to the hearer more than he actually says by way of relying on their mutually shared background information, both linguistic and nonlinguistic, together with the general powers of rationality and inference on the part of the hearer. To be more specific, the apparatus necessary to explain the indirect part of indirect speech acts includes a theory of speech acts, certain general principles of cooperative conversation, . . . and mutually shared factual background information of the speaker and the hearer, together with an ability on the part of the hearer to make inferences. (pp. 60–61)

To explain more precisely how speech acts could succeed, Searle identified "felicity conditions," necessary and sufficient conditions that must hold in the real world for a speech act of a particular class to be recognized. These were not only logical conditions but also descriptions of the speaker's and hearer's desires, intentions, and level of sincerity. For example, if I promise my friend Fritz that I will bring my famous curried bean dip to his potluck, my utterance of that promise might take a number of different forms—from the direct, "I promise to bring my famous curried bean dip," to the more indirect, "I would be happy to bring my famous curried bean dip"—but Fritz would still recognize the utterance as a promise as long as certain conditions held. Paraphrasing Searle (1965), these conditions are shown in table 6.1. Likewise, we could come up with similar descriptions of the conditions under which an apology, a request, a warning, an offer, and so on could count as having been made. Searle's proposal provides an account of interpretation that rests neither on pure logic nor strictly on linguistic structural rules for its derivation.

TABLE 6.1 Felicity Conditions for a Promise

Preparatory condition	• I am able to bring the curried bean dip. • Fritz would prefer that I bring the curried bean dip (if he would not prefer it, the speech act becomes a threat!).
Sincerity condition	• I intend to bring the curried bean dip.
Propositional content condition	• The text of my utterance predicates my bringing the curried bean dip.
Essential condition	• By my utterance I intend to put myself under an obligation to bring the curried bean dip.

H. Paul Grice

A third pragmatist whose work is traditionally associated with speech act theory is Grice. Like Searle, Grice's concern was also with the conditions surrounding the interpretation of indirect speech acts. He proposed that conversants were aware of a cooperative principle, which he formulated as follows: "Make your conversational contribution such as is required, at the stage at which it occurs, by the accepted purpose or direction of the talk exchange in which you are engaged" (1975, p. 45). He then outlined a framework of conversational maxims to explain how a listener could determine a speaker's intentions, reprinted in table 6.2.

Routinely, however, speakers "flout" these maxims to achieve particular goals. The result of these manipulations is what Grice called "conversational implicature," for which the interpretation of a speech act requires more than a knowledge of the conventional linguistic meaning. Instead, listeners assume that the cooperative principle is in force and make inferences, taking into account the context of the conversation and their knowledge of the world to derive an interpretation.

A few examples from Grice will help to illustrate how the maxims might be flouted to convey an indirect meaning. Regarding the maxim of quantity, Grice cites the case of "damning with faint praise," as in a letter of recommendation written by a professor of philosophy for a student: "Dear Sir, Mr. X's command of English is excellent, and his attendance at tutorials has been regular. Yours, etc." (p. 52). Assuming that the writer is cooperative, the inadequate quantity of relevant information in such a letter is striking. Grice explains: "[The writer] must, therefore, be wishing to impart information that he is reluctant to write down. This supposition is tenable only on the assumption that he thinks Mr. X is no good at philosophy" (p. 52).

TABLE 6.2 Grice's Maxims

Maxim of quantity	• Make your contribution as informative as is required (for the current purpose of the exchange). • Do not make your contribution more informative than is required.
Maxim of quality	• Do not say what you believe to be false. • Do not say that for which you lack adequate evidence.
Maxim of relation	• Be relevant.
Maxim of manner	• Avoid obscurity of expression. • Avoid ambiguity. • Be brief (avoid unnecessary prolixity). • Be orderly.

Source: Grice, 1975, pp. 45–46. Reprinted with kind permission from Academic Press.

A second example is one in which the maxim of quality is flouted. If A says, "X is a fine friend" (p. 53), when both A and the listener (B) know that X has betrayed A, then B, rather than taking the utterance literally and assuming A is lying or confused, will assume that A is flouting the maxim of quality. The conversational implicature is that the statement is ironic; A believes the opposite of what he or she literally says.

In summary, the pragmatists' emphasis on the function of language rather than its form can be seen in much discourse analysis work. The importance of context to interpretation is also taken for granted in most later treatments of discourse analysis. Regardless of the tradition of discourse analysis one follows, it is widely held that the structural form and propositional content of an utterance alone are insufficient for its interpretation, and this belief can be traced to speech act theory.

Intonation and Illocutionary Force

There is no question that the intonation of an utterance contributes to its illocutionary force, or what the speaker intends to communicate. Austin (1962) himself discussed "tone of voice, cadence, and emphasis," as among the devices that can serve as alternatives to explicit performatives (pp. 73–74). Situations commonly occur in which what is grammatically one type of speech act may, via its intonation, be interpreted as another. For example, both of the rising pitch boundaries—high-rise (↑) and low-rise (↗)—tend to carry a directive illocutionary force, that of a question, request, or demand. This is not surprising, given that rising pitch boundaries are "forward-looking" (Pierrehumbert & Hirschberg, 1990) for their interpretation; thus, they anticipate a subsequent constituent for their resolution—often a recipient's response. Cases in which the grammar suggests one speech act but the intonation conveys another have traditionally been described as indirect speech acts. However, in the current framework, where intonation is presented as a system of linguistic meaning (that is, part of the locution), I argue that this view is too simplistic. It may be more accurate to say that the illocutionary force conveyed by intonation can be direct or indirect—just as the illocutionary force conveyed by the lexicogrammatical structure can be direct or indirect—with respect to a given context. Moreover, it may be necessary to characterize some utterances as simultaneously having more than one illocutionary force.

Rising Pitch Boundaries as Directives

Consider the following conversation (from Corpus 2) on the topic of the
invasion of Nepal by the Gorkas:

1	C	NÉPALI pe- folks about 200 YEARS ago⌄ they (.3)
2		INVÁDED↓ (4.9)
3	T	The GÓRKAS↓ (.6)
4	R	Hmm. (.7)
5	M	The- the ⁺GÓRKAS⁺↑=
6	T	=GÓRKAS↓ (.1)
7	M	ꜛRÉALLY↑ (2.7) NO KÍDDING↓ (.6)
8		They wear those ₚₐₙₜₛ all the TIME↑ (4.5)
9		↳You know ᴡʜᴀᴛ ₚₐₙₜₛ I'm TÁLKING about↑=
10	C	=Uh ha ha sure ha ha ha ha ...

Of interest in this excerpt is the utterance from M in line 8, "They wear
those pants all the time?" shown in figure 6.1. Grammatically, the utterance is a statement, or "representative" speech act; but intonationally,
having a high-rising pitch boundary at the end, it is a question, or "directive" speech act. It comes in reaction to the claim that the Gorkas invaded
Nepal, which is evidently a great surprise to M—she questions *Gorkas* in
line 5 and continues to express surprise using a high key in line 7 on *really*
and *no kidding*. In line 8 she seeks to confirm her understanding that a
previously held schema of the Gorkas as a people clad in folkloric pants
is really to be matched with the invaders of Nepal. Receiving no response,
she perseveres in line 9 with a second request for information, "You know

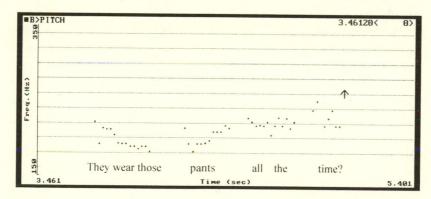

Figure 6.1 The high-rising pitch boundary (↑) conveys a question while the
grammar is that of a statement.

what pants I'm talking about?" Finally, in line 10, C responds to M's speech act as if it were a request with "Sure," amid laughter.

We can analyze this utterance further within Searle's framework of felicity conditions: the preparatory condition for requests is that the speaker does not have what is requested but believes that the hearer is able to provide it. In this case, what is requested is confirmation that the Gorkas with the folkloric pants of M's imagination are indeed the invaders of Nepal T has mentioned. The sincerity condition stipulates that the speaker actually wants what is requested—here again, the confirmation. If this were a representative, the class of speech acts that includes statements of fact, these conditions would be different: M would already have the information and would not be desiring confirmation of it from others. Although we will never have access to M's true intentions, we do know that M has never been to Nepal, whereas both T and C have lived there and are presumably familiar with the history. Thus, it is more likely that the preparatory and sincerity conditions of a request, rather than those of an assertion, are in force: M lacks certainty with respect to the proposition, wants confirmation, and looks to T and C to provide it.

This analysis raises the question of whether the "pants" utterance can properly be called an "indirect" speech act when the intonation conveys the directive force of the request. Intonation, being part of the phonology of English, contributes to the locution. This example is a far cry from the canonical indirect speech act where "I'm cold!" is intended as a demand: "Shut the window!" In the latter example, pragmatic principles give rise to a conversational implicature: the maxim of relation leads listeners to the interpretation that the speaker wishes the hearer to solve the coldness problem by shutting the window. In the "pants" example, the illocutionary force of the request for information is conveyed more directly through the linguistic form.

Schiffrin (1994) further analyzes the illocutionary force of high-rising intonation attached to grammatical statements using Searle's framework. The following three sequences from Schiffrin (pp. 67–68) illustrate speakers using this intonation in a slightly different context: when they already have the information provided in the statement. (I retain Schiffrin's question mark symbol [?] to represent the high-rising boundary):

((Phone rings))
CALLED   Hello?
CALLER   yeh, hi. This is Debby, David's mother?
CALLED   Oh hi . . . how are you . . .

And in giving one's phone number:

D   One two four?
A   Um.
D   Three two?
A   Okay.
D   Nine four six six.

And finally, in clarifying the setting in a story before getting to the point:

Z   The following year, his son, who ha- was eighteen years old just
    graduating from high school.
    Was walking through the em . . . the fountain, Logan Square
    Library?
    Y'know that fountain?
D   Yeh.
Z   Bare footed, and stepped on a- a bare wire.

In the first example, it is obvious that the caller knows that she is her own
son's mother. She is not requesting confirmation of the proposition "I
am David's mother." Similarly, in the other two examples, the speaker
already has the information concerned. Nonetheless, Schiffrin argues that
there is a "directive" (questioning) force to the utterances, expressed in
the rising pitch boundary:

> [T]he function of final rises comes very close to fulfilling the sincerity,
> preparatory, and essential conditions of questions. Final rising intonation
> marks S's [the speaker's] uncertainly about how information provided to
> H [the hearer] will be taken: what S is questioning is not propositional
> content per se, but the adequacy of propositional content for H's needs.
> Thus, what S wants is information about H's reception of information (the
> sincerity rule) that S does not have (the preparatory rule) and that S is
> attempting to elicit from H (the essential rule). (p. 68)

In these cases of statement grammar and rising intonation, Schiffrin concludes that both the intonation and the lexicogrammatical structure are
indicators of illocutionary force. In effect, more than one speech act is
performed at the same time: the lexicogrammatical structure enacts a representative (e.g., it provides the information that Debbie is David's mother),
while the intonation simultaneously enacts a directive (e.g., it questions
whether this information is sufficient for the recipient to identify her).

Rising Pitch Boundaries as Commissives

Still other investigations suggest that the high-rising pitch boundary can
add a mitigating force to statement grammar. In terms of speech act

theory, this might be described as a commissive illocutionary force in that it offers the listeners the option to disagree. Lakoff (1975), who studied the phenomenon across genders, found the high-rising pitch boundary more prevalent in women's speech than in men's. She interprets it as a mark of insecurity—a mitigating device in the face of male dominance. McLemore (1991) researched the use of this boundary among sorority sisters at a university in Texas where it was used to elicit approval and, more generally, to convey a "connective" meaning. However, she disagrees with Lakoff's claim that the rising pitch boundaries are characteristic of those of lower social status because the *senior* members of the sorority used this intonation the most. McLemore actually traced changes in the speech of newer members to the sorority over time: as they adopted the speech patterns of the more senior members, the younger women's use of the rising intonation became more frequent.

Ching (1982) discusses the rising pitch boundary in a Southern American dialect in Memphis, Tennessee, where, in a corpus of interviews with 14 speakers, he found it heavily used among both women and men. Ching's findings point not so much to social status as to politeness as the motivation behind this intonation: in many cases, the rising boundary was used to add a deferent, nondefensive, and even apologetic force to an utterance whose propositional content might otherwise offend or contradict someone. By presenting hard facts with a rising intonation, the speaker could politely offer the recipient an opportunity to disagree. As an example, Ching describes a situation in which his wife, an attorney, used the rising intonation during a trial in the following utterance (p. 106, I retain Ching's question mark to convey rising pitch):

I believe that's hearsay, your honor?

Ching explains:

Because she was late in stopping the testimony of a witness, she could not, normally, according to legal procedure, stop the witness's statements from being put on the record. However, by intuitively mitigating what she said with a question intonation—by asserting, but also at the same time appearing to request for confirmation in the role of a supplicant—she found that the judge sustained her objection. (p. 106)

To generalize, the rising pitch boundary—in the current model either high- or low-rising—tends to be affiliative, conveying a sensitivity to the recipient's point of view and the adequacy of one's contribution to it. We have seen examples in which it had a directive force—to question whether the listener had sufficient information—and a commissive force—to politely offer the listener an out and thereby mitigate the force of a grammatical assertion.

Intonational Idioms

Further evidence for the direct illocutionary force conveyed by intonation comes from the work of Liberman and Sag (1974) and Sag and Liberman (1975), who attempt to isolate entire intonation contours that typically, or we might even say "idiomatically," convey particular speech acts. Liberman and Sag introduce one such idiom, the "contradiction contour," with the following, rather cute, exchange (p. 422). The response is represented musically in figure 6.2:[1]

> MARK Hey Ivan, how about on your way to school this morning you drop off my pet whale at the aquarium?
>
> IVAN (Kazoo or slide whistle; ad libitum)

Liberman and Sag comment (p. 422):

> Without having any idea of the content of his utterance, we know from the melody performed by the second speaker that he objects in some way to the first speaker's request. What propositional content might he have meant to attach to this intonational superfix? A few possibilities might be:
> a. You don't have a pet whale!
> b. I'm not going to school today!
> c. I don't want that monster wiggling around in my car!
> d. They don't want him at the aquarium!
> e. I'm not taking orders from you any more!

In other words, although the propositional content of the response may vary, the tune itself holistically suggests the illocutionary force of a contradiction. In the current model of intonation, it makes the most sense to characterize these contours as "intonational idioms." Just as certain

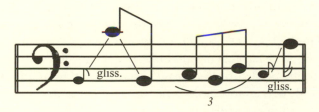

Figure 6.2 A musical representation of the "contradiction contour."

collocations of words become familiar as lexical idioms, certain combinations of tones are so frequently used that they become recognizable as "idiom chunks of the intonation system" (Pierrehumbert, 1980, p. 105). The contour itself is a kind of speech act.

I would analyze the case of the contradiction contour as ˥L+H* L* ↑, as in, for example:

˥You <u>DON'T</u> <small>HAVE A PET WHALE</small>↑

The initial high pitch is the result of high key (˥) commonly found at the onset of contradictions, as they are at odds with the prior utterance. Next, the negative word is associated with L+H* pitch accent to further indicate the contrast with the first speaker's order. Thereafter, L* pitch accents are associated with the other lexical items in the utterance, accessible through the mental representation formed from the initial utterance. Finally, the high-rising boundary (↑) at the end of the contradiction contour indicates that the utterance as a whole is forward-looking and begs a response, perhaps a retraction of the original order. This also gives the contour a combative feel—a challenge that requires an answer.

Sag and Liberman (1975) introduce other intonation contours with holistic meanings. The "surprise-redundancy" contour is used when the speaker wishes to express that an assertion is either surprising or extremely obvious ("redundant" in the discourse). They construct two contexts to illustrate these two meanings (pp. 491–492). In the first, the speaker walks into a classroom, sees to his surprise that the blackboard is painted orange, and exclaims:

(˥) The <small>BLÁCKBOARD</small> is painted <u>ÓRANGE</u>!↓

In the second context, the speaker is asked what color the blackboard is and quips, exasperated:

"I've told you a thousand times!" or "Just open your eyes and look—
(˥)The <small>BLÁCKBOARD</small> is painted <u>ÓRANGE</u>!↓"

The surprise-redundancy contour is reconstructed in figure 6.3.[2] I analyze the underlying tonal sequence of this intonational idiom as (˥)L* L+H*↓. The high key (˥), which I have indicated in parentheses as optional, conveys the fact that the utterance is at odds with expectation. Next comes L* pitch accent on *blackboard*, a standard item in any classroom and obviously perceivable in this one. It need not be added to the mental representation of the discourse but can be assumed accessible. *Orange* is associated with L+H* pitch accent, because it contrasts with the ex-

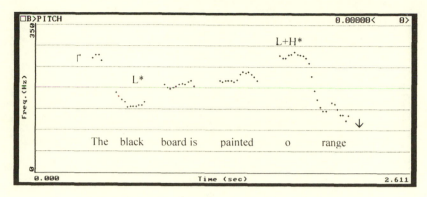

Figure 6.3 The "surprise-redundancy" contour.

pected "black" blackboard. The final low pitch boundary (↓) indicates the relative independence of this utterance with respect to what might follow—it is a self-contained exclamation. An additional influence on these utterances, within the contexts provided by Sag and Liberman, is that the speaker is in an emotional state, either surprised or exasperated. Thus, the pitch range as a whole may be somewhat exaggerated due to the emotional overtones (see chapter 8 for more examples of this sort).

Sag and Liberman (1975) also consider idiomatic intonation contours associated with certain types of questions. Their interest lay in comparing the intonation of "real" questions to that of questions used indirectly to accomplish other speech acts. Their efforts came in response to a remark from Searle in a 1974 talk. According to the authors: "Searle suggested that the indirect versions of such sentences are intonationally different from the direct versions in some way and asked for help from linguists in pinning the differences down" (p. 487). Sag and Liberman contend that real WH-questions commonly have an intonation pattern that they refer to as the "tilde contour." The tilde contour is described as having an initial high pitch on the WH-word, followed by a fall and ending in a final rise. I have done my best to convert their transcription of this contour (they use a line drawing) into the current intonation coding system as ⌐L* (L*) ↑ in reporting their examples (p. 487), as in:

⌐Who ópened the réstaurant↑

The tilde contour is reconstructed in figure 6.4.[3] Here, the context is one of a speaker merely expressing open-ended curiosity about a new restaurant. This is easily interpreted within the current model of intonational meaning: the main content words of the utterance, *opened* and *restaurant*, are associated with L* pitch accents because, as noted in chapter 2, propo-

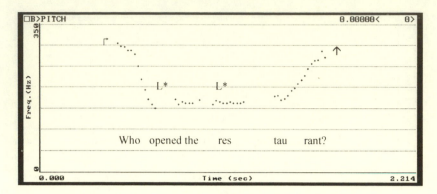

Figure 6.4   The "tilde" contour is typical of "real" questions.

sitions expressed in questions are often meant to be withheld from the mental representation of the discourse until the answers are provided. The utterance ends with a final high-rising pitch boundary to indicate that the speaker is waiting for subsequent discourse—the answer—for a complete interpretation. Indeed, Pierrehumbert and Hirschberg (1990) specifically call the L* ↑ sequence "a typical interrogative contour" (p. 277). The only difference between their description and that of Sag and Liberman's tilde contour is that the latter has a high onset. I interpret this as a high key (⌐⁺) because the utterance comes out of the blue rather than as a continuation of a thought expressed in a prior utterance.

In contrast, the authors present indirect versions of questions—as accusations, suggestions, or commands—for which the tilde contour is inappropriate. If the speakers are co-owners of the restaurant, the example uttered with what Sag and Liberman call a "hat contour" (H* H* ↓) (p. 488) would have a negative, accusatory implicature, as in:

Who ÓPENED the RÉSTAURANT↓

as in "What fool opened the restaurant" (on a Sunday morning when it is supposed to be closed).

Another context for which the tilde contour sounds inappropriate is when a grammatical question is used as a suggestion. The following utterance (p. 488), when uttered as a real question, is likely to have the tilde contour:

⌐⁺Why DON'T YOU MOVE TO CALIFÓRNIA↑

However, when used as a suggestion, the same intonation sounds odd (as I have indicated by the # symbol):

Hey Baldwin, the climate here is really bad for you! I've got a suggestion—
#↱Why ᴅᴏɴ'ᴛ ʏᴏᴜ ᴍᴏᴠᴇ ᴛᴏ ᴄᴀʟɪꜰÓʀɴɪᴀ↑

Finally, contexts are constructed to compare the appropriateness of the tilde contour in a real question versus a command, associated with the utterance "Would you stop hitting Gwendolyn" (p. 494):

Real Question:
    ᴘsʏᴄʜɪᴀᴛʀɪsᴛ Are you willing to make some sacrifices so that we can proceed with your therapy?
    ᴘᴀᴛɪᴇɴᴛ I'm not sure.
    ᴘsʏᴄʜɪᴀᴛʀɪsᴛ Well, for example—
    ↱would ʏᴏᴜ sᴛᴏᴘ ʜÍᴛᴛɪɴɢ ɢᴡÉɴᴅᴏʟʏɴ↑

Command:
    ᴛᴇᴀᴄʜᴇʀ You children are behaving very badly. Myra, please stop running around. And Lennie, I'm not going to tell you again—
    #↱would ʏᴏᴜ sᴛᴏᴘ ʜÍᴛᴛɪɴɢ ɢᴡÉɴᴅᴏʟʏɴ↑

In the second, command context, Sag and Liberman (p. 493) suggest that the tilde contour sounds inappropriate—a teacher would be more likely to intone the command as a declarative:

Would you STOP HÍTTING GWÉNDOLYN↓

To study these contours empirically, Sag and Liberman asked subjects to read short skits from scripts constructed in two versions, one that established a context for a direct reading of a question, and the other an indirect version. Tape recordings of these skits were analyzed to determine what kind of intonation contours the readers associated with the test utterances in each version. A second experiment involved asking subjects to listen to pairs of identical questions intoned in different ways and to choose an appropriate context from a list. The findings of Sag and Liberman's study confirmed their intuition that the tilde contour was characteristic of a direct question. However, the authors were not able to make definite claims about contour shapes for the indirect versions because there was less consistency among the subjects on those items.

To summarize, the evidence suggests that particular intonation contours, or "intonational idioms," are used so routinely that they can be said to have holistic meanings. The existence of intonational idioms is in keeping with the view that a sequence of tones can be a locution in its own right and can be recognized in many contexts as a particular kind of speech act.

Pragmatics Can Override Intonation

This brings us to another important point about the role of intonation in speech acts: it is not the claim that intonation always directly conveys the illocutionary force of an utterance; it is also possible for the force of an utterance to be interpreted indirectly with respect to its intonation. This is exemplified in "queclaratives," which Sadock (1974) describes as "questions . . . used with the force of assertions of opposite polarity" (p. 79). The following are two examples from Sadock:

> Does anyone study Aristotle anymore?
>
> Haven't I been good to you?

These, he points out, have approximately the same illocutionary force, respectively, as:

> No one studies Aristotle anymore.
>
> I have been good to you.

Having both the syntax and the intonation of yes/no questions, queclaratives function indirectly as assertions in cases where the speaker already knows the answer to the question to be the opposite of the proposition. Here is a naturally occurring queclarative from a conversation (from Corpus 3) about the decision to take estrogen during menopause:

```
1    K   . . . My- my MÓTHER↗ (.4) had a HYSTERÉCTOMY
2        ((material omitted)) and→ (.5) they IMMÉDIATELY PUT
3        HER ON ÉSTROGEN↓ (.2) NO QUÉSTIONS↓ (.2) She just
4        was jus- PSSSHT- YOU KNOW and THAT was in the
5        SÍXTIES↓ (.8) H- And she's TÁKEN it- (.2) NÉVER
6        QUÉSTIONED IT she's TÁKEN it for YEARS↓
7    B   She's STILL TÁKING IT NOW↗=
8    K   =YEAH↓=
9    B   =I CAN'T be [⁺LÍE:::VE⁺ it]↓
10   L              [for  HOW  ]  LONG↗ for THÍRTY
11       YEARS↗
12   K   YEAH!↓ She's seventy SIX↓ (.1)
13   L   Is that NÉCES [SARY↗    ]
14   K               [seventy] (.2) NO::!↓ (.2) I y- it's it's
15       in⁺SÁNE⁺↓
```

In this dialogue, K's point is that in the days when her mother started menopause, women were put on estrogen for the rest of their lives with no consideration for the long-term effects. Both B and L express incredulity at K's mother's acceptance of this life-long estrogen regimen in lines 7–11 ("She's still taking it now?" "I can't believe it!" "For how long? For 30 years?") The queclarative comes from L in line 13, "Is that necessary?" and is shown in figure 6.5. When the utterance occurs, it is already clear from L's previous contributions that she thinks the opposite: prolonged use of estrogen is unnecessary. The queclarative is an example of a speech act that is indirect with respect to both the grammatical and the intonational form. Only from the context, and with the assumption that the maxims of relevance and quality are in force, can this be interpreted as having the illocutionary force of an assertion of L's disapproval.

An empirical study conducted by Geluykens (1987) also deals with the relationship between intonation and pragmatics in illocutionary force. He looked at utterances that were grammatically assertions but had question intonation.[4] In his study, subjects listened to a series of test utterances with five different possible intonation contours. They were asked to judge the utterances as statements or questions. Another variable in the study, however, was the pragmatic value of the utterance, which was controlled by manipulating the lexicogrammatical structure. For example, the utterance "You feel ill" is pragmatically "question-prone," while the statement "I feel ill" is not. Geylukens explains this in terms of speech act theory by pointing out that Searle's felicity conditions for a directive (of which questions are a subclass) are more closely matched in "You feel ill" than in "I feel ill," because no speaker ever has direct knowledge of how another feels. Thus, the preparatory condition for questions, that the speaker does not know the answer, is fulfilled in "You feel ill," even when it has the grammatical form of a statement. Geluyken's finding was that the pragmatic variable overruled the intonation contour as the de-

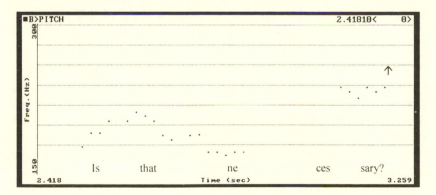

Figure 6.5   A "queclarative" is a question used as an opposite assertion.

ciding factor in how subjects judged the utterances. In other words, "You feel ill," and other pragmatically question-prone sentences like it, were judged as questions, even if their intonation contour had a low pitch boundary at the end, as would a typical statement.

Another empirical study with a similar result comes from Eaton (1988) on the topic of sarcasm. As Searle (1979) pointed out, sarcasm (or, irony for Searle) is a special kind of indirect speech act—the illocutionary force is not merely indirect, but the proposition expressed is actually the opposite of what the text directly conveys. Eaton's interest lay in the ability of children to interpret a sarcastic intention. She constructed twelve short dialogues for which the final line could have either a direct or a sarcastic reading. Subjects of different ages listened to tapes of these dialogues for which two variables were manipulated: background information and intonation. The background variable involved the amount of information supplied in the dialogue to cue subjects to possible reasons for sarcasm. The intonation variable was either a "flat, neutral tone" or "heavily sarcastic intonation" (p. 129). For example, one of the dialogues ran as follows, with four possible versions (sarcastic intonation shown in italics):

A   Hello, here's your shopping.
B   Thank you, keep the change.
Contextual information + intonation:
A   Oh thanks a *lot*, I can buy *so many* things with *one penny*.
Contextual information + no intonation:
A   Oh thanks a lot, I can buy so many things with one penny.
No contextual information + intonation:
A   Oh thanks a *lot*, I can buy *so many* things with *that*.
No contextual information + no intonation:
A   Oh thanks a lot, I can buy so many things with that.

In the versions with contextual information, it was explicitly stated that the amount of change was small—one penny. Subjects were then asked a set of questions to assess their interpretation of the dialogues. Eaton's results were, first of all, that age was a factor in the recognition of sarcasm: adults and eleven-year-olds were more able to recognize sarcasm than were seven- and nine-year-olds.[5] However, of most relevance to my discussion is the relationship between the intonation and background variables among adults and older children: background content was the stronger predictor of a sarcastic interpretation; that is, even when the intonation was neutral, utterances were judged sarcastic if the content suggested it, and even if the intonation was sarcastic, some subjects judged utterances as direct if the content was neutral. In both Eaton's and

Geluykens's findings, intonation, though certainly one cue to speaker intention, was not always given priority in the interpretation of direct versus indirect illocutionary force.

To summarize, intonation is one system, along with lexical and grammatical systems, that speakers use to convey their intentions. Often, when grammar and intonation are at odds, the intonation directly carries the illocutionary force of the speech act. This was shown in examples of grammatical statements uttered with high-rising pitch boundaries that were analyzed as questions rather than assertions. It is also possible for a single utterance to convey more than one illocutionary force, as when a statement with a rising pitch boundary functions as both an assertion and a request for confirmation that the utterance is sufficient for the listener's needs. Certain intonation contours have become so strongly associated with particular speech acts that I have called them "intonational idioms"— the tune of the contour suggests the speech act. However, I do not claim that intonation always carries the illocutionary force directly; we saw examples in which an indirect illocutionary force could be derived that was at odds with the intonational structure—for example, Sadock's "queclaratives." Empirical studies such as Eaton's and Geluykens's have also shown that pragmatic factors can override the intonational cues in the interpretation of a speech act.

Intonation and Implicature

This brings us to the more general question of how to integrate intonation into a speech-act framework—should intonational meaning be considered semantic or pragmatic? In considering this question, I return to Grice's (1975) classifications. Grice distinguishes that which is "said," directly, from that which is "implicated," indirectly. Implicatures are further divided into "conventionally" implicated and "nonconventionally" or "conversationally" implicated. Levinson (1983) provides a definition of the "conventional" category: "Conventional implicatures are non-truth-conditional inferences that are *not* derived from superordinate pragmatic principles like the maxims, but are simply attached by convention to particular lexical items or expressions" (p. 127). Grice presents the following example to illustrate conventional implicature: "He is an Englishman; he is, therefore, brave" (p. 44). Here the conventional implicature is that being brave is a result of being an Englishman, even though it is not part of what is directly said. Listeners arrive at this conclusion from the meaning of the word *therefore*, without invoking conversational maxims. In contrast, conversational implicature refers to a speech act that requires one to draw on context, knowledge of the world, and conversational maxims for interpretation.

In Grice's terminology, then, we can rephrase the original question as whether intonational meaning is part of what is said, part of what is conventionally implicated, or part of what is conversationally implicated. As will emerge from the discussion, the best fit for intonational meaning is probably in the realm of conventional implicature. Whether that is semantic or pragmatic depends on one's definitions of terms. I will now review work by Ward and Hirschberg (1985), Jackendoff (1972), and Martinich (1984), for these authors have used a framework of speech act theory to investigate this very question. In addition, I will draw on Levinson (1983), who thoughtfully clarifies much of Grice's philosophy with accessible examples.

Conventional Versus Conversational Implicature

Support for the claim that intonational meaning is conventional can be derived by comparing it to other types of meaning classified as conventional implicatures. We already saw one example from Grice ("He is an Englishman; he is, therefore, brave.") Here, the conventional meaning comes from semantic features of the word *therefore*, one of which involves "causation," and hence his being an Englishman is implicated as the cause of his bravery. We do not need pragmatic principles to interpret this. Levinson (1983) provides three further examples of what might count as conventional implicature. The nature of the meaning in these examples is strikingly similar to that of intonational meaning in that it involves discourse connections. The first example is from Grice (1961, in Levinson, p. 127): the words *but* and *and* have the same truth value, but the former is said to conventionally implicate a contrast whereas the latter is not. In parallel, the H* pitch accent (like *and*) is used to add a new item to the discourse whereas the L+H* pitch accent (like *but*) conveys the meaning of contrast with some item in the mental representation of previous discourse. Second, Levinson suggests that the meaning of "discourse-deictic items"—*however, moreover, besides, well, oh*, and so on (p. 128)—is conventional as well. These items are apparently equivalent to discourse markers (Schiffrin, 1987). As argued in chapter 5, paratones, the expanded pitch range associated with topic transitions, function in a similar way to discourse markers, indicating organizational shifts in the discourse. Third, Levinson cites the meaning difference between formal *vous* and informal *tu* in French as part of conventional implicature. In this case, the meaning encoded in the words has social value rather than propositional content. This to some extent parallels to the polite use of the ris-

ing pitch boundary to mitigate the force of an unpopular assertion, discussed earlier in this chapter.

Ward and Hirschberg (1985) also take the position that intonation
is part of conventional implicature. Their argument involves the "fall-rise"
intonation contour, which is composed of L*+H pitch accent and L- H%
boundary, or in my transcription system a low-rising pitch boundary (↗).
The contour is reproduced in figure 6.6 based on Ward and Hirschberg's
diagram (fig. 1, p. 748).[6] The context is:

A   Alan's such a klutz.
B   He's a good ʙᴀ́ᴅᴍɪɴᴛᴏɴ ᴘʟᴀ́ʏᴇʀ↗

As they explain, this contour "conveys uncertainty about the appropriateness of some utterance in a given context—specifically, about some
salient relationship between discourse entities, including (but not lim-
ited to) ... set-membership" (p. 756).[7] The discourse entities in question must be involved in a "scale," that is, a partially ordered set. Two more
examples (pp. 756, 767) help clarify the meaning of this contour:

1   A   You have a VW, don't you? (= Ladd's [1980] ex. 18)
    B   I have an ᴏ́ᴘᴇʟ↗
2   A   Have you ever been West of the Mississippi?
    B   I've been to ᴍɪ́ꜱꜱᴏᴜʀɪ↗

In these examples, B's intonation conveys uncertainty about how the
response will be accepted—whether it will "count" as appropriate in the
context. My analysis of the fall-rise contour into its underlying component parts is quite transparent: the L*+H pitch accent means that the
relevance of a lexical item is questioned in contrast to an alternative. In

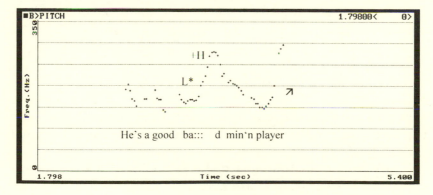

Figure 6.6 The "fall-rise" contour.

these cases, the alternative is a member of a scale already established in the first utterance: for example 1, this is a set of car makes for which there is a sense of ordering in just how exotically foreign a car might be; for example 2, it is a set of states in the United States west of the Mississippi River. Because Missouri borders the Mississippi, B's utterance posits it as perhaps at the very low end of the scale of Western states. The final low-rising boundary conveys an open-endedness for its interpretation—the speaker requests confirmation of whether the response will be accepted as appropriate for the scale invoked.

Ward and Hirschberg argue that the fall-rise contour passes Grice's tests for conventional implicature through "cancelability" and "detachability." Cancellability refers to the ability of an utterance's meaning to be cancelled by the addition of some contradictory premise. Detachability refers to the attachment between an implicature and its semantic content. If a semantically equivalent utterance of a different grammatical form can be substituted for the original without changing the implicature, then the implicature is said to be nondetachable. According to Grice, a conversational implicature should be cancelable but not detachable, whereas a conventional implicature should be detachable but not cancelable.

To clarify these concepts, we turn again to Levinson's (1983) helpful examples. The first example (p. 115) shows that in the case of conversational implicature, the meaning is cancelable:

John has three cows.

John has three cows and maybe more.

The first sentence carries a conversational implicature—that John has *only* three cows—by the maxim of quantity. In adding the information that he may have more cows, the second sentence cancels the meaning of the first without seeming contradictory. However, conventional implicatures cannot be cancelled without contradiction, as illustrated in the following pair (p. 115):

John has three cows.

#John has three cows, in fact none.

Here John's having three cows does not entail (and thus, conventionally implicate) that he has none, so the second sentence is contradictory and resultantly odd.

Now, returning to Ward and Hirschberg's argument, the claim is that the fall-rise contour behaves like Levinson's example of conventional implicature—it is not cancelable, as in:

A: Do you have a nickel?
a. B: I have a $_{\text{DIME}}\nearrow$
b. B: #You're in luck—I have a $_{\text{DIME}}\nearrow$

The meaning conveyed by the fall-rise contour is that of uncertainty about whether a dime will be satisfactory for A's purposes. However, by adding "you're in luck," B conveys a contradictory meaning—certainty that A will be satisfied with the dime. Thus, the (b) utterance is pragmatically odd.

The second part of their argument involves Grice's notion of detachability—whether the semantic content of an utterance can be detached from its linguistic form. Detachability is a characteristic of conventional, but not conversational, implicatures. As Levinson puts it, "[conversational] implicatures cannot be detached from an utterance simply by changing the words of the utterance for synonyms" (p. 116). Levinson's example (p. 116) is one of irony:

a. John's a genius
b. John's an idiot

If (a) is known to be false, then by the maxim of quality, (b) is the conversational implicature. That this is attached to the semantic content rather than the linguistic form itself is shown because any of the following alternatives (p. 117) to (a) lead to the same ironic interpretation:

John's a mental prodigy

John's an exceptionally clever human being

John's an enormous intellect

John's a big brain

In contrast, conventional implicatures are detachable—a truth-conditionally equivalent substitution can actually lack, or "detach," the implicature, as shown in (p. 116).

a. John didn't manage to reach the summit
b. John didn't reach the summit
c. John tried to reach the summit (p. 116)

Here, (a) and (b) are equivalent in their truth value. However (a) conventionally implicates (c), but (b) does not. Turning to intonation, Ward and Hirschberg argue that the fall-rise contour is also detachable because a truth-conditionally equivalent substitution does not necessarily preserve the implicature. They provide the following example (p. 766):

A: Is she taking any medication?
a. B: VITAMINS↗
b. B: VITAMINS↓

Although (a) and (b) are equivalent in their truth value, (a) with the fall-rise contour conveys the implicature that person B is uncertain about whether vitamins count as medication. However, in (b), which has H* pitch accent on *vitamins* and a low boundary tone, the uncertainty is not implicated.

To summarize the argument so far, the kinds of examples that have been used to illustrate conventional implicature resemble the discourse-level meaning conveyed by intonation. Furthermore, Ward and Hirschberg have identified a configuration of tones whose meaning is conventional, that is, to some extent independent of its context. The meaning resides in the form and can therefore be detached from the semantic content; it cannot be cancelled by the addition of a new premise without a pragmatically odd result. Intonational meaning is conventional rather than conversational in its implicature.

Saying Versus Implicating

What remains to be discussed is whether intonational meaning is properly an implicature at all. Much of the discussion of the distinction between saying and implicating has hinged on truth value, which, as Ward and Hirschberg (1985) and Martinich (1984) argue, is usually not part of intonational meaning. Martinich (p. 70) provides the following example, which he credits to Dretske (1972, p. 411), of three utterances for which the propositional content remains consistent even though the intonation changes:

> I have three friends who are variously misinformed about one of my recent transactions. The first wants to know why I gave my typewriter to Clyde. I set him straight by telling him that I did not *give* my typewriter to Clyde.
> 1. I *sold* my typewriter to Clyde.
> Somewhat later my second friend gives it to be understood that he thinks I sold my typewriter to Alex. In correcting him I say,
> 2. I sold my typewriter *to Clyde*.
> Still later the third asks me why I sold my adding machine to Clyde and, once again, I find myself saying,
> 3. I sold *my typewriter* to Clyde.
> How shall we describe the difference?

Despite the quaint, old-fashioned subject matter, the example is easily analyzed as one in which the placement of the L+H* pitch accent (in italics) varies depending on which lexical item in the sentence is being contrasted to the friend's misinformation. Although the propositional content remains the same in each case, the pitch accent placement changes what is presupposed.

Jackendoff (1972) also discusses the role of intonation in conveying the presupposition of an utterance. The following pair (p. 357) illustrates this:

1. Max doesn't beat his wife because he <u>LOVES</u> her↗
2. Max doesn't beat his wife because he LOVES her↓.

Misogynistic subject matter notwithstanding, in sentence (1), it is presupposed that Max does beat his wife, whereas in (2), it is not. If we interpret Jackendoff's claim within the current model of intonation,[8] the difference resides in the pitch accents and boundary tones of the utterances: in (1), a contrastive reading of *loves* presupposes that while loving his wife is not the reason he beats her, there is some alternative reason why he does beat her. In addition, the final low-rising pitch boundary conveys the meaning that subsequent discourse will be involved in the interpretation and therefore adds to the sense that there is an alternative explanation (for her bruises) on its way. I would add another component to this analysis by including the effect of the L* pitch accent. Although Jackendoff does not discuss the meaning of low pitch, for sentence (1) he uses Bolinger's (1965) "B contour," usually represented with a low "trough" prior to the focused word. I have transcribed this as follows in (1'):

1'. MAX doesn't <small>BEAT HIS WIFE BECÁUSE HE</small> <u>LOVES</u> her↗
2'. MAX DÓESN'T BEAT his WIFE because he LOVES her↓

In (1'), the beating of the wife is associated with L* pitch accents, indicating that it is accessible in the mental representation of the discourse—that he beats his wife is already under discussion—whereas in (2') (Bolinger's A contour), *beat* and *wife* have H* pitch accents as new elements in the discourse. This analysis adds to the strength of the argument that the presupposition is different for the two versions because L* pitch accent explicitly conveys a "you should already know this" meaning.

A second example from Jackendoff (p. 359) involves L+H* pitch accent versus a simple H* associated with a conjunction:

1. Both John <u>AND</u> Bill didn't go.
2. Both John AND Bill didn't go.

Here, the first sentence presupposes that only one of the men did not go. This is because the L+H* pitch accent sets up a contrast between *both-and* and another conjunctive relationship, *either-or*. In the second, it is presupposed that neither went because the H* pitch accent does not lead to a contrastive interpretation.

The examples so far are consistent with intonation in the realm of conventional implicature: it can affect the presuppositions associated with an utterance but not the propositional content. However, Jackendoff (p. 352) also points to cases where intonation can affect propositional content, as in the following quantifier-scope relationships:

1. <u>ALL</u> of the men didn't go↗
2. ALL of the men didn't go↓

Sentence (1) means that not all the men went but some did, whereas (2) means that none of the men went. These facts are easily explained: in the first sentence, *all* is associated with L+H* pitch accent of contrast. Thus, *all* presupposes some alternative quantity in the discourse—*all* didn't go, but *some* did. In the second sentence, the quantifier has H* pitch accent, which simply adds the quantity *all* to the discourse, in association with the noun *men*.

Ward and Hirschberg (1985) counter Jackendoff, by providing alternative contexts such as the following (p. 771) for which his quantifier-scope examples fail to yield the desired interpretations:

A The foreman wants to know which union meeting some of the men missed.
B <u>ALL</u> of the men didn't go to the last one↗

They claim that in this context, the B sentence, which Jackendoff argued as having only a narrow-scope reading, can actually have a wide-scope reading. They therefore argue that the context rather than the intonational meaning changes the propositional content.

Ultimately, the question of whether intonational meaning is semantic may boil down to one of definition. Martinich (1984), for example, draws the line between pragmatics and semantics with some nonpropositional aspects of meaning on the semantic side. He refers to that which is "indicated" (p. 67) (in contrast to "implicated") as nonpropositional meaning conveyed through linguistic devices—verb tense, mood, adverbial force, case endings, the tone of lexical items,[9] and, most relevant for this discussion, contrastive stress—the L+H* pitch accent of the current model. He considers indication to be in a different category from Grice's conventional implicature because the latter involves the conventions surrounding lexical meaning. For Martinich, an implicature must not be realized in any syntactic marking (p. 66).

Returning to the previous examples about the selling of the typewriter to Clyde, reprinted here, Martinich claims that the contrastive L+H* pitch accent in each case is part of the indication rather than an implicature:

1. I *sold* my typewriter to Clyde.
2. I sold my typewriter *to Clyde.*
3. I sold *my typewriter* to Clyde.

Martinich observes, in reference to the meaning distinctions of these sentences, "The difference is not . . . merely pragmatic, since the difference in the content of what is communicated is due to the phonetically different stresses of each sentence" (p. 70). So, for Martinich, intonational meaning has a semantic side to it, on par, for example, with the choice of passive instead of active voice or of verb tense. Rather than being an implicature at all, the contrastive meaning is indicated directly through the linguistic form—in this case the L+H* pitch accent. Martinich's view is not substantially different from Ward and Hirschberg's; he simply draws the line between semantic and pragmatic in a different place and evidently takes a narrower definition of conventional implicature, confining it to lexical meaning only.

To synthesize this long section on the place of intonational meaning in a speech-act model, it is clear, first of all, that the meaning conveyed by intonation is tied more to linguistic form than that derived through conversational implicature. As Ward and Hirschberg showed, intonation is detachable but not cancelable, as is characteristic of conventional, but not conversational, implicatures. Beyond that, it is probably safest to say that intonation is part of conventional implicature, if one accepts a narrow definition of what is "said" as only that which is part of propositional content and excludes presupposition. Although there do appear to be cases, as Jackendoff shows, for which intonation can affect propositional content, this is admittedly not its usual role. Instead, intonational meaning seems on par with other types of conventional meaning, as deictics, discourse markers, honorifics, and certain conjunctions, whose contribution to meaning is described at the discourse, rather than the propositional level.

Nevertheless, as Martinich's remarks attest, there is something dissatisfying about calling intonational meaning an "implicature" when it is phonological. Why should discourse-level meaning be excluded from the realm of semantics? I will leave the last word on this topic to Levinson (1983): "In a sense conventional implicature is not a very interesting concept—it is rather an admission of the failure of truth-conditional semantics to capture all the conventional content or meaning of natural language words and expressions" (p. 128).

Unresolved Issues

The writing of this chapter has posed a dilemma because so many of the discussions in the literature of speech act theory rely on constructed examples out of context. By including others' arguments and examples, I have had to sacrifice, to some extent, my commitment to the use of natural speech. However, this also means that there is ample room for research involving the application of speech act theory to natural contexts, for little work exists on the illocutionary force of intonation in this mode. I suggest several ideas for ways to investigate the role of intonation in discourse using a speech-act framework. By returning to issues such as politeness and sarcasm that typically involve indirect speech acts, and investigating their intonation in natural contexts, a better understanding of the role of intonation in speech act theory can be achieved.

What Further Evidence Can Prosody Provide in Discussions of Speech Act Theory?

In the latter part of this chapter, I discussed the status of intonation in a model of speech act theory, but this brief sketch needs to be augmented. The discussion of detachability and cancelability, for example, hinged on a single intonation contour, the "fall-rise" of Ward and Hirschberg (1985). The question of whether intonation can alter truth value was also addressed with a single case, Jackendoff's (1972) quantifier-scope example. I have not even touched on how other aspects of prosody might interact with speech acts. Nonetheless, I do hope to have demonstrated that prosody *belongs in the discussion* of speech act theory—that its meaning potential is too great to be ignored. Those who work in the framework of speech act theory are urged to consider the nature of the contribution of other aspects of intonation (and prosody overall) to the communication process and to draw evidence from natural speech. Is the illocutionary force conveyed by prosody to be properly described in the realm of pragmatics or semantics? Or do these terms need to be revisited if evidence from prosody in context is to count?

What Are the Characteristics of the Prosody of Sarcasm?

As reviewed earlier in this chapter, Eaton (1988) recognized that intonation was a cue to sarcasm and tested its effect on the subjects in her study. Although intonation was not the only factor in the subjects' judgments, it did appear to have an important influence. However, Eaton does little to describe sarcastic intonation other than to say that speakers have a "heavily intonated voice" (p. 126). It would be useful to search for sarcastic utterances in corpora of natural speech and analyze the prosody. Is there a particular pitch pattern of sarcasm? What are the pitch accents and boundaries like? Is there a durational component? Is there a loudness component? Though members of a speech community seem to agree that there is something that can be called "a sarcastic tone of voice," its prosody remains to be described in more detail.

What Is the Role of Prosody in Politeness?

Politeness typically involves indirect speech acts. Brown and Levinson (1987) have found that the intonation associated with an utterance can make the difference between politeness and rudeness, but it can vary with context. For example, exaggerated prosody can sometimes convey a positive emotional affiliation (p. 104), but it can also indicate a harsh, challenging attitude (p. 133). Furthermore, a rising pitch boundary associated with statements in speech can have a polite, mitigating effect by offering the recipient an option to disagree, ask for clarification, or confirm understanding (Ching, 1982; Schiffrin, 1994). I expect more to be discovered on the topic of prosody and politeness. The subtleties of how prosodic variables mitigate a negative illocutionary force are open for investigation. By revisiting the issue of politeness in naturally occurring discourse with an eye for the role played by prosody, one could gain a better understanding of this interesting border zone between semantics and pragmatics.

What Is the Role of Prosody in Illocutionary Force in Other Languages?

In English, the intonation system plays quite a large role as a bearer of discourse meaning, but this is not claimed as a universal. In a tone language like Chinese, for example, pitch conveys lexical meaning, and although discourse-level intonation exists, it has a smaller inventory (Shen, 1990). It remains to be investigated whether the role of intonation in illocutionary force in tone languages is different from that of English. Do other prosodic variables play more of a role in place of pitch? In general, the role of prosody in speech acts in other languages is of interest from both a descriptive point of view and to gain insights into cross-cultural communication. One method to approach this problem would be to search through discourse corpora for speech acts that are typically face-threatening and therefore more likely to be indirect, such as requests, commands, and jokes (see Brown & Levinson, 1987). Having identified these, one could determine whether prosodic variables mitigated these acts consistently.

Where Is the "Prosody" in E-mail Discourse?

Although it may sound like a contradiction in terms, e-mail discourse has its "prosody." For example, I was explicitly taught by friends to show emphasis in e-mail messages by using the star diacritic (I was *surprised* to hear your news) rather than capital letters (I was SURPRISED to hear your news) because the latter can "sound" overemotional or even harsh! One theory to explain why e-mail discourse can sound aggressive or angry is that, although it has the informal feel of a conversational genre, it lacks the usual mitigating factors—body language and prosody—that we rely on to soften our speech acts in face-to-face discourse.[10] To my knowledge, no studies exist on this topic, but research could be done on e-mail documents to determine diacritics in use, and people's reactions to different versions of e-mail text, with or without particular diacritics, could be assessed. Subjects could also be asked to read e-mail texts aloud to determine how particular diacritics "sounded" to them. Finally, following a more ethnographic approach, one could take instances of misunderstanding over e-mail as a starting point for the study of how prosody can affect interpretation. The documents could then be searched for possible causes of the misunderstanding and participants interviewed about the incident. Overall, one could attain a better understanding of how prosody "comes through" electronically to convey illocutionary force.

Sample Analysis

Turning now to a concrete research application, I present the chapter's sample analysis, contributed by Philip Gaines, whose interest in legal discourse is reflected in his 1998 dissertation. In this brief data analysis, Gaines argues that the illocutionary force of trial attorneys' key utterances can be manipulated through their intonation. Because the perlocution of courtroom discourse can be crucial, Gaines's analysis clearly demonstrates that the relevance of intonational meaning is more than just an academic question.

Intonation as a Marker of Illocutionary Force in Legal Examination Tag Questions*

The questions that attorneys ask in courtroom examination have been extensively studied from the standpoint of their use in controlling the responses of witnesses. Through looking at numerous trial transcripts, Bülow-Møller (1990), Danet et al.(1976), and Walker (1987), among others, have concluded that certain types of questions are relatively coercive in their response-eliciting illocutionary force. Among these types are sentences containing tag questions—short questions "tagged" onto the end of matrix statements:

A. You didn't really see a gun in the defendant's hand, did you?
B. You're the one who actually pulled the trigger, aren't you?

The inclusion of a tag question guarantees, of course, that the utterance will be an information-seeking speech act, but the point often made is that, because the question begins with a statement for which the questioner seeks confirmation by means of the tag, the question is relatively coercive.

As illustrated by these examples, tags can be either positive or negative, depending on the positivity or negativity of the matrix statement. In either case, however, the effect of the tag is to turn the statement into a question whose answer is inherently suggested. In A, for example, the tag has the effect of indicating that the (extended) answer to the question should be "No, I didn't really see a gun in the defendant's hand." In B, the suggestion is that the answer should be "Yes, I'm the one who actually pulled the trigger." Generally speaking, then, the illocutionary force of tags is to seek confirmation of the assertion in the matrix statement.

Although the coercive nature of tag questions in courtroom examination has been well established, a further distinction can be made among tags with regard to their illocutionary force—a distinction that emerges only through a close look at intonation. Tags virtually always have pitch accents with either rising or falling[11] intonation. The difference between the two generates a subtle but important difference in the illocutionary force of the question. Questions A and B will again be used to illustrate this difference. Consider the questions with rising intonation and then falling intonation on the tags:

A1. You didn't really see a gun in the defendant's hand, did you↗
    [rising]

*This section was contributed by Philip Gaines.

A2. You didn't really see a gun in the defendant's hand, did you↓
[falling]

B1. You're the one who actually pulled the trigger, aren't you↗
[rising]

B2. You're the one who actually pulled the trigger, aren't you↓
[falling]

In A1 and B1, an illocutionary effect of the rising intonation suggests that the confirming response being sought is important—perhaps even necessary. In A2 and B2, on the other hand, the force of the falling intonation suggests that the response is a foregone conclusion and is virtually redundant. All things being equal, either intonation pattern is perfectly appropriate; the choice of patterns is a product of the illocutionary and perlocutionary effects intended by the speaker.

I turn now to the analysis of an actual courtroom examination, using the principles already outlined. The case is the murder trial of O. J. Simpson. Early in the proceedings, the prosecution offered as a witness Ronald Shipp, who testified, among other things, that Simpson had told him of having dreams about killing Nicole Brown Simpson. The cross-examination, conducted by defense attorney Carl Douglas, was an effort to discredit Shipp's testimony by impeaching him as a liar and alcohol abuser motivated in his testimony by personal gain. In the examination segments analyzed, Douglas used 58 tag questions (11 positive, 47 negative) of the following form:

AUX (n't) P / E, (sir) ?

where AUX = auxiliary or linking verb; P / E = personal pronoun or existential word (*there* as in *isn't there?*); and the lexical material in parentheses is optional. In all cases, both rising and falling intonation are possible and equally appropriate, depending on the intention of the speaker and on the context. The following is a representative selection of the tag questions used by Douglas:[12]

You and Phil go back awhile, don't you?

You knew on that occasion that I was representing Mr. Simpson, didn't you?

You've lied a few times, haven't you, sir?

He was grieving that evening, wasn't he?

Well, you haven't just acted in schools and commercials, have you?

Your wife and you were invited, but you never went, did you?

That was when you visited there with some blond female, wasn't it?

Angela is a German woman, isn't she?

Of the 58 tags, rising intonation is used on 14 and falling intonation on the remaining 44. This clear preference (75%) for falling intonation suggests the observation that Douglas tends to use tag questions to suggest as strongly as possible that confirmation of the assertion in his matrix statement is expected. Again, in all cases where falling intonation on tags is used in this examination, rising intonation could have been used, performing exactly the same yes/no questioning function. The choice of falling intonation would seem to indicate Douglas's illocutionary insistence on acceptance of the assertions in the question.

One approach to understanding the purpose of the consistent use of more illocutionarily "insistive" tag questions is to consider the perlocutionary effects that Douglas might have intended. Recall that the purpose of this cross-examination was to discredit the testimony of Shipp. This discrediting, of course, is for the benefit of the jury. Using stronger, more insistive tag questions serves not so much to get certain answers from the witness but rather to communicate to the jury the attorney's perspectives. Thus, falling intonation not only instantiates the illocutionary force of more insistently seeking confirmation of the question's assertion but also produces the perlocutionary effect of communicating the perspective of the attorney to the jury to persuade them of the "truth" of that assertion.

This phenomenon is illustrated even more strikingly through an analysis of one specific aspect of the tag questions themselves. Of the 58 tags, 39 have "you" as the pronoun—for example:

> And you said that you no longer have an alcohol problem, didn't you?
>
> You haven't just acted in schools or in commercials, have you?
>
> You're not really this man's friend, are you, sir?

This is not surprising, of course, since the focus of attention in the cross-examination is the witness himself. What is of interest, however, is the fact that 34 of the 39 tag questions containing "you" (87%) have falling intonation, as opposed to only 5 with rising intonation. Consider further that the topic of 32 of these 39 questions is Shipp's attitudes or actions. The nearly exclusive use of falling intonation in tag questions dealing with the attitudes and actions of the witness suggests that, when it comes to the task of producing an unfavorable representation of the witness, the attorney is especially focused on generating the perlocutionary effect of persuading the jury of the truth of his assertions.

One could argue, of course, that cross-examining attorneys in general tend to produce falling intonation on tag questions and that Douglas's pattern is not distinctive. Should this prove to be the case, it would provide support for a claim that cross-examining attorneys tend to instantiate the illocutionary and perlocutionary forces under discussion here. Such an analysis could be supported by a much larger database of tag questions used in a wider variety of interactive contexts. In any case, a final note is that the subtle distinctions between speech act types discussed here show up only when intonation is considered; written trial transcripts conceal these distinctions. In view of the importance of trial transcripts in, for example, cases of appeal, it might be worth considering the possible significance of interactions in which intonation comes into play. Potentially consequential elements of intentionality and meaning may be routinely hidden from the view of decision-makers in cases wherein weighty matters hang in the balance.

Chapter Conclusion

In this chapter I have reviewed the early work of speech-act theorists who developed the notion of language as action, a basic premise of much discourse analysis today. The speech-act theorists also demonstrated the importance of pragmatics to interpretation, in particular by showing that there is no one-to-one relationship between the linguistic form of an utterance and its illocutionary force. Instead, interpretation can be obtained only by evaluating conditions in the real world. The influence of this thinking can be seen in more recent treatments of discourse analysis, where it is generally agreed that the context of an utterance needs to be taken into account in its interpretation.

From an overview of the literature, an utterance's intonation clearly conveys an important element of the speaker's intention, and it can be discussed independently of the contribution of the lexicogrammatical structure. We have seen many examples of intonation directly affecting the illocutionary force of an utterance. Rising pitch boundaries may add a directive force—statements become requests for confirmation or solicitations of evidence of listener satisfaction, or they may add a commissive force, offering others the right to another opinion. We have also seen examples of intonation contours whose illocutionary force has become conventionalized into intonational idioms—the tilde contour, associated with "real" questions, the contradiction contour, and the surprise/redundancy contour.

However, intonation does not resolve the interpretation of all speech acts. It is simply one part of the linguistic form that a listener takes into account in deriving a speaker's intention. Pragmatic principles and background information are also assessed in determining the illocutionary force of a speech act. Studies of sarcasm and statements used as questions confirm that subjects in experimental situations are more apt to be swayed by the background context than by grammar and intonation in deriving interpretations.

The chapter also reviewed arguments over the place of intonation in a model of speech act theory. I concluded that, given a definition of semantics based on propositional content, intonational meaning is best considered part of "conventional implicature." Although intonation can alter propositional content in some cases, its meaning is generally at the discourse level—on par with lexical nuance, word order, and verb tense—rather than at the propositional level. Based on Grice's notions of detachability and cancelability, intonational meaning was argued to have a more stable, conventional form-meaning correlation than what has been described as conversational implicature. Ultimately, it would be wise to reevaluate some of these terms, factoring intonation into the equation.

Finally, I presented several ideas for further research on the relationship between intonation and speech acts. I recommended that the question of the place of prosody in a model of speech act theory be investigated further, using naturally occurring discourse in a variety of languages. Language functions that are typically conveyed indirectly, such as polite requests, demands, and ironic language, are a likely starting point to search for the mitigating force of prosodic forms. I also suggested that the illocutionary force of e-mail discourse, which lacks the mitigating effects of prosody, be researched. In the sample analysis by Gaines, the language of the courtroom, wherein persuasion can be critically important, was a key site for the study of intonation's illocutionary, and perlocutionary, force.

7

PROSODY IN THE STUDY
OF CONVERSATION

In this chapter, I turn to the question of how prosody contributes to informal "ordinary" conversation. Several approaches to the analysis of conversation are touched on in the chapter, including those of Gumperz (1982), Fiksdal (1990), and Eggins and Slade (1997). The school of thought I draw from the most, however, is conversation analysis (CA), which stems from the work of sociologists Garfinkel (1967) and Sacks, Schegloff, and Jefferson (1974). In CA, a tradition of discourse analysis, everyday talk is regarded as a highly organized social achievement. By zeroing in on minute details of talk, preserved on audio- or videotape, conversation analysts attempt to discover how members of a culture display their knowledge of how to conduct daily affairs under their particular social order. Many conversation analysts consider conversation the most fundamental genre of speech; its very "ordinariness" makes it revealing as an object of study. As Goodwin and Heritage (1990) write:

> Conversation constitutes the primordial site of language use in the natural world and is the central medium for human socialization. Thus ordinary conversation is the point of departure for more specialized communicative contexts (e.g. the legal process, the educational system, the medical encounter), which may be analyzed as embodying systematic variations from conversational procedures. (p. 289)

Also crucial to CA is the fact that face-to-face talk is "emergent"; that is, with each new contribution to the discourse, participants are simultaneously demonstrating their orientation to the context established by the prior turn(s) and projecting a subsequent context (Goodwin & Heritage, 1990, p. 288). Hence, the sequencing of conversational events is an important concern in CA, as is the reaction of each speaker to the previous one in the developing context. Conversation analysts use empirical methodology: instead of speculating about a speaker's intention in an utterance, a conversation analyst would more likely examine the recipient's actual reaction, deriving an interpretation directly from the details of the conversation.

It is not surprising that prosody is an important focus of the microanalysis that has traditionally been characteristic of CA. In the introduction to an important anthology on CA and prosody, Selting and Couper-Kuhlen (1996) stress the central role of prosody in interaction:

> What are the cues that help to make social interaction more than the mere exchange of words, namely a real-time encounter between conversationalists who establish and negotiate units of talk as situated meaningful activity? It is our conviction . . . that at least some of the cues in everyday live speech events are prosodic in nature, involving auditory parameters such as pitch, loudness and duration and the categories they jointly constitute. (p. 1)

In particular, conversation analysts have always paid close attention to the timing of talk. One of the most important observations offered in the CA tradition is that there is relatively little silence in conversation. Although it may vary somewhat from culture to culture, even a second's silence may begin to sound like an awkward pause in the context of a lively conversation. Participants are skilled at synchronizing their turns so that, for the most part, one speaker has the floor at a time, with one turn latching on to the next or overlapping only slightly. Thus, with a strong research focus on the junctures between turns of talk, pause length has always had a high priority as an object of study in this tradition of analysis.

Other traditions of research on conversation reflect a similar interest in prosody: a glance at the transcription coding systems used in the analysis of conversations by researchers from a variety of backgrounds shows that prosodic variables are taken seriously. To name just a few, Coulthard and Montgomery (1981), Gumperz (1982), Schiffrin (1987), Tannen (1984a), and Tsui (1994) are all discourse analysts who have elaborate systems to encode prosodic phenomena in their transcripts. These coding systems include symbols for syllable and pause duration, tempo, volume, stress, and various intonational phenomena, all recognized as central to the study of conversation.

With the coverage of prosody that already exists in many traditions of conversation study, the goal of this chapter is to examine aspects of prosodic analysis that are perhaps less commonly explored. The chapter will address four major topics: the first is the role of pitch boundaries and their interaction with pause placement in the mechanics of turn-taking. I argue that the alignment of pitch boundaries, syntactic boundaries, and pauses can be manipulated strategically to achieve interactional goals. Second, I discuss the potential role of pitch accents in the flow of conversation. As presented in chapter 4, pitch accents perform a cohesive function, helping to integrate what is verbalized into participants' mental representations of a discourse in progress. An analysis of pitch accents has a potential to reveal evidence of the assumptions underlying the ongoing discourse context as it is developed and negotiated among participants in conversation. A third area to be covered involves "tone concord," the degree to which the pitch range choice, or "key," between two speakers matches across turns. This has potential value in questions of the power balance and rapport among participants in conversation. Finally, I discuss the role of rhythm as a regulating element in turn-taking. That speakers are aware of rhythm in the timing of their turns is consistent with the premise of metrical phonology, discussed in chapter 3, that rhythm is a universal organizing force in the phonologies of languages of the world. The chapter concludes with several ideas for further research in which prosodic analysis may be applied to conversation data. The sample analysis, contributed by Susan Fiksdal, investigates the relationship between timing and face in academic advisor/advisee encounters. At certain places where the conversational rhythm is irregular, Fiksdal has found, interactional problems tend to appear. Fiksdal's contribution provides an example of how subtle prosodic contextualization cues mirror the participants' interactional footing in conversation.

Prosody in Turn-Taking

One of the most central research questions in conversation studies has always been how participants in conversation are so easily able to synchronize their turn-taking—in *real time*—with little gap or overlap. As Sacks observes in a 1967 lecture (in Jefferson, 1995): "One person can start up talking within one tenths, two tenths—that order of speed—of a second after another had done what is, upon much later reflection by an analyst, something that seems to be a sentence" (p. 650). Thus, much of the focus of research on turn-taking involves the timing of the events surrounding the "transition relevance place" (Sacks et al., 1974) at which the floor may optionally shift from one speaker to another. Sacks emphasizes the role of syntax in turn transitions, pointing out that speakers routinely anticipate the endings of others' utterances prior to their completion, latching on without an interruption in the syntactic structure. This he takes as evidence of real-time syntactic processing during conversation:

> Such a fact as that persons go about finishing incomplete sentences of others with syntactically coherent parts would seem to constitute direct evidence of their analyzing an utterance syntactically in its course, and having those results available to them during the production of such a sentence so that they can use that to complete it. (p. 651)

However, syntactic processing is by no means the only factor in the anticipation of turn completions. Sacks et al. also cite the role of intonation in the determination of transition relevance places:

> Clearly, in some understanding of "sound production" (i.e. phonology, intonation, etc.), it is also very important to turn-taking organization. For example, discriminations between *what* as a one-word question and as the start of a sentential (clausal or phrasal) construction are made not syntactically, but intonationally. (pp. 721–722)

It is reasonable to expect that intonation can be analyzed "on line" just as syntax can due to three physical properties of the intonational phrase: first, intonational phrases are the domain of declination, the gradual downward slope of the baseline of the pitch melody that restarts at each new breath intake. Second, the effect of a pitch boundary is in force from the final pitch accent of the intonational phrase to its conclusion (Pierrehumbert, 1980). This is manifest in the form of a pitch boundary's directional movement (rising, partially falling, remaining flat, etc.). Last, final lengthening of the syllables before the boundary is manifest before the end of the intonational phrase (Klatt, 1975). Listeners can perceive these cues slightly in advance of a turn's end. Furthermore, it is feasible that rhythm contributes to the anticipation of a turn completion. Once a regular rhythm is established, the duration of the intervals becomes predictable, and the uptake of a turn can potentially occur on beat. Therefore, as with syntax, there is every reason to believe that prosody contributes to conversants' ability to anticipate the completion of a turn before it actually occurs and to latch on with little intervening silence.

Several empirical studies confirm the sensitivity of conversants to prosodic and other nonsyntactic cues in turn-taking, though not all agree in their findings. In a study of videotaped conversation, Duncan (1972) identified six features that tended to cluster around transition points to a next speaker: syntactic, intonational, and gestural completion; decrease in loudness; drawl on utterance-final stressed syllables; and the presence of lexical discourse markers. His statistical finding was that, although no one feature was a guarantee of turn transition, the greater the number of these features, the higher the likelihood of uptake by another speaker. The finding points to a set of cues that define the "canonical" turn completion.

Schaffer (1983) played tapes of a series of utterances excerpted from naturally occurring conversations to listeners asked to judge them as turn-final or turn-medial. Half of the utterances were filtered so that only the prosody could be heard. Her results showed that rising pitch boundaries were more likely to lead to judgments of turn completion than were level or falling boundaries. I speculate that this is because the rising boundaries were judged to be affiliated with yes/no questions. Also, even in filtered speech, utterances with no pitch boundaries (that is, the speech simply stopped with neither pitch movement nor final lengthening) were perceived as turn-medial rather than turn-final.

A different result was obtained by Cutler and Pearson (1986), who also asked participants to judge utterances as turn-final or turn-medial. Instead of filtering the speech to control for syntax, they used only syntactically complete utterances but varied their intonation. Their finding was that a "downstepped" intonation contour (presumably a low boundary [↓] in my model) was more likely judged as turn-final, whereas "upstepped" contours (presumably high-rising [↑] or low-rising [↗] boundaries) were judged as turn-medial. In view of the discrepancies between this and Schaffer's study, I would avoid concluding that certain intonation contours *always* indicate a specific turn-taking intention.

Auer (1996), in a study of German conversation data, controlled for syntax by focusing on a particular syntactic configuration: syntactic expansions—points where speakers added on new material after a syntactic completion. He found that "prosodic packaging" (p. 82) was instrumental in distinguishing how closely integrated the expansion was with the prior utterance. If an expansion was a separate, independent thought, it was likely to have a separate intonation contour, as well as an increase in loudness and/or tempo, interrupted rhythm, and a possible pause. On the other hand, an expansion meant to be more closely integrated with prior material could be added within the same intonation contour with no marked prosodic changes. Auer also cautions, however, that no single prosodic cue could be taken as a foolproof indicator of speaker intention. Prosodic cues varied in context and could even be ambiguous to listeners who sometimes overlapped a syntactic expansion.

Pause may also be associated with turn boundaries, but again it is not always a reliable cue. Speakers may pause midturn for strategic reasons, such as to secure an interlocutor's gaze and, hence, attention (Goodwin, 1981), or to "generate the impression of thoughtfulness" (Good & Butterworth, 1980, p. 51). Local and Kelly (1986) document the fact that phonetic cues directly *before* a pause, rather than presence of the pause itself, can indicate the speaker's turn-taking intentions. In their turn-taking study, two phonetically distinct types of pauses were identified: the "trail-off silence" occurred with open glottis and was preceded by out-breath, vowel centralization, diminished loudness and tempo, and sometimes lower pitch. This was an indication that a speaker had completed his turn. Less likely to be associated with turn completion was the "holding silence," conducted with closed glottis, no final lengthening, and no drop in pitch. This is presumably equivalent to what I have called "no pitch boundary" or "cut-off intonation," often used to convey a speaker's intention to keep the floor in mid-utterance.

The placement of pauses can also be manipulated strategically with respect to other linguistic variables to achieve interactional goals. Eggins and Slade (1997), who use a systemic functional approach to the analysis of conversation (Halliday, 1985; Martin, 1992), discuss the "run on" (p. 189), whereby a speaker combines one or more syntactic units under a single intonation contour. The following is an example, provided by Eggins and Slade (pp. 170–171), of a run on by Fay, the middle speaker:

DAVID   This conversation needs Allenby.
  FAY   Oh he's in London so what can we do?
 NICK   We don't want—we don't need Allenby in the *bloody* conversation.

As they explain: "Here Fay rushes straight on from her first clause to produce a second, coordinated clause. Although the second clause is grammatically independent and each clause selects a different mood, prosodically the two clauses are packaged as a single discourse unit and are therefore treated as a single move" (p. 189).

Schegloff (1982) similarly documents the "rush-through," a floor-keeping strategy whereby speakers speed up through syntactic boundaries and then pause in the middle of a syntactic or intonational phrase rather than at its end. Here is an example (from Corpus 3) of a rush-through in which L replies to a question about whether she intends to use hormone therapy when she reaches menopause:

L   . . . THATS- (.3) a SÓMEthing that I- (.7) I've HEARD a lot
ABÓUT and I KIND of FEEL like- (.4) ɪ'ʟʟ sᴏʀᴛ ᴏꜰ CROSS THAT
BRIDGE when I COME to it↗ which is how I d- (.4) DEAL with
ÉVERYthing ɪɴ ᴍʏ ʟɪꜰᴇ↓ · · ·

In this sequence, L pauses at points where the syntax projects continuation, after *that's, I,* and *feel like,* while speeding through syntactic completions. The last pause actually occurs after a word boundary at the beginning of *deal.* Moreover, all four of these pauses are located in the middle
of intonational phrases—the intonation is cut off in midcontour without
a pitch boundary (the "holding silence" of Local & Kelly, 1986). This
behavior diminishes the chance of interruption because the canonical
turn transition cue of an aligned intonation and syntactic boundary followed by a pause is absent.

The observation of such creative alignments of pause, syntax, and
intonation in turn-taking served as an impetus for two similar statistical
studies of these variables in natural conversation data, Ford and Thompson (1996) and Wennerstrom and Siegel (2001). Ford and Thompson
investigated the interaction of syntactic completion points, pitch boundaries, and pragmatic closures. For this study, intonation was classified into
two categories, "final" (high-rising and low boundaries, in my terms) and
"nonfinal" (all other boundaries or no boundary). Some interesting statistics were derived from their data: 99% of all final pitch boundaries
coincided with syntactic completions, but only 54% of syntactic completions were aligned with final pitch boundaries. What this means is that
speakers could convey an intention to keep the floor *in spite of* a syntactic
completion through nonfinal intonation. The turn was most likely to shift
when syntactic completion, final intonation, and a pragmatic closure were
all aligned, a configuration that Ford and Thompson call the "Complex
Transition Relevance Place."

Wennerstrom and Siegel (2001) conducted a statistical analysis of two
15-minute conversations (Corpora 2 and 3), in which syntactic boundaries, pitch boundaries, and pauses were identified as potential points of
turn transition and entered as independent variables into a logistic regression analysis. The dependent variable in the analysis was whether the
turn shifted or whether the same speaker continued. This statistical model
tested the influence of each of the independent variables (the type of
syntactic boundary, the type of pitch boundary, and the pause length) in
predicting whether the turn shifted, while holding all the other variables
constant.

According to the analysis, pitch boundary type and pause length were
both significant predictors of whether the turn shifted, whereas syntax was

not. This does not necessarily mean that syntax was unimportant but rather that the information conveyed by the syntax was redundant once intonation and pause were taken into account. The most frequent site of turn-shift was at low (↓) or high-rising (↑) pitch boundaries when these were aligned with points of possible syntactic completion. This is the expected configuration at a transition relevance place—both the intonation and the syntax conspired to signal turn closure. Another finding was that midturn pauses commonly occurred at points where neither a syntactic boundary nor a pitch boundary was present. It is "safer" to pause in midphrase than at a phrase boundary if one wishes to avoid interruption. Perhaps more interesting, however, were a set of findings that indicated listener sensitivity to prosody *at odds with* syntax. Of a total of 539 potential syntactic completion points in the data, 395 occurred within turns—that is, the same speaker continued to speak after the syntactic completion. Of course there could many reasons for long turns of several syntactic constituents—the pragmatics of the situation, the topic, personal style, and so forth—but of the 395 cases, a full 266 (about two-thirds) were situations in which intonation gave a signal of continuation that overrode the completion cue of the syntax. Four intonation possibilities were used in this manner. The most common possibility was that two or more syntactic units were "packaged" into one intonational phrase with no intervening pitch boundary. An example of this "run on" situation has been shown from Eggins and Slade (1997). A syntactic boundary in the middle of the intonation contour was not a frequent site of turn shift.

The second possibility was that a plateau boundary (→) could signal a speaker's intention to keep the floor in spite of a syntactic completion. This situation occurs in the following example (Corpus 2), where T is describing a traditional feast in Nepal:

1	T	Then they have a BIG FEAST↘ and they DRINK they
2		'ave these BIG (.2) JARS↘ (.2) FÚLLA this (.5)
3		mm→ (1.5)
4		ᴛꜱ ʟɪᴋᴇ FERMÉNTED WI- er FÉRMENTED RICE↓ (.4)
5		ᴛꜱ ʟɪᴋᴇ THICK ʏ'ᴋɴᴏᴡ RI- ⌈CE
6	M	⌊RICE WINE↗ (.3)
7	T	↱ It's <u>NOT</u> like WI- ɪ ᴍᴇᴀɴ ɪᴛ'ꜱ ɪᴛꜱ' <u>NOT</u> like WINE→ it
8		doesn't <u>TASTE</u> ʟɪᴋᴇ ᴡɪɴᴇ but it's (.5)
9	M	FERMÉNTED↓ =
10	T	=WHITE and MÍLKY but its ⌈FERMENTED↓
11	M	⌊OH yeah↓

In line 7, the word *wine* completes a syntactic clause, but the plateau boundary indicates that more is to come in T's series of statements characterizing this strange milky beverage that seems to defy description. The juncture is shown in figure 7.1.

A third possibility for a pitch boundary conveying a floor-keeping intention despite a syntactic completion was the low-rising boundary (↗). The following example (Corpus 2) shows T using this configuration in an explanation of illnesses among natives of Nepal:

1   T   . . . ɪ ᴍᴇᴀɴ they DON'T get VÍOLENTLY ɪʟʟ ↗ (.4) but
2   SOME of them <u>DO</u> ɪ ᴍᴇᴀɴ⁻ (.1) while I was THERE↘ I-
3   ʏ'ᴋɴᴏᴡ⁻ (.2) TWO DÍFFERENT PÉOPLE I KNEW had
4   <u>TÝPHOID</u>↓ (.2)
5   M   ↳ °OH FUCK↓

As shown in figure 7.2, T's first utterance is a complete clause, ending with *ill*. However, the low-rising boundary conveys his intention to follow up with another utterance.

Finally, a partially falling boundary (↘) could be used to keep the floor after a syntactic completion. As shown in chapter 2, this boundary has a downward slope but does not reach the bottom of the speaker's range. Here is an example (Corpus 3) in a conversation about menopause in which several partially falling boundaries are used:

1   K   . . . A:::nd→ (.7) and <u>MINE</u> was sort of
2   CÓMPLICATED in a SENSE↘ (.2) because (.4) I was
3   PÉRI_ᴍᴇɴᴏᴘᴀᴜsᴀʟ through my mid-<u>FÓRTIES</u>↘ (.4) but
4   when I was FÓRTY↘ (1.5) <u>FIVE</u> FÓRTY-<u>SIX</u>↘ (1.3)
5   I had a PÁRTIAL HYSTERÉCTOMY↓

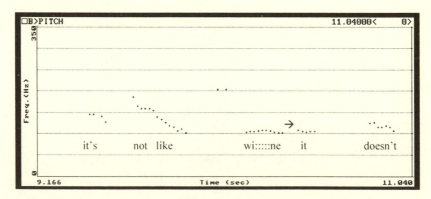

Figure 7.1 The word *wine* coincides with a syntactic completion and a plateau pitch boundary (→) within the same turn.

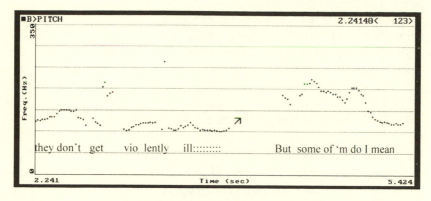

Figure 7.2   The word *ill* coincides with a syntactic completion and a low-rising pitch boundary (↗) within the same turn.

In this excerpt, K uses four partially falling pitch boundaries, after *sense*, *forties*, *forty*, and *six*, all of which are followed by pauses. Although in the first two cases, these are aligned with possible syntactic completion points, the boundaries indicate that she intends to continue her turn. The sequence in line 2 containing the word *sense* is illustrated in figure 7.3.

   To summarize, these examples show successful floor-keeping maneuvers in which intonation indicates a speaker's intention to continue despite the presence of a syntactic completion and in some cases a pause. More broadly, the studies reviewed in this section illustrate how conversants manipulate the alignment of a number of linguistic cues to achieve particular interactional goals—to minimize the chance of interruption,

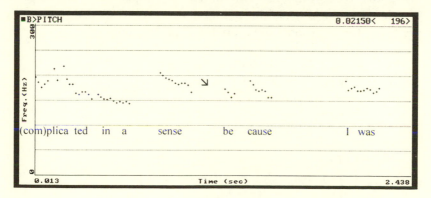

Figure 7.3   The word *sense* coincides with a syntactic completion and a falling pitch boundary (↘) within the same turn.

to gain the listener's attention, to relinquish the floor, and so on. The contribution of prosody to this complicated process appears to be significant, for in research on cases in which prosodic cues are at odds with syntax, the prosody is frequently attended to above the syntax.

The Pitch Accent and Conversational Cohesion

In this section, I move away from questions about the mechanics of conversation to consider its content. How does prosody contribute to the display of participants' priorities and goals, their inferences and assumptions, and, in general, to the coherence of conversation? Gumperz (1982) emphasizes the importance of the "flow" of pitch accents throughout an extended stretch of conversation, which, he says, "allows us to trace speakers' thought processes, and their strategies in developing a theme" (p. 114). His words hark back to the discussion in chapter 4 on the role of pitch accents in the cohesion and coherence of discourse and in how participants develop mental representations of a conversation as it progresses. To review, H* pitch accents are associated with lexical items a speaker wishes to add to the mental representation of the discourse; L+H* pitch accents associate with contrastive items; L* pitch accents associate with items that are not to be added to the mental representation of the discourse, in some cases because they are believed already accessible; and L*+H pitch accents associate with items whose relevance is being questioned.

The following example, from Gumperz (1982), shows how a series of accented words can be analyzed to derive the structure of an argument between two college students on the topic of relationships among subdisciplines in anthropology. The students are apparently discussing the fact that, in prior days, anthropologists were not as specialized as they are today, for everybody "did everythin'" in those days:

```
1     A   . . . I mean everybody started out
2         people who were in nineteen hundred
3         they did everythin'
4         right?
5     B   yeh but that's THEN
6         that's not NOW
7          ⎡now
8     A   ⎣but ultimately it they it . . .
9         so it's all spread out NOW
10        but it all CAME from somewhere
11        right? (p. 105)
```

Rather than attempting to convert Gumperz's transcript into my system, I have coded only the intonation of the words that are central to the example. Gumperz characterizes *then* in line 5 as "stressed" (p. 115), (I have coded it with H* pitch accent) and *now, now,* and *came* in lines 6, 9, and 10 as having "accents" and a "rise fall tune" (p. 116) (I have coded these with L+H* pitch accents). In Gumperz's view, these strongly accented items emphasize the temporal aspect of the argument being made—that the field of anthropology has changed *over time.* Gumperz warns that an analysis of isolated utterances and specific contrasts between word pairs would not do justice to the situation; rather, these contrasts are part of an overall discourse strategy to build an argument over a series of turns.

Sacks (in Jefferson, 1995) places a similar emphasis on the role of pitch accents in "tying" in conversation (his term for cohesion). Citing Gunter (1966), he is interested in how contrastive pitch accents (L+H* in my terms) are used to tie utterances together in conversation, which he considers a crucial interactive device in the display of understanding across speakers. He exemplifies this with a discussion of how these pitch accents associate with pronouns:

> If you have an utterance in which you have a possessive pronoun, e.g., "mine," "ours," "your," "their," etc., if that possessive pronoun bears the heaviest accent in the utterance, that is a pretty sufficient signal that the utterance is tied, and tied via a *contrast* of that possessive pronoun or the speaker of it, and some other: "Let's take my car." "No, let's take *my* car." The emphasis of the second "my" is a way that the tied character of that utterance to the prior one, and the contrast involved, are done. (p. 736)

He goes on to emphasize the global nature of the meaning of accents: "[T]he accent a word is assigned may be a feature not only of its position in an utterance, but also the position of that utterance in discourse. Which is to say that one can't account for accents comprehensively without studying more than a single utterance" (p. 736).

An illustration of Sacks's very point comes from Schegloff (1998, p. 248). The following is a portion of a conversation[1] between two college girls from California who are discussing a potential blind date that one of the girls, Hyla, might go on. Evidently a friend of Hyla ("she" in the first line) wants to match-make her with a male friend who will soon be visiting from Minneapolis. Hyla is lukewarm about the idea:[2]

```
1     HYLA   't'k YOU know she says eez a veewy NICE guy↓ eez
2            a REA:L↘ (0.7)
```

```
3                     't good PERS'    ⎡n↓
4        NANCY                         ⎣Ri:ght↓=
5        H    ='t 'hhh
6             (0.7)
7             A:nd→ YIHknow       s ⎡o↘
8        N                         ⎣That sounds GOO:D↓
9             (0.2)
10       H    EH:::↘=
11       N    =A'RÍ:: ⎡GHT↘
12       H          ⎣Gimm⎡e sumpn  ⎡tih do   ⎡one night⎤
13       N               ⎣YE::H    ⎣except   ⎣then yu'll⎦
14            like HIM en hill go back
15            ⎡tuh MINNEÁ ⎤P'LIS↓=
16       H    ⎣Hhhh Hhhhh⎦
17       H    =' eh En ah'll ne(h)ver hear fr'm HIM a ⎡gai:n↘    ⎤
18       N                                           ⎣Nihh hnh⎦ –
19            heh
20       ( )  'e-=
21       N    ='hihh ⎡hhhh
22       H          ⎣'hihhhhhh
```

Schegloff calls attention to the intonation in Nancy's utterance in lines
13–15, shown in figure 7.4,[3] which he interprets as a compliment from
Nancy to Hyla. Although we might expect H* pitch accent to be on *like*,
L+H* pitch accent (or in Schegloff's terms, the "nuclear stress") is instead associated with the pronoun *him*. The compliment, though never
directly stated, resides in the contrast invoked by this L+H* pitch accent:
Nancy presents the idea that Hyla might actually fall for the guy as the
contrastive, unexpected case, whereas the opposite, inferable assumption is that "he" (the boy) will of course like "her" (Hyla). In support of
Schegloff's analysis, I would also consider the role of the L* pitch accent,
which, from the figure, I take to be associated with the word *like*. Thus, I
would retranscribe the compliment as follows:

then you'll $_{LIKE}$ HIM and he'll go back to MINNEÁPOLIS↓

Despite no direct mention of "liking" in the conversation so far, the L*
pitch accent indicates that Nancy assumes the idea to be accessible in
Hyla's mental representation of the discourse. The assumption is not
unwarranted because the question of whether one's romantic feelings will
be returned is an age-old part of any dating schema. Therefore, the L*
pitch accent helps the utterance function as a compliment—that *liking*
will go on (on the boy's side) is presented by Nancy as given. Schegloff
goes on to analyze Hyla's response ("and I'll never hear from HIM again")

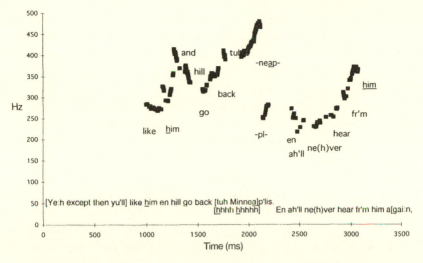

Figure 7.4   The intonation in this turn conveys a compliment.

as a deflection of the compliment. This time the L+H* pitch accent allows *him* to be interpreted as a contrastive element among members of the set of first dates who have rejected her (there was him and him and him, and now HIM!). Thus, Hyla conveys the cynical meaning that rather than being the adored, she will no doubt be left behind heart-broken while the boy stereotypically "keeps on trucking" back to Minneapolis.

This example reinforces three points about prosody in discourse that I have tried to make throughout this volume:

1. The lexicogrammatical structure alone could not achieve what is achieved by the intonation. If *him* did not have L+H* pitch accent and *like* have L*, the "compliment" meaning would be lost ("then you'll LIKE him" would convey a different meaning).
2. A cohesive tie need not be a direct one to previous items in the text; it may be made with reference to what one speaker believes to be in the other's mental representation of the discourse in progress. Here it involves a schema about dates and relationships common to American college girls.
3. The coherence is developed across two speakers, demonstrating the inferences made as they attend to each other's utterances and continuously readjust their mental representations of the discourse.

To summarize more generally, I am suggesting that the analysis of pitch accents as cohesive devices in conversation is a potentially powerful tool to obtain information about the development of the thread of the conversation, the relationships among the participants, the cultural assumptions underlying the conversation, and the inferencing process. One vehicle for studying cohesion is through contrastive L+H* pitch accents, as Gumperz, Sacks, and Schegloff have suggested. By tracing the points of highest focus in the conversation, an analyst can follow the chain of development: how each new idea is being juxtaposed with what has come before. A second contribution of pitch accent analysis is that of L* pitch accents in making manifest what each conversant assumes to be salient but already accessible in the others' mental representation of the discourse. As we saw in Schegloff's data, the placement of certain pitch accents revealed not necessarily a direct link to previous text but a link to what was assumed about the context of conversation. The analysis of pitch accents can be an enhancement to prior studies of conversation, potentially leading to new insights about cultural knowledge and values.

Tone Concord in Conversation

At this point, I turn to a third aspect of prosody of particular relevance in the analysis of conversation—key and tone concord. To review, high key ($\nearrow$) at the onset of an utterance indicates that it is contrary to expectation; mid key ($\rightarrow$) is a neutral choice, a simple addition; and low key ($\searrow$) means that an utterance is a foregone conclusion. A central issue is that of how one speaker's key matches the previous speaker's pitch termination, a phenomenon that Brazil (1985) refers to as the "tone concord" (p. 86). Concord is described as a supportive situation in which the pitch level at the termination of one speaker's turn is met with the same relative pitch level in the onset of the next speaker's turn.[4] In such cases, the two conversants agree about how they are interpreting and reacting to the context of the conversation. However, a mismatch of pitch range level, "concord breaking," may also occur with a less harmonious result. Brazil says that "we shall expect concord-breaking to occur at moments when there is a discrepancy between the ways the two parties assess the context of interaction" (p. 86). Brazil warns that a high key in response to a mid or low termination can have "distinctly querulous overtones" (p. 77).

A study by Günthner (1996) also provides evidence of high key conveying a discordant meaning, although Günthner herself does not use the term "key." In a corpus of German conversation data, she identified two distinctive meanings for *why* questions, each with a different intonation pattern. The first were genuine information questions about cause.

The second type she categorized as "reproaches," where *why* was not a neutral request for information but a challenge to the interlocutor. I believe that English also allows the possibility of reproaches delivered in a *why* question, for Günthner's examples translate only too well as reproaches—for example, "Why do you always let her in (p. 271)?" and "Why the hell don't you ask her directly then (p. 272)?" She found that the reproach type of question was uttered with a higher global pitch than the informational question, which, in terms of this discussion, translates into a high key, out of concord with the prior utterance. Günthner also found that the reproaches tended to be associated with a louder volume and a pitch accent on the finite verb.

A related finding comes from Selting (1996), also from German conversation data, where requests for repair could be prosodically unmarked—delivered in tone concord with the prior utterance, in my terms—or, delivered in a high key. The first type were neutral requests for repair whereas the latter were heard as astonished or surprised—this can't be right!!—and therefore required more elaborate repair work from the original speakers. Although neither Selting nor Günthner mention the term "key," their findings both appear to be in line with Brazil's general claim that high key is used for that which is contrary to expectation and can have a discordant reading. In Günthner's case, this was associated with reproaches and in Selting's with astonishment.

Another study on the topic of pitch range and interaction was conducted by French and Local (1986). This was a study of interruptions in natural English conversation data. When an interruption point involved a competition for the floor, both speakers raised their pitch and volume until one succeeded in obtaining the floor as sole speaker. Again, the authors do not mention "key" as a term, but I believe their results are in line with this discussion. Speakers used high key competitively in a power struggle to assert their right to the floor, rather than engaging in a more smoothly flowing cooperation.

Pickering (1999), who does use "key" in exactly Brazil's terms, points out the potential for misunderstanding in cross-cultural interactions between international teaching assistants and their American undergraduate students. She documents cases where speakers of Indian English, in which high-pitched onsets for intonational phrases are a normal part of the phonology, were perceived by American students as sounding aggressive. Pickering maintains that it was the perception of a high key in response to a neutral one that led to this conclusion. That is, the American-English speakers associated a negative social message with the concord breaking, which for the speakers of Indian English had no such meaning. Similar key-based misunderstandings also occurred between American students and Chinese teaching assistants in Pickering's data and will be discussed in chapter 9.

So far we have looked at examples of high key in concord breaking; however, it is also possible to find mismatches of key where a low key is crucial to the interaction, as in the following case documented by Schegloff (1998). The excerpt below (p. 245), also shown in figure 7.5,[5] is the beginning of a telephone conversation between two young women we've met before, Hyla and Nancy (I've added coding symbols for high [↱], mid [→], and low [↳] key to Schegloff's original transcript, although he does not use the term *key*):

```
1    N    →    H'llo::↑
2    H    ↳    HI:→
3    N    ↱    HI::↓
4    H    ↳    HwARyuhh=
5    N    = ↳  FI:NE how'r YOU↗
6    H    OKA:  ⎡Y↘
7    N          ⎣Goo:d↘      (.4)
```

As Schegloff describes the situation, the first speaker, Nancy, uses a high key in line 3 to display an enthusiastic stance upon recognizing her friend's voice. However, this is met in line 4 with Hyla's low-keyed "how are you," which can be heard as much more restrained. Immediately

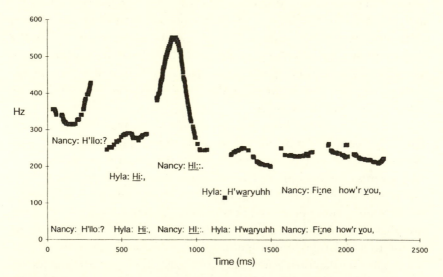

Figure 7.5 Two speakers negotiate their key at the beginning of a telephone conversation.

thereafter, in line 5, Nancy drops back down to match the low key of Hyla. Schegloff interprets these key choices as a negotiation over stance in which Nancy makes the adjustment to Hyla's lower key (p. 245). I analyze this as an instance of key functioning to assert what is, in this case, Hyla's social power: the low key conveys a kind of "put down" (you are less of a big deal to me than I evidently am to you), which leads Nancy to modify her initial exuberant stance. The concord breaking is again a reflection of a social discord, but, in this case, the mismatch of key goes from high to low rather than from mid to high.

The final example illustrates a somewhat more complex manipulation of key involving an interplay of both tone concord and concord breaking in a humorous sequence. In the excerpt (from Corpus 2), four participants collaborate to achieve social cohesion in a joking mode. In prior talk, T has described an illness in which he lost a lot of weight. Others are now discussing how and when he will gain it back. The humor begins in line 10 when R offers T some ice cream:

```
 1    M    ↱ So are you GÁINING WEIGHT↑ (.4)
 2         → I MEAN⁻ (.3) y- you LOST a lotta WEIGHT↘
 3         RIGHT↗ =
 4    T    = → YEAH↗ WELL I THINK I AM↗ (.9) → It's HARD to
 5         TELL↓ (1.0)
 6         →I MEAN I FEEL like I'm eating FULL MEALS↘ (.4)
 7    M    →You        ⎡WILL gain WEIGHT↓
 8    T               ⎣→NOW I'm just STÚFFING myself YOU
 9         KNOW⁻ (.8)
10    R    ↳ Want some ÍCE CREAM↑ (.3)
11    T    Uh ha ha ha ha ha ↳ No ↓(1.0)
12    R    ↳ We GOT some↓ (.4)
13    M    ↳ Y' want some LARD↑ (.2)
14    S    ↱ Y' want some CAKE↑ =
15    M    = ↱ CRÍSCO↑ (.8)
16    R    ↳ °CAKE 'n ÍCE CREAM↓ (1.0)
17    M    → GOD how WÓNDERFUL to be so SKÍNNY you
18         could just STUFF YOURSÉLF↓
```

The humor continues in lines 11–16 in which participants make ever more ridiculous suggestions for high-fat foods that T might like to eat to gain weight. The sequence provides a good example of the collaborative manipulation of key across several speakers' turns. Part of what makes this a humorous frame is the fact that some of the speakers associate a low key (↳) with their contributions, conveying the idea that the offers of food are made as casual asides. The low key is initiated by R, a male speaker, who in general has participated little in this conversation. Instead of taking active conversational roles, his style is to slip in occasional comments from the sidelines. His low-keyed offer in line 10, "Want some ice cream?" can be heard as an attempt at deadpan humor. T (also a man) declines the offer in a similarly low key in line 11. T's laughter indicates that he accepts R's contribution as humorous. R then continues with low key, "We got some," in line 12. M (a woman) joins in in line 13 with yet another low-keyed offer, "Y'want some lard?" These low-keyed offers are shown in figure 7.6. In the figure, M's contribution is slightly higher in pitch than R's and T's, but it is low with respect to her own pitch range. So far, two points about the use of low key in this initial sequence should be noted: first, it conveys an "offhandedness" whose effect is humorous (and oh, by the way, do you want some lard?). Second, it is used in concord by three different speakers—the humor is collaborative, reinforcing the social cohesion of this group. Moving on, in line 14, S (a woman) introduces a high key to offer "some cake." This concord breaking continues to be humorous because instead of a casual aside, her offer now sounds more serious and a little aggressive—a parody of the brightly smiling hostess in a restaurant. M makes her next offer of Crisco in a similar manner in concord with S—two brightly smiling hostesses! Figure 7.7 shows the shift in key: M's key changes from low in her offer of lard to high in her offer of Crisco, matching S's "hostess" style in her offer of cake. At this point there is a .8-second pause—the humor value of these repeated offers of food has almost run its course. However, in line 16, R gives it one more try, returning to a low key and low volume to offer "cake 'n ice cream" in his original offhanded style. No more offers are added after this. The joke is more than the sum of its individual parts; it is a

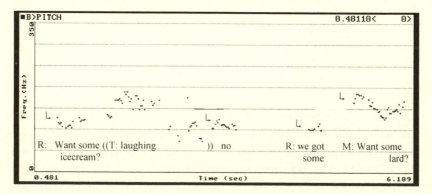

Figure 7.6   Several speakers use low key (ꓡ) adding an offhanded sense to their offers of food.

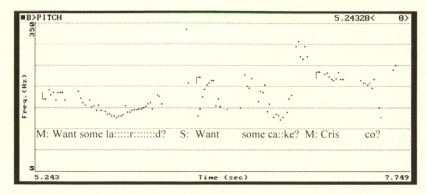

Figure 7.7   Speakers switch from low key (L) to high key (Γ) in this humorous sequence.

collaboration in which four people participate and the humor accumulates with each new offer. The manipulations of key create an image of multiple food giving "from all sides," whereas the idea of T (the one who needs to gain weight) actually eating all those food items becomes ever more repulsive and humorous.

These are just a few examples of a valuable tool to study power and solidarity moves in conversation. Key offers the analyst a turn-by-turn pulse of speakers' reactions to each other. We have seen that concord breaking can occur in conversations when there is a discrepancy in the agreement or stance of the speakers. We have also seen a case of tone concord among several participants in collaboration to achieve social solidarity through humor. Because there is relatively little research available on tone concord, it would be an excellent topic for future investigation.

Rhythm and Conversation

To begin the discussion of rhythm in conversation, I turn to Gumperz's theory of contextualization, which assigns a primary status to the role of rhythm in social interaction. As noted in chapter 3, I take this to be theoretically compatible with the body of research in metrical phonology showing that rhythm is the basis of phonological structure (Hayes 1984, 1995; Liberman, 1975; Liberman & Prince, 1977; and numerous other treatments). I discussed "rules of eurythmy" (Hayes, 1995) that tend to align stressed syllables into beats of equal duration for an overall rhythmic balance. According to Gumperz (1982, and elsewhere), rhythm is one of a number of "contextualization cues" upon which participants in conversation rely to infer how a particular social dynamic is to proceed. These cues may be lexicogrammatical, phonological, prosodic, paralinguistic, and even nonverbal and are largely unconscious. By both producing and interpreting these cues, participants negotiate their decisions about the goals of an interaction, its level of formality, its seriousness, and even what speech activity is taking place—whether they are "discussing politics, chatting about the weather, telling a story to someone, . . . [or] lecturing about linguistics" (Gumperz, 1982, p. 166). Part of our ability to conduct these negotiations is based on our knowledge, as members of a culture, of what Gumperz calls "interpretive frames," that is, sets of expectations that form a template for the communicative options available in a given context. Gumperz believes that rhythm is part of the coordination needed for successful involvement in interaction. In his words:

> I would like to suggest that the signaling of speech activities is not a matter of unilateral action but rather of speaker-listener coordination involving rhythmic interchange of both verbal and nonverbal signs. In other words, a successful interaction begins with each speaker talking in a certain mode, using certain contextualization cues. Participants, then, by the verbal style in which they respond and the listenership cues they produce, implicitly signal their agreement or disagreement; thus they "tune into" the other's way of speaking. Once this has been done, and once a conversational rhythm has been established, both participants can reasonably assume that they have successfully negotiated a frame of interpretation, i.e. they have agreed on what activity is being enacted and how it is to be conducted. (p. 167)

He goes on to say that a change in rhythm can reflect a change in frame: "Speakers continue in the same mode, assigning negotiated meaning to contextualization cues, until there is a perceptible break in rhythm, a shift of content and cues, or until a mismatch between content and cues suggests that something has gone wrong" (p. 167). From this statement, we can see that, although rhythm is not the only factor involved in the dynamics of interaction, Gumperz regards it as a basic signal of successful conversational involvement. If a frame has been negotiated and the conversation is going smoothly, the rhythm is regular. It then becomes of empirical interest to investigate the situations in which rhythm is or is not regular. Are there functional distinctions between these two situations?

Indeed, the regularity of rhythm in certain stretches of conversation, even across speakers, has been fairly well confirmed in empirical studies (see Auer et al., 1999; Couper-Kuhlen, 1992, 1993; Erickson & Shultz, 1982; Fiksdal, 1990, this volume; Goodwin, 1981; Hellerman, 1997; McClave, 1994; Uhmann, 1992, 1996). A study by Erickson (1992) is a case in point: His finding was that, in a conversation over dinner, a family of several mem-

bers collaboratively maintained a high level of rhythmic synchrony throughout the meal. This was especially evident in a listing sequence when participants added items to the list rhythmically over a stretch of several turns.
The rhythmic synchrony was manifest not only in the timing of the main
beats of the stressed syllables of noun phrases on the list, but also in the
gestures and even the eating behaviors, which were coordinated in regular alignment. Erickson views rhythm as a mechanism of social order, used
effectively by this group to accommodate each other in the social act of a
dinner conversation.

As an illustration of the phenomenon of cross-speaker rhythmic synchrony, I have drawn an excerpt from Couper-Kuhlen's study of rhythm
and tempo (1992) in which regular rhythm is maintained across turn
boundaries. To review from chapter 3, rhythm is typically manifest in the
stressed syllables of content words. These prominent syllables tend to be
aligned in time whereas unstressed syllables and function words are sand-
wiched in between. If a sequence of speech does not happen to contain
a regular alternation of strong and weak syllables, speakers tend to make
adjustments in syllable alignment so that the overall result is more rhythmically balanced, or "eurythmic." In the transcript here (p. 342), the slash
(/) indicates the rhythmic interval, the carat (^) indicates a silent beat,
and the small circle (°) indicates quieter speech. I have also added accent marks (á) to show the most prominent syllable of each beat in accord with Couper-Kuhlen's description of the data:

1	T	I/dídn't even		/
2		/knów him in		/
3		/ní:neteen		/
4		/twenty thrée,		/
5		/did I Érnest.		/
6		/ ^		/
7	L	/ ^	he	/
8		/wásn't		/
9		/bórn in		/
10		/ní:neteen		/
11		/twénty		/
12		/thrée!		/
13		/ ^		/
14		/ ^		/
15		/ ^		/
16	E	/whó.		/
17	L	/yóu	((faster, double time))	
18		weren't		
19		°born°.	/	

```
20    E   /Í wasn't,      /
21        /nó.            /
22    L   /nó
```

The excerpt illustrates several common characteristics of rhythmic exchanges. First, the sequence is structured with regular intervals, and the rhythm is maintained from one speaker to the next. Also, the fact that speech is approximately, rather than absolutely, rhythmic is not problematic for the claim of human sensitivity to rhythm, because people process rhythmic sequences holistically as "auditory gestalts" (Couper-Kuhlen, 1993, p. 69). Here, slight irregularities in rhythm do occur, as in line 10 where the stressed vowel of *nineteen* is lengthened, and in lines 4 and 5 where the prominence of the beat is delayed; yet the basic rhythmic structure is picked up again immediately after these irregularities. Furthermore, a pause does not necessarily count as a rhythmic disruption: conversants appear to be aware of the silent beats as the new speech resumes with the same synchrony as the previous. Finally, in the latter part of the conversation when E joins in, the tempo actually doubles with respect to the rhythmic pattern begun by T and L. Couper-Kuhlen (1992) explains this change in pace as associated with a "side sequence" between E and L, departing temporarily from the main topic and, likewise, from the main rhythmic structure (p. 345). Returning to the question of how participants in conversation time their turn-taking with little gap and overlap, it is highly plausible that rhythm plays a role. Once a rhythmic sequence is established, conversants can attune their judgments about the timing of turn-taking to the interval length currently in force.

Other studies have focused on changes or irregularities in rhythm or tempo. The thrust of this research has been to identify functional or interactional motivations for these irregularities. In a study of conversation by Uhmann (1992), side sequences were identified whose tempo was faster than that of the rest of the conversation. These included repairs, parentheticals, afterthoughts, summaries, and other turn-exit devices. Uhmann concludes more generally that sequences of higher relevance to the topic tend to be slower in tempo than sequences of lower relevance. This coincides with the doubled tempo in Couper-Kuhlen's data in the previous example. Uhmann's conclusion finds additional support in another tempo study by Local (1992), who found that parenthetical, or "self-interrupting," talk was characterized by an acceleration of tempo. Couper-Kuhlen (1992) also found that repairs were often associated with accelerated tempo. She theorizes that the desire to preserve face in conversation is sufficiently strong to motivate people to accomplish repair work as quickly as possible and resume the main conversational thread.

The one interesting exception to her finding, however, was that repairs involving sheer audibility (one person misheard the other), were not associated with faster tempo; instead, slower tempo was more appropriate for this type of clarification repair.

On the topic of rhythmic disruption, Müller (1996) analyzed the prosody of backchannels, or "continuers" (such as "uh huh" in English), of moderators in Italian radio call-in shows. He found that if these were "affiliative," they were constructed so as to "fit" with little disruption into the flow of the caller's speech, integrated rhythmically into the pauses. The volume and pitch of these affiliative continuers were also coordinated with those of the caller, the pitch contour of the continuation echoing that of the prior utterance and matching its volume. "Disaffiliating" continuers, on the other hand, were found to be out of synchrony with the flow of speech: They were delivered rhythmically early or late, with a lower volume, or with a lower pitch and little pitch variety (this is similar to the tone concord breaking mentioned in the last section). Radio moderators were skilled at using these subtle disaffiliation signals cumulatively over several turns to lead a caller toward a close.

To summarize, participants in conversation tend to establish a regular rhythm that can continue for several utterances and across turns. Changes in that rhythm occur when there is a sea change in the interaction. These may accompany a frame shift (Gumperz, 1982), a side sequence (Uhmann, 1992; Local, 1992; Couper-Kuhlen, 1992), an interactional manipulation (Müller, 1996), or even, as we will see in the sample analysis in this chapter by Fiksdal, social discord.

Unresolved Issues

What follows are several issues involving the role of prosody in conversation that remain underexplored. There is a need to replicate prior studies involving prosody with new data and to reopen old research questions with prosodic variables added. In general, it has been the durational features of prosody—pause, rhythm, and tempo—that have been analyzed the most in studies of conversation, whereas while the role of other prosodic cues, especially intonation, deserves to be expanded.

Can the Results of Prior Studies of Prosody in Conversation Be Replicated?

Research on prosody in conversation, especially multiparty conversation, is very labor intensive. Prior studies have often relied on rather small corpora; for example, the Wennerstrom and Siegel (2001) study of turn-taking depends on two corpora of about 14–15 minutes each, which resulted in over a thousand potential points of turn shift, each of which had to be coded for intonation, syntax, and pause length. To make generalizations beyond these particular conversations, it would be useful if others would attempt to replicate these studies. Conducting similar studies using different data would provide evidence for whether prior claims were generalizable or merely artifacts of a particular conversation. Many of the studies referenced in this chapter would be suitable to replicate. For example, Müller's (1996) study of backchannels in Italian radio call-in shows could be replicated for call-in shows in other languages; or Fiksdal's study (this chapter) of "uncomfortable moments" where the rhythm breaks down in academic advising sessions could be replicated in other "gatekeeping" situations.

Can the Addition of Prosodic Variables to Previous Studies of Conversation Shed New Light on Old Questions?

By revisiting the research questions of earlier conversation studies with the addition of prosodic variables, we may find new insights. For example, of interest in the CA tradition have been studies of topic initiation and change, openings and closings, adjacency pairs, interruptions, repairs, and so forth. In such studies, prosodic features often take a backseat to questions of syntax, lexical choice, discourse sequencing, laughter, and even the meaning of "little noises" (as are often encoded in transcripts). Where research methodologies of earlier studies have ignored prosodic features, they could be revisited to take pitch accents, tone concord, pitch boundaries, rhythm, tempo, or volume into account. An example of this type of project is French and Local's (1986) study of interruptions. Although overlapping speech has always been a popular topic in studies of conversation, their research, with its focus on pitch and volume, resulted in a sharper definition of an interruption and new classifications of overlapping speech.

How Do Pitch Accents Contribute to the "Flow," or Cohesion of Conversation from One Speaker to the Next?

By studying where conversants associate their pitch accents, one can learn more about the cohesion and thematic "flow" of conversation. As a conversation progresses, how are conversants able to construct coherent interpretations and make relevant contributions? This is a topic for which little prior work has been done. One approach to a study of cohesion would be to determine which lexical items were associated with different types of pitch accents. As H* pitch accents are associated with those items added to the discourse as new, an examination of the H* pitch accents would reveal the development of new themes of the conversation. A similar investigation of L+H* pitch accents would reveal the contrasts in the conversation. How are ideas juxtaposed? What sets of ideas constitute the basis for a contrast? Finally, an analysis of the L* pitch accents would provide insights into what is considered accessible in the mental representation of the discourse. As discussed in chapter 4, the cohesive pitch accents L* and L+H* may associate with lexical items that do not have explicit antecedents in the text itself. Instead, they may be interpreted based on what is assumed to be in the schema invoked by other aspects of the text or context. An analysis of these pitch accents, then, can provide insights into personal or cultural schemata held by the participants in a conversation. In general, the study of pitch accents contributes to the understanding of what makes conversation coherent, how inferences are made, and how meaning is created.

What Can Tone Concord and Concord Breaking Tell Us about the Structure of Interaction?

In this chapter we saw examples of a high key used to introduce material slightly out of kilter with the expectations projected by a prior utterance in a mid key. This "concord breaking" was presented as a negative phenomenon—I even cited Brazil as having used the word "querulous" to describe concord breaking. However, I also analyzed a passage in which tone concord and concord breaking were manipulated to achieve a playful, humorous effect. Could low key also play a role in understatement, deadpan humor, snide remarks, or to make the speaker sound "cool"? To say the least, there is room for more research on the possible nuances of key. Further conversations could be examined to investigate the circumstances under which tone concord is maintained or broken and the consequences in the subsequent conversation.

Is There Evidence in Conversation Data of Rules of Eurythmy?

As I pointed out in the section of this chapter on rhythm, the finding that rhythm is regular in many stretches of conversation is consistent with theories of metrical phonology that posit underlying rhythmic structure in spoken language. However, the traditional methodology for metrical phonologists has been to use introspective data (that is, constructed examples). A useful "applied phonology" project would be to search for

evidence of rules of eurythmy in naturally occurring conversations, especially across turn boundaries. One way to go about this would be to investigate instances of overlapping speech and latches—predictable sites for
coordinated rhythm. To my knowledge, little or no empirical research
has been done with actual conversation data in the framework of metrical phonology. This is therefore a useful topic for further analysis.

Sample Analysis

The sample analysis for this chapter is one of tempo and rhythm in interaction, provided by a guest contributor, Susan Fiksdal. The analysis is
drawn from her book, *The Right Time and Pace* (1990), for which she used
video technology to investigate the discourse of academic advising sessions. By replaying the videotapes, she was able not only to hear the conversational rhythm but also to observe the associated postural shifts and
gestures. Reported here is an investigation of sequences where the conversational rhythm became disrupted. Fiksdal refers to such instances as
"uncomfortable moments," when a lack of synchrony in rhythm—quick-
ened tempo and extensive pauses—corresponded to social discomfort.
Fiksdal (1990) observes that uncomfortable moments "cause a disturbance
in the flow of discourse, and they call for a heavy reliance on the rapport
system" (p. 115). Participants confirmed in follow-up interviews that they
felt uncomfortable at these arrhythmic moments. Fiksdal's data are especially intriguing because they involve a markedly unequal distribution
of power, between American academic advisors and their international
student advisees. Evidently the ethnicity factor did not prevent the participants in these conversations from establishing a synchronized rhythm.
Instead, face-threatening situations—power struggles over decision making and the like—accompanied the arrhythmic sequences. This suggests
a universal aspect to rhythmic synchrony in interaction and to the factors involved in its disruption.

A Time-Based Model of Conversation*

This sample analysis illustrates a time-based model of conversation. This
model responds to three research traditions: cultural differences in conversational interactions, ritual behavior and its relationship to turn-taking,
and findings about the rhythmic structure of talk. The notion of time in

*This section was contributed by Susan Fiksdal.

the model draws its definition from the two words for time in Greek—
chronos and *kairos.* Chronos is the notion of time that passes moment by
moment on clocks or calendars; kairos is the appropriate time to do something, such as when we say, the "time to bring that up just never came"
or "my timing was off in that interview." Each of these aspects of time
relates to an underlying organizational structure for conversation.
Chronos, or clock time, underlies the turn-taking system as shown by
Erickson and Shultz (1982). By measuring stressed syllables and nonverbal gestures with a metronome, they discovered a regular underlying
tempo or beat that speakers collaboratively created during their talk. This
close adherence to an underlying tempo explains how speakers can oc-
casionally begin to speak at exactly the same moment. Strikingly, they
found that when disruptions occurred in this tempo (either a faster tempo
or momentary arrhythmia), an uncomfortable moment occurred in the
discourse.

Kairos, or the appropriate time to say something, is the basis for the
face system each speaker draws upon. Face as a system worthy of careful
exploration by Western researchers was first proposed by Goffman (1967)
as he examined ritual behavior in ordinary social interaction. He drew
on a number of previous researchers including Hu (1944) to define the
concept of face. Face is the line or approach a speaker takes in a conversation; in Goffman's words, it is "an image of self delineated in terms of
approved social attributes" (p. 5). The time-based model of conversation
builds on Goffman's ritual model of conversation (1981) as well as Brown
and Levinson's (1978) politeness theory to explore face as a system, particularly in the way it builds cohesion.

Both of these systems are fundamental to every conversation. To
understand the conventions and constraints speakers use, one might look
at repair in the conversation within the context of the talk. How do speakers maintain the face system when something goes wrong? In the study
reported here, data come from nine interviews between Taiwanese students and their American advisors and six interviews between those same
advisors and native English speakers foreign to the United States from
Canada, England, and Ireland. All interviews took place at a large Mid-
western university. Interviews were videotaped in advisors' offices when
students came to discuss immigration issues, from the minor questions
of getting practical training in the United States after graduation to seeking permanent residency status. These are, then, natural conversations.
The advisors had long experience in helping students negotiate the regulations of the Immigration and Naturalization Service (INS), which students respected. Unlike many bureaucracies in the United States, the INS
has no clearly written directions for attaining a particular status; instead,

it has policies that can be interpreted in many ways. For this reason, the advisors' knowledge was important to every student but crucial to the Taiwanese students trying to stay indefinitely in the United States.

The Taiwanese speakers use a deference face system, or what Brown and Levinson term *negative politeness*. The native English speakers (Canadian, English, and American) use a rapport face system, or *positive politeness*. (Note that positive and negative refer to opposite poles of politeness, not to connotations of a particular approach to politeness.) Each of these face systems draws on different strategies to repair the talk. To investigate these systems from the speakers' point of view, I asked each participant to take part in individual playback sessions in which they had the opportunity to comment on what happened in the interview.

In the following example drawn from an interview between a female Taiwanese student and a female advisor, the advisor is giving the Taiwanese student a long explanation about the difficulties in applying for permanent residency while the student has a particular visa status. She has tried to cover several possible approaches, each of which is rather complicated. Here she experiences an uncomfortable moment even though the student tries to help her save face (S = student; A = advisor; >> = faster tempo; << = slower tempo):

```
1     A  They're sent off to the (.) regional (.) office (.) in (.)
2        Lincoln Nebraska
3     S  ((laughs))
4     A  I know it's ri  ⎡diculous ((nods))
5     S               ⎣((leans back))
6     S  It must be spring there already  ⎡((laughs))
7     A                                   ⎣((laughs))
8     A  ⌐Oh no it's (.) it's a crazy sort of set up and I'm ((nods,
9        laughing))
10       >> trying to figure out (.)
11       y'know you need to lay out a time schedule about
12       << when you're going to cease to be
13       a student
```

Even though there is laughter from both speakers that seems to align them in the understanding that the problem the advisor has outlined is ridiculous (see lines 1–4), the next move by the student in line 6, "It must be spring there already," causes a disruption in this alignment. In line 8 the advisor's immediate response is "Oh no." It is spoken at a louder volume and higher pitch and as she nods and laughs signaling something is amiss. Indeed, her tempo quickens in lines 10 and 11, indicating a rhythmic disruption in the discourse, in this case, an uncomfortable moment.

In the playback session when asked about the student's statement, "It must be spring there already," the advisor indicated this was an uncomfortable moment: "Unless she was thinking of Nebraska being south, maybe it was the noise [there was loud music coming into the office through an open window], maybe I don't know. That threw me at the time." When asked why she made that statement, the student said, "It's a Chinese proverb. Spring brings hope." The student, then, recognized the difficult situation she could be in, given the advisor's explanation, but thought the location of the INS office, particularly its being well south of the university, might be beneficial to her situation. Her contextual link using a proverb was appropriate for Taiwanese culture. The advisor, however, could not make this connection, given her cultural background, so she experienced an uncomfortable moment.

Speakers experience uncomfortable moments for many different reasons. In this case, the advisor is giving a complicated explanation, and momentarily she is not certain if the student understands what she meant when she talked about documents being sent to Nebraska. Her strategy for moving back to the explanation is to step outside the explanation to remind the student of what she is doing in her explanations. Speakers accomplish this stepping outside when they use a metastatement such as "what I'm trying to say is." In lines 8–11 the advisor uses this strategy: "I'm trying to figure out (.) y'know you need to lay out a time schedule about when you're going to cease being a student." In this study, advisors commented on the interaction using a metastatement about what they were doing to reach agreement about the topic of the conversation. In this case, the point was not Nebraska, but rather the timing of applying for one status while being in another.

This move to reach agreement on the topic is a move to repair an uncomfortable moment in the talk. In Brown and Levinson's (1978) politeness theory, it is a strategy to create common ground, a rapport strategy. Coming to agreement, which is a form of creating common ground, was a strategy native English speakers used often to repair a moment. The Taiwanese students, on the other hand, drew on deference strategies when something went wrong in the conversation.

In the next two examples, with a male Taiwanese student and a male advisor, the student uses a deference strategy. The advisor suggests that he process the student's practical training application by sending it to the INS and that in the meantime the student begin to negotiate the renewal of his passport. The problem is that the Taiwanese government may not renew the passport so many months in advance of its expiration, and, if not, the application for practical training will have to be resubmitted. The student wants to begin his practical training within two weeks as he has accepted a job offer in Texas. Here is part of that interview containing the advisor's first suggestions and the student's deference strategies of delay.

```
 1    A   Well we can go ahead and send it in if you like=
 2    S   =uh huh
 3    A   Uh and in the meantime cause we don't need to send
 4        your passport
 5    S   Yeah
 6    A   we could send in the application (.) you could begin to
 7        negotiate
 8    S   Yeah
 9    A   with your government. About the revalidation of your
10        passport. If they do send it back then perhaps by that
11        time you would have gotten the passport renewed
12        and we could re-resubmit it to the office of
13        immigration
14    S   uh huh
15    A   Want-w-want to try that?
16        (1.96 sec.) or do you want to hold for a- few days until
17        you find out
18    S   (3.0) I go Texas probably I go Texas probably on
19        Thursday so I have to use Federal Express
20    A   Well
21    S   ((laugh))
22    A   why don't we go ahead and send it in.  ⌈that's
23    S                                          ⌊How long is
24        it going to take for the processing of practical training
```

In this example, the advisor makes a suggestion in line 1, "Well we can go ahead and send it in if you like," and repeats it in line 6, "We could send in the application." After each suggestion, the student gives a listener response ("uh huh, yeah"), but he does not seem to choose one. The advisor then asks in line 15, "W-want to try that?" The student makes a comment about going to Texas that does not seem to respond to that question, so the advisor again makes the suggestion, but this time in a more definite way in line 22: "Why don't we go ahead and send it in." The student clearly delays his response to the suggestion.

After this exchange, the student and advisor continue to talk and the advisor repeats, "well (.) why don't we send it in." The student again responds with a noncommittal "uh huh." Then the advisor launches into a detailed scenario of how this suggestion would work. At this point the student offers his own efficient solution to the problem:

```
 1    s   (2.8) Well I think (.) let me call the (.) the well it's the
 2        consulate in Chicago
 3    A   Is that where you deal with them  ⎡now for your
 4    s                                     ⎣yeah
 5    A   Ok
 6    s   If they say that I can renew the passport I just mail it
 7        today
 8    A   All right
 9    s   And I (.) then I mail them the (.) ten bucks
10        ⎡for the Ex-  ⎡Federal Express
11    A   ⎣ok          ⎣ok
12    s   and I can get it back on Wednesday
13    A   ok ((nods))
14    s   and submit it on Wednesday
15    A   (1.91) ((louder))
16        ⎡>>let me look over this over
17        ⎣((leans forward)) quickly
18        ⎡and see if  ⎡there's anything else
19    s   ⎣yeah       ⎣see (.)
20    A   <<that we need to be concerned about.
```

In this example, the student gives a good solution for resolving the difficulty in lines 1–14, but the advisor does not acknowledge it; instead, in line 15 he turns back to the paperwork before him and changes the topic. The student in the playback session noted this sudden change and said, "My-my ways was not good. I don't know how the Americans respond. When M say something that's opposite to your idea they will say no no no I will do what I (.) what I want." In fact, then, he understood very well how Americans respond to a suggestion they do not want to take; however, given his cultural tradition, he had to show deference to someone in authority and he could not explicitly reject a suggestion as he claims Americans do. In this case, his strategy was to delay rather than give a response to the advisor's many suggestions. He knew what approach he would take, but the situation became difficult when the advisor indicated they should take his own final suggestion ("Why don't we send it in?").

The advisor was made noticeably uncomfortable by the student's clear and simple strategy. In line 15 his tone of voice becomes quite loud after his long pause, and his muddled syntax ("let me look over this over quickly") and change of topic, posture, and tempo all indicate his discomfort, recognized by the student. Nevertheless, he did not indicate that discomfort in his playback interview: "I'm sure I felt that his looks were deceiving that he's quiet, but he did understand what it was about and that happens frequently." One reason this advisor did not admit to being surprised could be that he was offering suggestions for a relatively rou-tine task (practical training) rather than for the consequential task of applying for permanent residency. The consequence of the student's delayed response was that the advisor moved on to another task, signal-ing that this one was over.

In both these instances of uncomfortable moments, the trigger is dif-ferent, as is the consequence in the conversation. Nonetheless, both share common traits of disruption of rhythm and loss of face on the part of the advisors. In the first example, we see the advisor's use of coming to agree-ment, drawing on a rapport face system; in the next two examples, we see a Taiwanese student's use of delay, drawing on a deference face system.

This relationship between advisors and students is complex because the advisors play a gatekeeping role. On the one hand, they advise stu-dents based on information available to them about paths through the INS maze of regulations. On the other hand, they regulate most of the students' choices by verifying that they fill out all documentation fully and truthfully and reporting that information to the INS. The power relationships between the speakers, the face systems, and the rhythmic organization of talk are all integrally and contextually linked in this analy-sis, thanks to findings in previous research, improved technology, and the speakers' focus on their very real interests in the interviews.

Chapter Conclusion

I have argued in this chapter that the analysis of prosody is highly com-patible with research on conversation. Indeed, many analysts have always taken prosody seriously as a meaningful aspect of the dynamics of inter-action. The timing, the rhythm, the tempo, the duration of both syllables and pauses, the intonation, the volume—all are available resources in the complex social process of orchestrating a conversation.

One important aspect of prosody in conversation is its function in the determination of transition relevance places by conversants in turn-taking. Intonation, rhythm, syntax, pauses, and even nonverbal cues can work together to send a clear signal of turn relinquishment. However, there is seldom a perfect correspondence among these variables. Instead, conversants manipulate their alignment strategically to convey many subtle turn-taking intentions. Interlocutors are sensitive to these manipu-lations as they anticipate their upcoming turn.

A second topic that has received relatively little attention is the role of pitch accents in cohesion, or "tying" (Sacks's term) in conversation. How conversants build a coherent structure can be explored through the study of pitch accents in context. By looking at H* and L+H* pitch accents throughout a conversation, one can see how the participants' focus of attention progresses and how the theme of the conversation develops. An investigation of L* pitch accents can lead to a better understanding of the participants' underlying assumptions about what is accessible in the mental representation of the discourse. This, in turn, can shed light on what kinds of cultural schemata form the background for the interaction and how participants make inferences to arrive at a coherent interpretation.

The third main topic of this chapter was tone concord, the extent to which key is matched from turn to turn. Tone concord occurs when participants adopt a similar perspective on the context of the conversation and are fulfilling each other's expectations. Concord breaking, the mismatch of key, can indicate a difference in stance with respect to a first speaker's projected expectation, or even a discordant reaction. Studies were reviewed in which a high key was associated with reproaches, astonished requests for repairs, and competitions over the floor. Another analysis involved a high key met by a low one conveying a lack of enthusiasm. An example was also discussed in which key was manipulated collaboratively among a group of conversants to create a humor sequence. Thus, it appears that key can be used in interesting ways as conversants continually react to each other's contributions in the context of the conversation.

The last topic involved the regularity of rhythm in conversation. There is evidence in the literature that, once speakers establish a conversational footing within an agreed upon frame of interpretation, they tend to follow a regular rhythm, even across turns. However, at places in conversation when tempo changes or rhythm breaks down, researchers have found that shifts in frame, side sequences, or even interactional problems tend to be evident.

Because traditional approaches to the analysis of conversation have focused on the microlevel details of interaction, they provide a natural framework for future studies of prosody. Several research areas have been proposed in this regard, involving tone concord, the flow of pitch accents, and the regularity of rhythm. Given the labor-intensive nature of studying prosody in conversation, there is a need to replicate past studies, as well as to investigate topics of prosody with new data. Fiksdal's sample analysis of rhythm in advisor/advisee encounters has provided an illustration of how one such project was conducted and, in particular, how videotaping might be used in similar circumstances. As Fiksdal's analysis and the other research cited in this chapter demonstrate, a scrutiny of the minute prosodic details in ordinary conversation can contribute to a better understanding of human social behavior.

8

PROSODY IN
ORAL NARRATIVES

In the oral narrative, as in other discourse genres discussed in this volume, the phonological functions of prosody will again play a role. For example, storytellers use paratones to mark component shifts in narratives just as lecturers do to delineate topics. However, this chapter also emphasizes the paralinguistic aspects of prosody. Within the genre of the oral narrative, I will argue that intensified prosody can bring particular story events to the foreground. Certain key words, for example, may be uttered with a higher-than-usual pitch; vowels may be lengthened; pauses may be used strategically to provoke tension; volume may be increased at crucial points for a crescendo effect. The use of such prosodic "performance features" (Wolfson, 1982) is not an all-or-nothing choice but a matter of degree, depending on the speaker's level of emotional involvement with the text, the situation, the audience, and the norms of the speech community. Unlike the phonological aspects of intonation, which have a finite inventory of forms and corresponding functions, pitch, volume, voice quality, and timing can be manipulated to achieve an infinite variety of emotional, attitudinal, and stylistic effects. Such effects may occur in any spoken text, but they are especially likely in the oral narrative, a genre of discourse that by definition includes "evaluation"—a presentation of the teller's point of view and frequently an emotional investment. As Wolfson points out, in informal situations, storytellers may engage in almost theatrical performances of story events to enliven the experience for the audience. By using performance features, such as repetitions, gestures, sound effects, quoted speech, and, I argue, other prosodic manipulations, tellers attempt to draw the empathy of the audience to their own evaluation of the events. In Wolfson's words: "performance features . . . have the double function in stories of enabling the listener to see the events being recounted through the eyes of the narrator and of making these events seem more authentic, thereby supporting the narrator's viewpoint of the moral judgment which is the central theme of the story" (p. 29). The oral narrative, then, provides a lively domain for this chapter's focus on paralinguistic prosody.

I begin with an introduction to Labov and Waletzky's (1967) and Labov's (1972) model of narrative structure and an examination of certain features of intonation that play a role within that framework. Then I discuss the performative nature of narratives, reviewing work done specifically on prosody as an evaluative device. After an explanation of the relationship between prosody and emotion, I include several examples from actual narratives to illustrate how speakers manipulate prosodic variables to enliven or intensify key elements of text. Exaggerated prosodic forms may occur in conjunction with the enactment of high points of plot or other forms of evaluative language, although this depends on sociolinguistic and individual variation. Several unresolved questions are then raised in connection with the prosody of narratives. The chapter concludes with a sample analysis of the use of quotation in the oral narratives of both native speakers (NS) and nonnative speakers (NNS) of English, drawn from Wennerstrom (1997). The analysis shows how prosodic variables can count as evidence that quoted speech is evaluative—a performance feature—rather than merely reiterative, an attempt to accurately replicate original utterances.

Prosody and Narrative Plot Structure

In 1967, Labov and Waletzky published an analysis of oral narratives told informally by black teenagers in impoverished urban areas of the United States. The analysis came to be a model for innumerable subsequent works, partly because of its social relevance and partly because it demonstrated that narrative analysis could transcend the boundaries of literature and folktale and approach the genres of informal, everyday speech. At the time, Labov and Waletzky's concern was to demonstrate that the language of the children they interviewed, Black English Vernacular (BEV), was a dialect of English, with systematic structures every bit as complex as those of the local prestige dialect, Standard American English. At the time it was commonly believed that BEV was a failed attempt to speak English rather than a dialect in its own right. Labov (1972) published both a grammar and a phonology of BEV, but I am most interested in his analysis of narrative structure—a simple model of components in informal stories, summarized in table 8.1.

It is not necessary that every component in this model appear in every narrative, nor must they always occur in order. Labov (1972) emphasizes that the abstract and coda are optional and that evaluation can occur at any point in the story. Young (1991) notes that in narratives with complex episodic structure, Labov's components may recur for each episode, beginning with a new orientation and ending with an evaluation. Küntay and Ervin-Tripp (1997) point out that, when all the participants in the storytelling event are familiar with the background, little or no orientation may be needed. Fleishman (1997) maintains that the resolution component may also be missing or difficult to identify. In view of these possible variations, I will take Labov and Waletzky's model as flexible, acknowledging that components may be optional, reordered, or reiterated. Nevertheless, I will use the model as a tool because it offers a departure point from which to discuss stories and provides a set of familiar terminology.

One of the more reliable aspects of Labov's structural model is that most narratives do contain one or more complicating actions. Something has to happen for there to be a story. Discourse analysts have identified the linguistic features that distinguish this component from the orientation material. Longacre (1983) provides evidence from several diverse languages of grammatical devices, such as verb tenses or lexical particles, that distinguish complicating actions from orientations. For English, Wolfson (1982) demonstrates that some speakers mark this transition with

TABLE 8.1 Components of Narrative

Component	Function
Abstract	An introductory element, often a brief summary, indicating that a narrative is about to be told.
Orientation	The setting and/or background for the narrative.
Complicating Actions	The events of the narrative's plot.
Resolution	The outcome of the narrative; the ending.
Coda	A final segment that links the narrative back to the present interaction.
Evaluation	An assessment of the narrative events.

Source: Adapted from Labov (1972).

a shift to the historical present tense, as in, "I *get* in, *turn* the key, BRRMM, and I *drive* home" (p. 28). Furthermore, deictic lexical content may mark this transition (as in "suddenly" or "then, when I turned sixteen").

In addition to these lexicogrammatical devices, English speakers also exploit prosody to distinguish orientations from complicating actions. Consider the following excerpt (Corpus 5) drawn from a story told by a male graduate student (H) in a discourse analysis class where students were asked to form small groups and tape-record personal stories on the topic of "a mistake my parents made in raising me" (O = orientation; CA = complicating action; + = extra high pitch; << = tempo slows):

```
 1   H   [O]   Ahh→ they were ₁ᵤₛₜ ⁺RÉ:ALLY⁺ STRICT↘ (.3) and
 2               VÉRY TRÁDITIONAL↗ and (.5) there was this BIG
 3               ÉLEMENT of RÉSPECT↑. (.1) A:::nd→ (.6) ᵧ'ᴋɴᴏw,
 4               you FÓLLOWED the RULES of the ʜᴏᴍᴇ↑ (.3) and
 5               you FÓLLOWED the RULES of your ₚáᴿᴇɴᴛₛ↑ (.9)
 6       [CA]   ⇑<< And ⁺THEN⁺ when I TU::RNED→ about
 7               ⁺SÍXTÉEN⁺↗ (.5) SÚDDENLY ᴛʜₒₛₑ RULES were
 8               ⁺LÍFTED⁺↓ (.6) and I no LÓNGER had to FÓLLOW
 9               these RÉALLY (.2) STRICT and DÍSCIPLINARY (.3)
10               TYPE of RULES↗
```

In lines 1–5, H gives an orientation describing his parents' traditional attitude. Three phrases in this orientation end with high-rising (↑) pitch boundaries: after *respect* in line 3, *home* in line 4, and *parents* in line 5. I interpret these as offers to clarify the scene for listeners if necessary ("are you with me?").[1] Continuing the story, we find in line 6 a shift to the complicating action component when H turns sixteen. This transition is marked lexically with the deictic word *then* and the adverb *suddenly*, as well as syntactically with the shift from the generic pronoun *you* to the personal pronoun *I*, specifically referring to H himself. The transition is also associated with prosodic changes: an increase in pitch and a slowing of tempo, shown in figure 8.1. As discussed in chapters 2 and 5, this corresponds to the paratone—a prosodically marked topic unit, which in this case associates with a component of narrative structure, the complicating action. The association between paratones and boundaries of complicating actions appears fairly robust: the study from which the excerpt was drawn (Wennerstrom, 1997) included seven similar oral narratives told by American graduate students. One finding was that all eight speakers entered the top 10% of their pitch ranges at the crucial transition point from orientation to complicating action in their stories (p. 198).

To summarize, structural components of narratives may have characteristic prosodic features. An orientation may contain high-rising pitch

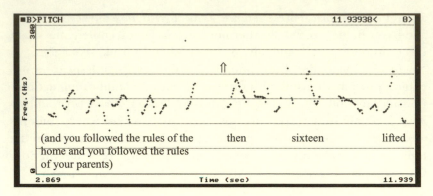

Figure 8.1   The transition from orientation to complicating action is associated with a high paratone (⇑) and a slower tempo.

boundaries as a speaker seeks confirmation that listeners are following, and paratones may be used to mark transitions between components of a narrative's plot structure. Of particular salience is the transition from orientation to complicating action, a shift linguistically marked in many languages. Prosody's role in this transition is not unexpected, as we have already seen that intonation performs an organizational function in other genres of discourse. At this point, however, I turn from structural to attitudinal functions of prosody in oral narratives and consider how they can be manipulated to enhance the performance of the story.

Evaluation and Narrative

Since Labov and Waletzky's (1967) seminal analysis, the study of oral narratives has continued to expand among discourse analysts (Polanyi, 1985; Tannen, 1984b; Toolan, 1988; Wolfson, 1982; Young, 1991), ethnographers (Bauman, 1986; Bauman & Sherzer, 1989; Briggs, 1997; Linde, 1993; Mishler, 1986), child development specialists (Blum-Kulka, 1997; Feldman et al., 1993; Peterson & McCabe, 1983; Snow, 1991), and even psychologists (Bruner, 1986; Feldman, 1991; Freeman, 1993). Common among these disciplines is the view that narrative, more than a mere report of past events, includes what Labov and Waletzky termed "evaluation"—the teller's assessment of the events, or why the story is worth telling. As Labov explains, "Evaluative devices say to us: this was terrifying, dangerous, weird, wild, crazy; or amusing, hilarious, wonderful; more generally, that it was strange, uncommon, or unusual—that is, worth reporting. It was not ordinary, plain, humdrum, or run-of-the-mill" (1972,

p. 371). Stories thus offer windows into their tellers' attitudes and value systems. What is presented as reasonable versus shocking behavior? How are a character's motivations critiqued or justified? What self-image does the teller project to the recipients? What does a story's point reveal about its teller's world view? As Labov (1997) points out, certain stories have "entered into the biography of the speaker" (p. 398) or become, as Linde (1993) phrases it, "life stories," stories told repeatedly as a means of self-definition and presentation. How a storyteller chooses to construe a set of real-world events and his or her role among them becomes a testament to his or her sense of position in the world and a defense of moral choices (Tappan, 1997; Wolfson, 1982). And finally, even beyond the individual, we can ask how a story reflects the values of its teller's culture as a whole. How do the norms of a speech community constrain a storytelling event? (Bauman, 1986; Bauman & Sherzer, 1989; Polanyi, 1985) It is this aspect of narrative—the attitude, the world view, the "slant"—that has broadly been termed "evaluation" in the narrative literature.

Labov (1972) describes both external and internal types of evaluation. External evaluations are individual clauses in which storytellers suspend story events momentarily to express their points of view. For example, from a woman's story about a frightening airplane trip, Labov (p. 371) cites the following as external evaluations:

- And it was the strangest feeling because you couldn't tell if they were really going to make it.
- But it was really quite terrific.
- But it was quite an experience.

In contrast, internal evaluations are defined as grammatical, lexical, and phonological mechanisms embedded within the clauses of the story events themselves that indicate the teller's perspective. For example, tellers can use superlatives, expletives, "loaded" lexical items, quoted speech, sound effects, and the like to add a special evaluative status to certain parts of a narrative. Although Labov does not dwell on the role of prosody in evaluation, he does discuss "expressive phonology" (p. 379) as an intensification device. By lengthening the stressed vowels of key words, the teller calls special attention to them. Labov's examples of vowel elongation fall within the durational parameter of prosody. In other studies (e.g., Bauman, 1986; Erickson, 1984; Peterson & McCabe, 1983; Selting, 1994; Wennerstrom, 1997, 2001), exaggerated volume and pitch have also been shown to play a role in signaling to the hearer those elements of the story that are particularly important. Because prosody is simultaneous with lexical content, a speaker is afforded the possibility of adding intensity to an internal story clause to render it evaluative, or of intensifying an external evaluation even further. Thus, often a cluster of evaluative devices works together, including marked lexicogrammatical structure *and* intensified prosody.

In the following sections, I will consider the question of how lexicogrammatical devices interact with prosody in evaluation. As we will see, speakers use intensified prosodic forms to dramatize climactic event sequences and, more generally, to highlight language that is already evaluative. Before beginning that discussion, however, I review functions of prosody I discussed earlier to better delineate the relationship between prosody and emotion.

Prosody and Emotion

So far, I have taken a phonological approach to intonation. I have claimed that within a foundational rhythmic structure, pitch accents associate with various constituents of text to convey their status in the information structure of the discourse; that phrase-final pitch boundaries are important in the segmentation of the discourse, as well as in indicating hierarchical relationships among constituents of discourse at the phrase level; and, finally, that initial pitch boundaries (paratones and key) indicate the degree of integration of a new constituent with the previous one.

Within the constraints of this phonological system, however, prosodic features may be further manipulated—exaggerated, diminished, sped up, slowed down—to convey emotion and attitude. Consider the following utterance drawn from the orientation component of the story we looked at earlier about a young man's strict upbringing. The superscripted text (+) means higher-than-usual pitch, defined in Wennerstrom (1997) as points where the speaker entered the top 10% of his pitch range:[2]

> Ahh→ they were ₁ᵤₛₜ ⁺RÉ:ALLY⁺ STRICT↘ (.3) and VÉRY
> TRADÍTIONAL↗

To begin, we can analyze this utterance in terms of its basic intonational structure. It has four content words with H* pitch accents—*really, strict, very, traditional*—which introduce new ideas that the teller wants the audience to add to their mental representations of the discourse so far. Although he has just met the audience, three fellow graduate students in a seminar class, he can assume that they belong to a common speech community of young North American academics. They have a schema for child raising that includes a range of strict versus permissive parenting behaviors. The teller in this case wants the audience to understand that his own parents were on the strict, traditional end of the spectrum. Next, the pitch boundaries—after *ahhh, strict,* and *traditional*—indicate how the utterance is to be segmented into intonational phrases and, in this case, that the three phrases are interdependent. The plateau boundary on the hesitation sound *ahhh* serves to hold the teller's place as he formulates his thoughts; the partially falling boundary after *strict* sets up a close link between the two rather balanced phrases that describe his parents—they were (1) really strict and (2) very traditional. The low-rising boundary after *traditional* again indicates a connection between the two-part description of his parents and additional characteristics of his home life that are to follow. Last, the key from one intonational phrase to another remains in a mid range; the speaker is simply adding new elements in his description. There is no paratone during the excerpt.

Beyond this basic intonational structure, however, the teller also uses prosody as an intensifier. Figure 8.2 shows that the teller exaggerates the pitch and duration of the word *really,* from which listeners may deduce that he has particularly strong feelings about his parents' strictness. This is what is meant by intensified or exaggerated prosody: whereas the basic intonation structure offers a finite inventory of choices, the exaggeration or diminishment of prosodic features within that structure can indicate the attitude and emotion associated with certain parts of the text. Selting (1994) describes this manipulation of prosodic variables as an "emphatic speech style,"

> an expression of and/or manifestation of a speaker's heightened emotive involvement, which is expressed and signaled by linguistic cues, be this for reasons of high(er) contrast or unexpectedness, high(er) positive or negative emotional load, animatedness, etc. Emphatic style

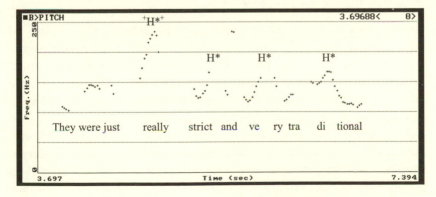

Figure 8.2 Although this utterance contains several H* pitch accents, the word *really* has an extremely high pitch for extra emphasis.

is used to highlight any particular activity or any particular kind of emotive expression with which it occurs. It suggests and triggers interpretive frames of "emphasis" or "emphatic involvement." (p. 383)[3]

For Selting, this speech style is characterized by higher pitch peaks and/ or increased volume, and a higher density of accented, in proportion to unaccented, syllables.

Yet to say that one raises one's pitch and volume in anger or excitement is not to say that human beings universally yelp like hyenas with unrestrained emotional outbursts. Instead, children are taught from an early age the constraints regulating the display of emotion in their culture (Couper-Kuhlen, 1986; Selting, 1994). Our friend describing his parents is well within the limits of acceptability for his speech community in showing his emotion: although he exaggerates the word *really*, he still remains within a conversational pitch range. Furthermore, as Couper-Kuhlen warns, it is a mistake to attribute all emotional expression to prosody. Lexical and grammatical features convey emotion as well, as in "I'm sick and tired of that dang cat being in the house!" which, regardless of its prosody, tends to convey an element of displeasure. Similarly, intonation can suggest an attitude even when it is not exaggerated. Couper-Kuhlen offers "Shut the door↓" versus "Shut the door↑" in which the pitch boundary conveys a definite attitude in the former but a tentative one in the latter (p. 182). In other words, exaggerated prosody is only one mechanism among many to display emotion and attitude. As we will see in the upcoming sections, however, it tends to occur in conjunction with language that is already expressive through its lexical content or grammatical structure.

Prosody and Evaluative Language

Let us return, then, to consider the association between prosody and other evaluative devices in oral narratives. One category of internal evaluation discussed by Labov (1972), marked lexical items, add intensification to the story without departing from the story line. We have already seen an example of this in figure 8.2 where the storyteller described his parents as "*really* strict." The following example (from Corpus 2) shows a similar use of intensifying pitch peaks associated with lexical items in an assessment of cleverness. The point of this story is that, despite the common belief that only Western visitors get sick in Nepal, Nepali natives themselves often get sick too. As evidence for this claim, the teller (an American woman) describes how a Nepali man

(Geeven) is immediately familiar with the appropriate remedies that will help her American husband (Travis) stricken with parasites:

```
1    c   But- (.4) GÉEVEN↘ the GUY who brought them
2        BACK↘ knew ⁺EXÁCTLY⁺- (.4) He and I went out
3        ⁺IMMÉDIATELY⁺↘ while TRÁVIS ₛₒᵣₜ ₒf SPRAWLED
4        on the BED↗ (1.3) ⁺IMMÉDIATELY⁺ and got
5        ⁺THREE⁺ ₐíffₑᵣₑₙₜ THINGS↘ that they ÁLWAYS
6        USE↘ when they're SICK↘ (.1) which is QUITE
7        ÓFTEN ᵢ ₜₕᵢₙₖ↓
```

This segment contains four pitch peaks in lines 2–5. The first three, *exactly* in line 2 and *immediately* in line 3 and again in line 4, are evaluative adverbs of intensification; the fourth word, *three* in line 5, can also be interpreted as evaluative, for, arguably, to a Western audience, *one* remedy might be considered enough to treat an illness. The example again shows that evaluative devices tend to cluster together, with prosody, in this case pitch, functioning as a spotlight on evaluative adverbs and adjectives.

Another category of evaluative device in Labov's scheme is marked syntax. The following is an example (from Corpus 5) of a speaker manipulating the syntax to highlight an event, while compounding the evaluative intensity by using a pitch peak as well. In this story, the teller's mother has ignored her complaint of an injured ankle and sent her to bed with no supper as a punishment for whining:

I have NO ᵢₐéₐ WHYhh↗ or WHAhT HÁhhPPENED↗ (.6) but
I ⁺DID⁺ ₉ₒ ₜₒ ᵦₑₐ↘ and I CRIED myself to SLEEP↘

In this excerpt, instead of simply reporting the event, (as in "I went to bed") the teller chooses to use the auxiliary *did* to emphasize this action as a contrast to what one might reasonably expect from a child whose ankle was broken and who should instead be taken to a hospital. The pitch peak on the marked form *did* heightens the contrast even more. The excerpt is also distinguished by the laughter syllables in the middle of *why* and *what happened* in the first two phrases.

A third type of internal evaluation on Labov's list of intensification mechanisms is quotation. By quoting another's words, the teller makes the story world in the hearer's mental representation more realistic. Quotations may not always represent the exact words originally spoken; their purpose is often to combine story action with a strong evaluative function (Young, 1991, p. 45). Wolfson (1982) also discusses quotation as a performance feature that enables the hearer to see through the eyes of the teller and thereby better support his or her moral judgment. Empirical support for the link between quotation and prosody comes from Grosz and Hirschberg (1992), who demonstrated statistically that quotations were initiated in a higher pitch range than other utterances in the reading of news stories. Moreover, subjects' labeling of written transcripts as they listened to these stories showed that they perceived expanded pitch range as a cue to quoted speech.

Additional evidence for the function of prosody in quotation is supplied by Bauman (1986) in an ethnographic study of humorous anecdotes told by rural west Texans. One common trend was for the punch line of a story to be rendered in a direct quotation, even in repeated tellings by the same person over a time span of several years. Bauman reports that quoted speech was often set off by pauses and could sometimes involve altered voices, with higher pitch, louder volume, and other paralinguistic features. From a practical standpoint, prosodic changes are one mechanism to assist in keeping track of who is speaking. Bauman explains:

> Reported speech, especially quoted speech, involves special problems of communicative management, because the narrator is actually speaking for other people in addition to himself. Accordingly, there is a need for ways of marking the difference between the voice of the narrator in the present storytelling context and the reported speech of the action in the original event being reported (one of whom can be the person who later tells the story, but in a different voice), and of marking speaker change within the conversational dialogue that is the core of the narrated event. (p. 66)

The topic of high pitch in quoted speech is revisited in the sample analysis of this chapter drawn from Wennerstrom (1997), where more examples are provided.

Another evaluative function of prosody in narrative is to call attention to what the teller deems climactic in the story, Longacre's (1981) "peaks of tension," where "the flow of discourse seems to quicken and grow more turbulent" (p. 347). Longacre describes several linguistic features that storytellers use to mark such peaks of tension, including changes in verb tense, shifts into dialogue, a dense packing of minute details, and changes in sentence length. As the following example from Eggins and Slade (1998) demonstrates, prosody can also be manipulated at tension peaks. The excerpt is a reaction sequence in an anecdote told by an Anglo-Australian woman about an embarrassing incident. Eggins and Slade define anecdotes as stories designed by the teller to draw a specific reaction from the other participants. The reaction sequence forms the crux of the anecdote and may be marked by "an outburst of laughter, a gasp indicating horror or fear, or an expression of amazement" (pp. 247–248) by the teller and often audience members as well. The woman in this story has described a situation in which she was taking an important exam when suddenly a cockroach crawled over her foot. Despite strict rules demanding quiet during the exam, she screamed, leaped onto a chair, knocked over a bench, and scattered another student's papers. After relating these events, the teller continues to dwell on this climax in the following reaction sequence (p. 246):

> And I was standing on this chair
> screaming
> and the exam supervisor came
> running over "what's going on there!" ((laughs))
> and I said "there's a cockroach
> down there!" ((laughs))

This sequence is characterized by quoted speech, laughter, the use of a progressive tense, and lexical items that emphasize the unusualness of the behavior (screaming, running). We also note Longacre's (1981) dense packing of details. Eggins and Slade mention the "amplification" leading up to and during this sequence (p. 247), which I take to mean an increase in volume as well.

There is also evidence that shifts in rhythm can associate with an evaluative sequence. For example, Auer et al. (1999) cite the role of altered rhythm to introduce dramatic points, or "hot news" (p. 203). These presumably coincide with Longacre's "peaks of tension." Moreover, as reviewed in chapter 3, Uhmann (1996) discovered that at highly dramatic points in stories, German storytellers would deliberately introduce stress clash—the alignment of several strong rhythmic beats in a row. Even unstressed syllables and function words could occupy a single rhythmic beat to provide extra emphasis. We saw instances of this in English in two sentences reprinted below from chapter 3 (Corpus 3). The speaker, a Mormon woman, is emphasizing how extremely relieved she will be to reach the age of menopause when she will no longer be able to have children (slashes indicate the rhythmic intervals):

1. / FÍVE   /
    / KÍDS   /
    / Í   /
    / CÁN   /
    / NÓT   /
    / ⁺WÁIT⁺   /

2.   / Í   /
     / DÓN'T   /
     / WÁNT   /
     / Á   /
     / NÓ   /
     / THÉR   /
     / B'ə   /
     / HÁY   /
     / BÉE   / ("baby")

In these highly emotional and evaluative utterances, the function word *can* and the unstressed syllables in *another* and *baby* occupy full rhythmic beats.[4]

So far, we have seen examples in which exaggerated prosody intensifies evaluative material already manifest in the lexicogrammatical structure of the text. In some cases, however, the prosody itself adds an emotional element in the absence of any other evaluative devices. For example, in the following excerpt (Corpus 5), the teller conveys her excitement at going to a friend's house as a child and being delighted that her friend is free to play. She says:

> So I WENT over↘ (.7) and uhh (.2) SHE was AT the DOOR↘
> AND I SAID "ASK your MOM↗" and SHE did↘ (.2) and she could
> come ⁺OU:::T⁺↓

The word *out* is not in itself especially value-laden; yet, as we see in figure 8.3, its pitch is quite high in contrast to the rest of the text and its vowel relatively long. Indeed, the context indicates that this phrase is important because it sets up the motivation for the primary complicating action of the story: because of her extreme excitement, the teller runs and jumps, falls, and breaks her ankle.

Another example (from Corpus 5) comes from a male speaker who has just described a terrifying film that he saw as a child about the Antichrist. He continues:

> And uhh→ (.3) ↾ ⁺I⁺ was about ⁺EIGHT⁺↗ and ⁺THIS⁺ was-
> (.5) ⁺EXTRAÓRDINARILY⁺ (.3) FRÍGHTENING ₜₒ ₘₑ.↓

The words themselves in the clause "I was about eight" simply state the teller's age. Were it not for the extremely high pitch peaks, it might seem as if he were merely providing further orientation material. However, the exaggerated pitch on *I* and *eight*, along with the high key of the phrase, adds an evaluative sense: eight is an impressionable age at which to be

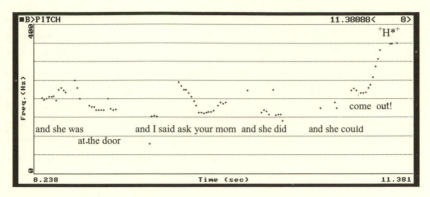

Figure 8.3 The word *out* has an extremely high pitch, which gives it an evaluative sense.

viewing such films. The second clause is an external evaluation describing the emotional impact of the film at the time—"extraordinarily frightening"—where both lexical meaning and pitch act as evaluative devices.

To summarize, evaluation has been discussed in the literature as a functional category that involves the expression of a teller's emotions and attitudes toward a narrative in progress. Many speakers exaggerate their prosody in evaluation. Examples have shown a clustering effect, whereby prosody intensifies material that is already made evaluative through other devices, such as marked lexical content, syntactic structure, quotation, or plot structure. I have also shown that prosody itself can render relatively neutral language evaluative. In the next section, I discuss variation in how speakers manipulate prosody to achieve a particular storytelling style.

Prosody and Storytelling Style

I do not wish to imply that there is a universal emphatic storytelling style. Rather, as Selting (1994) emphasizes, story genres are regulated by "display rules" of the speech community in which they occur. The expression of emotion in stories varies with genre (a comedy routine versus an informal gab session), ethnicity, gender, geographic region, class, personal style (a Peewee Herman versus a Groucho Marx), and other pragmatic factors. For example, Erickson (1984) identifies a participatory storytelling style sanctioned in the African American community, reminiscent of the call-response pattern found in other genres of both West African and African American speech communities (Abrahams, 1970; McCrum, Cran, & MacNeil, 1986). In this style, the speech of a primary speaker and audience respondents undergoes similar changes as episodes culminate in a crescendo of emotional force. These climactic sequences are characterized by heightened volume and pitch and a high instance of repetition of key phrases. There is also an increase in audience participation toward the climax, during which the primary speaker and members of the audience maintain an alignment of pitch and rhythm across turns. The following (p. 142) is part of an extended reaction sequence in a narrative about a poll watcher in Chicago, who was thrown out of the polling place for trying to prevent interference as black citizens attempted to vote. The "curtains" in line 3 refer to those of the voting booth, which can be closed to ensure a voter's privacy:

```
1     JIM   That's all they- because
2           once they get behind the
3           curtains, see (.) ain't nobody sposed to
4           mess with, ain't nobody sposed to
5           be back there with them (.)
6     ED    No no they  ⌈ain't supposed to   ⌈be back there
7     JOE               ⌊they ain't
8     AL                                     ⌊they ain't (.)
9                 ⌈sposed to but they do
10    JIM         ⌊ain't sposed to be there but they do
```

In this sequence, Jim occupies the role of primary speaker. The phrases "ain't sposed to," "be back there," and "but they do" are repeated back and forth among the other three speakers and again at the end by Jim. According to Erickson, these repetitions are characterized by matched pitch across speakers. Within my model we can call this "tone concord," as discussed in chapter 7—a matching of key from one speaker to the next to indicate rapport and agreement. The speakers also synchronize their rhythm as they overlap each other's contributions.

Storytelling style may also vary by geographic region, as Tannen's (1984a) study of a dinner party conversation between New Yorkers and Californians demonstrates (there was also one person from England in attendance). The display rules for the New Yorkers, it appears, allowed for much more variation in the prosodic forms than did those of the other speakers. In Tannen's examples, the New Yorkers used a variety of performance features: they exploited their pitch ranges to a much fuller degree, going from a very high pitch to a very low pitch even within a single phrase (p. 85); they spoke more loudly and with more variation in overall volume; the tempo was quicker with fewer and shorter pauses; and there was more speaker overlap. The New Yorkers also made liberal use of altered voice qualities to develop stylized voices and to mimic others.

In the following example (pp. 113–114), a male speaker mimics a little girl's "squealing" voice in a story about one of his pupils in the school where he teaches:[5]

> s . . . Can YOU imagine? She's SÉVEN years old, and she SITS in her chair and she goes . . . . ((squeals and squirms in his seat)).
>
> D Oh: Go:d. . . . She's only ⁺SEV⁺ en?
>
> s And I say well . . HOW about let's do SO-and-so. And she says . . . ↱⁺⁺Okay↗⁺⁺ ((squealing)) . . . →JUST like that.

The point of the story is how even young children in American society are immersed in their gender roles. The teller never spells out his point explicitly; instead, he conveys it by mimicking the girlish voice quality with an exaggerated pitch and volume and squirming body movements. In contrast to this "high-involvement" style of the New Yorkers, the Californians' style was more restrained. They were more likely to use lexical detail to make their points rather than to perform them. This storytelling style led to a judgment by the New Yorkers that the Californians were plodding along rather than getting to the point. Meanwhile, the Californians thought New Yorkers' style was aggressive and even somewhat rude. Tannen describes a situation in which a New Yorker asked a question with a loud volume and high pitch. The Californian interlocutor reacted with surprised silence to what he considered to be an "outburst," and the conversation actually ground to a halt (p. 84).

The prosody of a storytelling style may also depend on the formality of the speech situation. Kirshenblatt-Gimblett (1989) describes several subgenres of storytelling in the Jewish community for which the level of prosodic involvement differentiates the informal from the more formal genres. In formal settings such as weddings, professional storytellers are often hired to tell stories as part of the program. In this formal storytelling genre, the teller is sanctioned to include "special prosodic and paralinguistic features" (p. 307) to a greater extent than in more informal, conversational storytelling genres. These professional stories are also characterized by fewer interactions between the teller and the audience than the more informal genres.

Finally, individual style and circumstance affect the nature of prosodic variation in a story. Johnstone (1996) coins the term "linguistic individual" to refer to the way in which each person creates a unique set of styles for self-expression, drawing on phonology, syntax, discourse features, and, of course, prosody. Johnstone's central message is that, although traditional sociolinguistic variables play a role in how one speaks, there is also more at stake:

> When we study individuals' speech . . . and when we concentrate on
> what happens in stories or speeches or conversations, it becomes clear
> that no two people talk alike and that it is more enlightening to think
> of factors such as gender, ethnicity, and audience as resources that
> speakers use to create unique voices than as determinants of how they
> will talk. (p. 56)

Although Johnstone does not dwell on prosodic variation, she does cite
particular instances of speakers using prosody as part of a unique style.
For example, the storytelling style of a white, male gas-station owner from
the American Midwest is described as "clipped, like poetry recited a line
at a time" (p. 38). Johnstone attributes this to the teller's use of intonation and pause: he uses "relatively small bursts of words" (p. 38.), organized into intonational phrases that do not always contain complete
clauses. These short phrases typically end with low ($\downarrow$) pitch boundaries
and are followed by a pause.

Mimicry is also important in individual style, and prosody can contribute to its distinctive character. In the following example (Corpus 2),
a female speaker draws on a more feminine, higher-pitched voice to mimic
herself in a story we have seen before about illness in Nepal ("he" refers
to her husband):

1	c	I $^+$KNEW$^+$ he was gonna GO on this THING an'- (.6)
2		an'- I- an'- he was RÉALLY SICK↘ (.1) but I didn't
3		want to be ₗᵢₖₑ (.5) the MÁMA and say don't go↓
4		↱ "$^+$GO AHÉAD$^+$!↗ You'll have a GOOD TIME↘ It's
5		ALL RIGHT↓" (.6)
6		→ NEXT DAY he was ESCÓRTED HOME by→
7		ha ha (1.6)
8		⎡he was
9	w	⎣on a ₛₜₐₑₜ𝒸ₕₑᵣ↑ (.4)
10	c	JUST ABÓUT↓

Here, the teller (C) chastises herself for agreeing to let her husband go
camping even though she knew he was sick. She hits an extremely high pitch
at the onset of a quotation in line 4, shown in figure 8.4, about her acquies-
cence in her husband's plans. In quoting herself, she mimics the high voice
of a stereotypical "nice wife" instead of a more sensible and maternal version of herself ("the mama"), who would have warned her husband not to
go camping when he was obviously showing signs of an illness.

A last example is another illustration of a variation in personal style
that might be termed "deadpan," in which extraordinary events are uttered with a relatively low pitch. The storytelling activity, again from

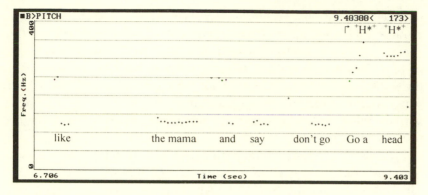

Figure 8.4   A woman mimics herself in this high-pitched quotation.

Corpus 5 of "mistakes my parents made," took place during the second session of a discourse analysis class when students were not yet well acquainted. In such circumstances, it would not be unusual for some of them to be nervous. Thus, I interpret this young man's choice of deadpan style as an attempt to be "cool," protecting his emotions in telling a personal story to relative strangers.

In this particular story, the teller describes how naïve his parents were about his bad behavior as a teenager. His opinion is that they should have put more limits on him, or as he puts it, "They thought I was too good of a kid." The plot builds with several examples of unruly behavior to which his parents barely react. He utters these descriptions of bad acts with little prosodic distinction. For example, in the following excerpt (Corpus 5) the lexical items describing his bad behavior are all delivered within a narrow pitch range:

    1   I WRECKED the CAR↘ (.8) at SIXTÉEN and- (.6)
    2   >>they ₛₒᵣₜ ₒF LAUGHED it OFF . . .
    3   ((portion omitted))
    4   . . . Uh I ⁺REMÉMBER⁺ my GÉTTING↘ (.6) HÁVING-
    5   (.2) my- (.2) PÁRENTS HÁVING COMPLÉTE TRUST
    6   ᵢN ME↓ an'- an'- as a RESÚLT↘ (.8) uh (.5) I became
    7   PROGRÉSSIVELY MORE- (1.) um (1.4) DEMÓNIC↗
    8   (hh) ₒᵣ WHAT(HH)EVER↓ ((others laugh)) uhh→ (.4) ↑ 'ts
    9   ⁺ALMÓST⁺ to the- (.2) ⁺WELL⁺ to the ⁺POINT⁺
    10   where I was ARRÉSTED↘ at- (.2) 'bout EIGHT - (.3)
    11   ⁺NO⁺ it ⁺WÁSN'T⁺↓ (.2) t'SEE↓ I was NOT→ (1.3) I
    12   was STILL a JÚVENILE↓

In lines 1 and 7, respectively, the phrases "wrecked the car at sixteen" and "progressively more demonic" are uttered without any distinguishing pitch. Nor are louder volume or vowel elongation associated with these phrases. Likewise, in line 10, the complicating action verb *arrested*, the climax of his story, is relatively short and low in pitch and volume. A segment of this is shown in figure 8.5, where the cursor marks the center of the word *arrested*. The speaker does not avoid pause, however: significant pauses occur throughout the passage, and, in particular, an extended, partially filled pause of almost three seconds occurs prior to the adjective *demonic* in line 7.

It is also of interest to consider the words for which the teller does use his highest pitch (albeit, given his narrow range, it is never terribly high). All words within the top 10% of the teller's pitch range are marked with superscripted (+) signs in the transcript: *remember* in line 4; *almost, well,* and *point* in line 9; and *no* and *wasn't* in line 11. Rather than naming the climactic events themselves, these items surround his assessment of them. He "remembers" his parents' particular behavior, which was "almost to the, well, to the point"—in other words, he calls attention to the misplaced nature of his parents' naïve trust, which had reached an extreme "point" by the time of the arrest. *No it wasn't* is part of a self-repair of the teller's age at the time of the arrest—an important one in this case because in the United States, 18 is the cutoff age at which one is considered an adult by the courts and can therefore be sentenced to a more severe punishment.

The deadpan storytelling style, then, involves conveying rather shocking events unemotionally within a narrow pitch range, with little vowel elongation or volume increase. The highest pitch is reserved for the evaulation of these events rather than the events themselves, which are rather understated. Deadpan style invests a certain power in the teller—he is able to tell calmly of arrests and other "demonic" acts as if they were nothing unusual in his worldly experience.

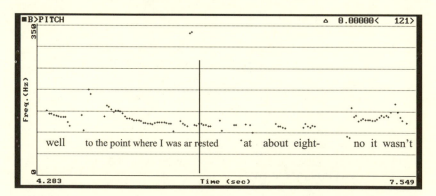

Figure 8.5 The word *arrested*, shown by the cursor, has a rather low pitch despite its dramatic meaning.

To sum up, in the telling of stories, prosody can be manipulated to call attention to certain key events, to highlight evaluative language, and, in general, to display the emotional priorities of the teller. Variation in how extreme a prosodic display can be depends on the norms of the speech community, the circumstances surrounding the storytelling event, and the individual's own creative choices. We have looked at one particular style in which a storyteller actually suppressed emotional display to achieve a worldly aura, and doubtless many other styles as well involve different manipulations of prosody.

Unresolved Issues

In a special issue of the *Journal of Narrative and Life History* (Bamberg, 1997), 48 scholars of narrative were asked to assess the 30-year impact of Labov and Waletzky's (1967) foundational analysis of conversational narratives. Scanning those articles, I noticed that not one is devoted directly to any topic of prosody, although a few authors do mention it in passing. Research on prosody in narrative is thus an open field. The following questions need answers.

What Is the Relationship Between Prosody and Narrative Structure?

As Longacre (1983), Wolfson (1982), and others have found, languages of the world often have particular linguistic devices whose function is to distinguish important events, or "complicating actions," from orientation and other narrative material. As I discussed in this chapter, prosody may also function in this way: the Americans in my 1997 study exploited paratones to mark this transition. Moreover, high-rising pitch boundaries were associated with orientations for one teller as he established a connection with listeners before introducing the complicating actions. These examples notwithstanding, the role that prosody plays in the structure of stories has not to my knowledge been researched in any depth. As my own study involved such a small number of storytellers, it would be useful to replicate it using additional narrative data. Likewise, other structural components of stories—codas and abstracts, for example—could be investigated for distinctive prosody.

How Does Prosody Contribute to Individual Storytellers' "Style Profiles"?

We have seen one example in this chapter of an individual style that I referred to as a "deadpan" style, characterized by understatement, displayed through a low degree of prosodic intensification associated with extraordinary events. I also discussed a "clipped" style from Johnstone, and a use of mimicry in another storyteller's style. Other styles could also be described in terms of their prosodic features. By describing the social variables affecting individual storytelling events—who were the participants; what was their gender, class, ethnicity; what were the relationships among them; what was the purpose of the storytelling event; what was the topic; and so forth—one could build a repertoire of the variation in styles available within a speech community. Within this range of options, individual creativity could also be explored: how do storytellers draw on these resources to develop their own unique style?

How Can the Study of Prosody Enhance the Methodology of Ethnographic Studies?

I have always considered it an emotional disadvantage not to have been raised in a speech community where members are encouraged to wail at public funerals. In my speech community, women may sniffle and perhaps whimper a little, but beyond that you'd better step into the ladies' room. Men have fewer options in these public events: they are allowed silent tears and perhaps a nose blow. Despite these constraints, we also acknowledge the importance of letting grief out, through loud, body-wrenching crying in private or with an intimate. This is considered a cleansing, healing experience. People who do not release grief run the risk of neurosis in later life.

Thus, the prosody of crying—the loudness and pitch of this mode of expression—provides an entry point to the value system of the Northern European American culture I describe. This leads to other questions about ways of displaying emotion; notions of what is public versus private; the metaphor of grief as "contained" in the body; gender-based norms; and so on. Investigations of how cultures regulate the expression of emotion could be conducted with a focus on exaggerated prosody as a point of departure. Although here I have used crying as an example, laughter and other expressive prosody would also merit study. As we have seen in numerous examples in this chapter, high pitch, louder volume, and elongated vowels tend to be associated with expressive language. Thus, for ethnographers who analyze the texts of a culture, exaggerated prosody may offer an additional tool—a "red flag" located at the most value-laden parts of a text.

Can We Trace the Development of Expressive Functions of Prosody in Childhood?

From early infancy, children's cries begin to take on functional differences (as in the tired cry versus the gas pain cry versus the hungry cry).

Eventually, even before the onset of speech, some of these sounds become symbolic rather than actual bursts of discomfort. A certain whine, for example, rather than being a pure expression of frustration, might direct a nearby adult to help reach for a toy. In this chapter, I have entertained the assumption that adults' expressions of emotion are culturally restrained versions of emotional outbursts, manifested through, among other things, the exaggerated prosody associated with their speech. If this assumption is correct, an interesting research question emerges: at what stage of childhood development does the cultural influence take shape? The answer to this question is particularly important in light of recent research on child development (Brown, Donelan-McCall, & Dunn, 1996), which suggests that emotional language may be linked to social and cognitive development. By tracing exaggerated prosodic features in child discourse, one could perhaps better understand the child's emotional priorities and development.

How Is Prosody Used as a Performance Feature in Other Genres of Discourse?

In these discussions of the role of prosody in emotion, I do not mean to imply that narratives are the *only* genre in which prosody can be manipulated to convey self-expression, attitude, and emotional priority. I have simply chosen narratives as a potential site for the extensive display of emotional language by a single speaker in one self-contained text. However, the investigation of prosody and self-expression can certainly be extended into conversation data, classroom interaction, pubic speaking, and other genres of discourse. The prosody of emotion has often been considered "beside the point" by phonologists and phoneticians because it is not in the traditional realm of linguistic theory. Yet, to get a full picture of spoken communication, theories that ignore the relationship between prosody and emotion fall short.

Sample Analysis

At this point I turn to the chapter's sample analysis, an investigation of pitch extremes in a set of narratives told by Americans and Asian learners of English. The analysis is drawn from my dissertation (1997), and a version of it also appears in Wennerstrom (2001). For this chapter, I have focused mainly on one particular subset of the results of those prior studies concerned with the relationship between pitch extremes and quoted speech. Speakers in the study routinely raised their pitch in direct quotations, regardless of gender or nationality. These results offer further support for the claim made throughout this chapter that pitch can be considered a performance feature—storytellers use animated quotations to bring to the audience a more vivid picture of the original scene.

Pitch, Evaluation, and Quoted Speech

Most prosodic analyses in the literature start from the text and work "up" to the prosodic features of interest. For example, in French and Local's (1986) analysis of interruptions, the authors scanned conversations to identify interruptions and then measured their pitch and loudness. In Selting's (1994) analysis of climactic points in narratives, she began first by locating the climactic points in the texts and then assessing the characteristics of the prosody. In my 1998 analysis of paratones and lecture structural components, I began by coding the boundaries of the structural components and then measuring the pitch at those junctures.

However, in the following analysis the approach was the opposite: to start with the prosody and work "down" to the text in an investigation of pitch peaks in oral narratives. Of interest was the question of where in the text storytellers' very highest pitch peaks would be located. Behind this question was the assumption that in an extended text such as an oral narrative, the highest pitch peaks would represent a teller's emotional priorities. A second question was whether there would be cross-cultural differences between native and nonnative speakers of English in the distribution of pitch peaks in the stories. I hypothesized that language background would not be a distinguishing factor because the use of pitch in emotion is paralinguistic, rather than part of a language-specific phonology of intonation.

Methodology

Oral narratives from eight NSs of Standard American English and eight NNSs were transcribed for analysis. Six of the NS stories were told in small groups in a graduate seminar on discourse analysis in which students in the class were asked to tell about a mistake their parents had made in raising them (Corpus 5). The final two NS narratives were taken from a naturally occurring conversation among a group of friends (Corpus 2). The NNS stories were collected in an advanced English as a second language (ESL) conversation class by the students themselves (Corpus 6). Volunteers included seven Japanese students and one Korean student who were assigned to tell a story from their own life that was either embarrassing or scary. They told these stories to the class and finally submitted them to the instructor on cassette tapes. All stories ranged from 150 to 500 words. Using a CSL machine, I measured the stories to determine where in the texts the highest pitch peaks were located. Specifically, two measurements were identified for each speaker: (1) the highest 10% of all pitch peaks and (2) the top three highest pitch peaks. That is, if a story had 200 words, the twenty words with the highest pitch were selected for analysis in the 10% category, and the top three words were selected for analysis in the second category. Henceforth, the term "pitch peak" will refer only to words in these two categories.

Next, a functional analysis was conducted of all pitch peaks to determine whether they played a structural role, an evaluative role, or some other role in the stories. The structural role was defined in terms of Labov's (1972) narrative component boundaries—abstract, orientation, complicating action, resolution, and coda (see table 8.1)—and it was determined whether the first content word of a new component was a pitch peak. The category also included episodic and other deictic shifts. The evaluative role was identified using Labov's criteria for lexical intensifiers and syntactic evaluative devices. These included superlatives, expletives, and other value-laden lexical items (such as *really, terrible, idiot,* etc.), and certain syntactic manipulations: clefts, questions, negatives, projection verbs (such as *I guess* or *I believe*), and quotations. The "other" category referred to instances where storytellers made repairs or dealt with questions, interruptions, or outside distractions. Tabulations were then made to determine how pitch peaks were distributed with respect to these functional categories.

Results

The majority of the pitch peaks in the stories were associated with evaluative language for both NSs and NNSs of English. The percentages in each functional category for both groups for the top 10% of pitch peaks are shown in the graphs in figure 8.6; the percentages for the top three pitch peaks are shown in figure 8.7. As these graphs show, there was indeed a high degree of association between pitch peaks and evaluative language. For the top three words only, this trend was even more evident. The result was similar for NSs and NNSs, as expected.

Within the evaluation category, a further tabulation was done to determine which of Labov's (1972) evaluative devices were most frequently associated with the top three pitch peaks, calculated as a percentage of total evaluative devices. Four categories were used to make this tabulation: external evaluations, and, among internal evaluations, syntactic

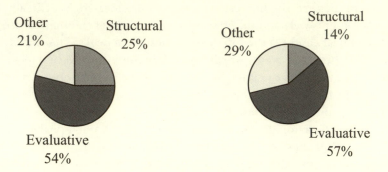

Figure 8.6   The distribution of the top 10% of pitch peaks in each functional category for native ($n = 191$ tokens) and nonnative ($n = 264$ tokens) speakers of English.

devices, lexical intensifiers, and quotations. These results are summarized in the bar graph in figure 8.8: NNSs relied on quoted speech more than did NSs in high-pitched evaluations. In fact, for some NNSs, all three of their top three pitch peaks occurred in quoted speech. This may have been due to the fact that the NNSs had fewer lexical and syntactic resources to draw from in English.

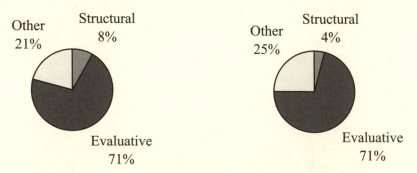

Figure 8.7   The distribution of the top 3 pitch peaks in each functional category for native and nonnative speakers of English ($n = 24$ tokens for each group).

Types of Evaluation

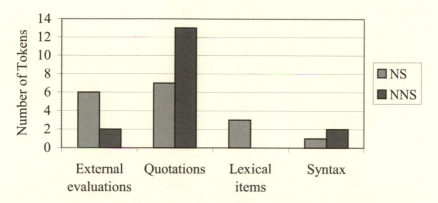

Figure 8.8 The distribution of the top 3 pitch peaks among different types of evaluation for native and nonnative speakers ($n = 17$ tokens for each group).

Discussion

Although the study had several interesting findings, for the purpose of this brief analysis, I will focus on the quotation result. This result was particularly intriguing because it did not appear that tellers were attempting to accurately replicate the original speech in the quotations. There were examples of speakers quoting themselves, their parents, and even of women quoting men, all at the top of their pitch ranges. Had a woman wanted to accurately render a man's voice, one would expect that she would have lowered, instead of raised, her pitch. Likewise, speakers quoting themselves would have no reason to exceed the pitch of their own normal voice range if exact rendition were the goal. Here is an example (from Corpus 6) of a Japanese woman quoting first a male friend and then herself. The man was urging her to hurry and get out of the car so that they could go swimming with their other friends, but the woman was too embarrassed to leave the car because she had forgotten to bring her shoes (plus signs [+] are used to indicate pitch peaks):

1   And→ (.6) one- (.4) one of my FRIENDS↘ (.6) came

2   to the CAR↓ (1.8) and asked ME↓ (.3) ↗ "What

3   +HÁPPENED+ to you↓ WE are +WÁITING+ for

4   you↓ +LET'S+ go to the (.3) to +SWIM+↓" →And↘

5   (.7) I said to HIM↘ (.4) ↗ "+OH+↘ I +CAN'T+ get out of

6   HERE↘ (.2) because I have no SHOES↗ (.6) I +LEFT+

7   my SHOES↘ (.4) BEHÍND . . . . "

In lines 2 and 5, the teller changed to a very high key to initiate the quotations of both the man and herself. There are pitch peaks on *happened, waiting, let's,* and *swim* in the man's speech, and on *oh, can't,* and *left* in her own. The first half of the excerpt is shown in figure 8.9, where the cursor marks the onset of the quotation of the man.

Another example (from Corpus 5) shows an American man quoting his parents. Although one might expect a lower voice to be attributed to parental authority figures, the teller instead slowed down and hit the very top of his pitch range in the following quotation (arrow symbols indicate faster [>>] and slower [<<]):[6]

1   I WRECKED the CAR↘ (.8) at SIXTÉEN↘ (.6) and-
2   >>they ₛₒᵣₜ ₒF LAUGHED it OFF ₐND ₛₐID (1.8)
3   << ⌐"WELL that's the ⁺WAY⁺ you ⁺LEARN⁺ and
4   GROW ₛₒN↗" (.1) >> ↳ ₒᵣ SÓMETHING LIKE THAT↓

Here, the quotation in lines 3–4 stood out above the normal range, even higher in pitch than the words associated with the complicating action of wrecking the car in line 1. This is shown in figure 8.10, where the cursor highlights the word *way.*

In the final example (from Corpus 6), shown in figure 8.11, a Japanese man quoted his father, who chastised him for damaging a stranger's car during a skiing accident. The text is as follows:

1   . . . and→ (1.3) ÁFTER THAT↗ (1.2) my FÁTHER
2   came to- (1.0) came to ME and said↘ (6.2)
3   ⌐ "⁺I⁺ thought ⁺WHO⁺ was↘ (.3) the STÚPID
4   (1.2) STÚPID ⁺BOY⁺↗ (1.5) → but→ (1.0) it was
5   YOU↓ ₘY ₛₒN↓"

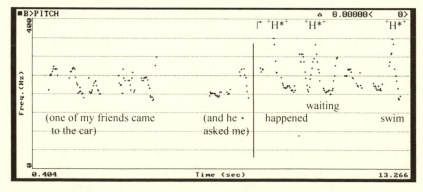

Figure 8.9 A female speaker hits the very top of her pitch range in quoting a man. The cursor marks the onset of the quotation.

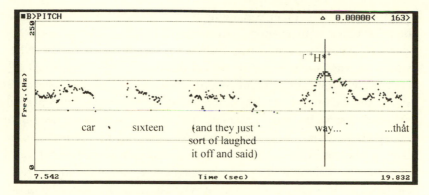

Figure 8.10   A male speaker hits the very top of his pitch range in quoting his parents. The cursor marks the word *way*.

Again, one might expect the older man's voice to be rendered in a lower, rather than a higher, pitch, but this was not the case.

It appears then that the high pitch associated with these quotations must be interpreted not as an attempt to accurately reiterate the original speech but rather as an intensification mechanism. Thus, the finding adds support to research that has already demonstrated quotation as an evaluation device (Bauman, 1986; Eggins & Slade, 1997; Labov, 1972; Wolfson, 1982). If quotations were merely attempts to accurately render what was uttered at the time, one would not necessarily expect storytellers to hit the very top of their pitch ranges. Instead, the evidence suggests that exaggerated pitch is yet another performance feature—a manifestation of the speaker's emotional involvement with these evaluative points of the text.

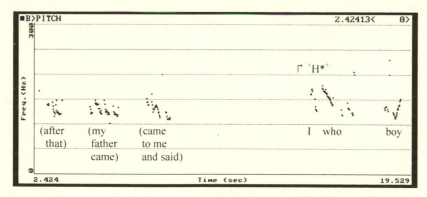

Figure 8.11   A male speaker hits the very top of his pitch range in quoting his father.

That this is an evaluative, paralinguistic function of pitch, beyond the phonological use of intonation, is also evident in the fact that NSs and NNSs placed their pitch peaks similarly. As shown in Wennerstrom (1994), NNSs do not always acquire the English intonation system easily or automatically; in that study, significant differences occurred between how NSs versus NNSs from Japan and other language backgrounds used intonation in oral reading and free speech tasks. The difference between the two studies is that in the 1994 study, the focus was on the use of particular intonational morphemes; whereas in this study, it is on the paralinguistic, emotional use of pitch. An obvious follow-up study would analyze Japanese- and Korean-language narratives in a similar way; it is possible that the speakers in this study had acquired American cultural norms for storytelling style.

To conclude, this small analysis supports a distinction between the phonological intonation system of English and the paralinguistic use of pitch for emotional expression. The latter tends to occur in association with other linguistic devices that have been characterized independently as evaluative. In delivering crucial events in altered voices, storytellers call attention to what is remarkable, unexpected, regrettable, amusing, touching, and shocking—in short, their emotional priorities.

Chapter Conclusion

The focus of this chapter has been on the various roles played by prosody in oral narratives. The chapter began with a presentation of Labov and Waletzky's model of narrative structure and a discussion of how prosody can distinguish certain narrative components. We saw high-rising pitch boundaries used in an orientation to a story as a teller checked whether the listeners were following. Then, as he moved from the orientation to the first complicating action, he used a high paratone. These facts support the findings of Longacre, Wolfson, and others that distinctive linguistic features coincide with narrative components.

The remainder of the chapter focused on the relationship between prosody and the expression of emotion. The expressive functions of prosody, in a sense, ride on top of the underlying phonological intonation system and can therefore be analyzed as separate phenomena. Exaggerated pitch, louder volume, elongated vowels, and tempo changes can be associated with certain parts of a text to intensify them. Because oral narratives are likely to include performance features that express a storyteller's values and emotions, and because they tend to be extensive enough for a rich analysis, they were judged to be an appropriate genre of discourse for a discussion of the expressive aspects of prosody.

I have presented evidence that exaggerated prosody does indeed reflect a storyteller's emotional priorities. Examples have shown that exaggerated prosodic forms frequently associate with the climactic points of stories and with other language that is evaluative through its lexico-grammatical content. In particular, quoted speech is often prosodically distinctive when it is used to convey a key event in the narrative plot. Such intensifying performance features serve a social function: they enliven the storytelling event, making it more realistic, and thereby encourage the audience to re-experience the original events and support the teller's point of view.

We have also looked at variation in storytelling style, assuming that speech communities hold norms for prosodic manipulations. As shown, ethnic group, geographic region, social setting, and of course, individual style influence variation. I have urged that analyses of a community's ways of speaking should include descriptions of how prosody can be manipulated to achieve expressive, attitudinal, and other stylistic effects.

I mentioned several areas where further investigation is needed into how prosody is used in oral narratives. In general, narratives have received less attention by prosody analysts than have, for example, conversation data. I recommended that the question of prosody in narrative structure be revisited and that the development of prosody in the expression of emotion in primary language acquisition be explored. I also suggested that ethnographic approaches include prosody in the analysis of narratives and of other genres as well. Because of the relationship between prosody and the expression of emotion, exaggerated prosody could serve as a "red flag" to the emotional priorities in a text. This was, in fact, the assumption underlying the sample analysis, in which the starting point was a determination of where in a set of narrative texts the very highest pitch peaks were associated. That analysis found that storytellers, both native and nonnative speakers of English, reserved their highest pitch for quoted speech, which other scholars have considered a performance feature in its own right.

Although the expressive functions of prosody are not often studied, I have attempted to argue that how we manipulate our speech to convey emotions—surprise, alarm, warmth, anger, fear—belongs in a description of language and social behavior. Therefore, I hope that this chapter has provided justification for an expanded role of prosody in future narrative research. For those interested in oral narratives—psychologists, discourse analysts, or ethnographers—there is structural, emotional, and cultural information to be gleaned from the way storytellers manipulate their prosody.

9

PROSODY IN
SECOND-LANGUAGE
DISCOURSE

In this chapter, I consider the discourse of adult learners of English from other native-language backgrounds. As previous chapters have shown, prosody is involved in information structure, topic organization, turn-taking, and other functions of language at the discourse level. Therefore, for those nonnative speakers whose goal is to participate in English-language speech communities, an understanding of the English-specific aspects of prosody will be an enhancement. Researchers with a theoretical interest in second-language discourse would do well to take prosody into account along with other features of language.

If the English as a second language (ESL) textbook market is any indication of current interests among second-language educators, prosody is a favorite topic. During the 1990s, authors of pronunciation textbooks for ESL students raised the status of prosody by including core units on rhythm, stress, and intonation as central components of their books (Bradford, 1988; Dauer, 1993; Gilbert, 1993; Grant, 1993; Hagen & Grogan, 1992; Hahn & Dickerson, 1999; Morley, 1993; Wennerstrom, 1991). A case in point is Linda Grant's pronunciation textbook, *Well Said* (1993), which includes chapter titles such as "Stress in Words," "Rhythm in Sentences," "Sentence Focus and Intonation," and "Phrasing, Pausing and Blending," while the material on vowels and consonants is relegated to appendices. Furthermore, textbooks aimed at ESL educators reflect a priority for topics of prosody. Wong (1987) outlines a systematic approach to the development of pronunciation materials based almost entirely on the interaction between rhythm and intonation; Celce-Murcia, Brinton, and Goodwin (1996) devote two out of their four chapters on the sound system of English to stress, rhythm, prominence, and intonation; Pennington (1996) includes a long chapter on prosody in a volume on phonology for English language teachers; and Kreidler (1997) allots five chapters out of twelve to topics of prosody in his introduction to spoken English for students of linguistics and second-language pedagogy.

The motivation behind this clear interest in prosody is based on language teachers' recognition of the difficulty adult learners face in acquiring the prosody of another language. Research also supports this commonsense view and provides evidence that prosody functions in the coherence of discourse, beyond the sentence level. A review article by Chun (1988) surveys the work of several theorists of intonation to show how it functions in communication. Her article provides a rationale for placing a higher priority on the research and teaching of intonation to second-language learners. In Chun's words:

> Intonation is fundamental to genuine communication because communicative competence is the ability not only to formulate grammatically correct utterances, but also to signal interactional strategies, such as interrupting, asking for clarification, taking the floor, changing the subject, concluding an argument, or constraining a hearer to reply. (p. 295)

In a review of research and pedagogical materials for the teaching of pronunciation, Pennington and Richards (1986) document a shift away from previous approaches based solely on segmental phonology to one that takes the discourse as a whole into account. They advocate a perspective on pronunciation that

> highlights the overarching role of context in determining phonological choices at all three levels—segmental, voice-setting, and prosodic features. Teaching isolated forms of sounds and words fails to address the fact that in communication, many aspects of pronunciation are determined by the positioning of elements within long stretches of speech, according to the information structure and the interactional context of the discourse as determined by speaker and hearer. (p. 218)

A more recent review article by Morley (1991) comes to a similar conclusion about the shift toward an emphasis on prosody in textbooks, references, research books, and journals in their coverage of ESL pronunciation. She describes this as "a redirection of priorities within the sound system to a focus on the critical importance of suprasegmentals (i.e., stress, rhythm, intonation, etc.) and how they are used to communicate meaning in the context of discourse, as well as the importance of vowel and consonant sounds and their combinations" (p. 493). In short, it has been recognized that prosody is as central to communicative competence as segmental phonology, that it functions to convey meaning at the discourse level, that its acquisition can be a stumbling block to an adult learner, and that it should be emphasized in teaching materials that address spoken communication for nonnative speakers of English. Clearly, prosody, not just a superficial flourish to be superimposed on "real" language, carries meaning in its own right.

From this perspective, this chapter reviews empirical research on nonnative speakers' prosody, its acquisition, and its effect on judgments of accent,[1] comprehensibility, and fluency. Thereafter, I call attention to a few of the many unresolved issues in the research on second-language prosody. The chapter ends with a sample conversation analysis, contributed by Heidi Riggenbach, of two nonnative speakers' pause patterns. Riggenbach argues that "conversational fluency" is characterized by these and other prosodic features.

Previous Empirical Studies

Descriptive Studies

By descriptive studies, I refer to research whose goal is simply to document prosodic features of nonnative speech in English without necessarily attempting to understand the process of acquisition. Such studies show which aspects of prosody might be more or less difficult to acquire, both in general and for particular language groups. In this category I will discuss my own work comparing the intonation of nonnative speakers to that of native speakers in both an oral reading and a free speech task (Wennerstrom, 1994); Hewings' (1995a, 1995b) studies of nonnative speakers and native speakers reading scripted dialogues; and interactional studies of cross-cultural miscommunications by Gumperz (1992), Pickering (1999), and Davies and Tyler (1994). All these studies focus on differences between intonation patterns of native speakers and nonnative speakers.

In 1994, I found differences in how intermediate speakers of English from Thai, Japanese, and Spanish language backgrounds used intonation in discourse tasks as compared with native speakers from the United States. For this research, I chose to focus on six intonational features of English that caused difficulty for ESL students. In terms of the intonation model presented in chapter 2, these were

1. Associating L+H* pitch accents with contrasts,
2. Associating L* pitch accents with accessible items,
3. Omitting pitch accents on function words,
4. Using ↗ low-rising pitch boundaries in mid-utterance position to indicate continuation,
5. Using ↑ high-rising pitch boundaries at the end of yes/no questions, and
6. Using ⇑ paratones, or increased pitch range, at topic shifts.

Subjects in the study were asked to read a special passage constructed to contain these intonational features associated with certain test words and phrases. They were also prompted to describe a picture of a street scene in their own words. By making tapes of ten intermediate level ESL students from each language background and ten native speakers as they conducted these two tasks, I was able to single out the particular intonation patterns and measure their pitch and loudness on a Visipitch machine.[2] I then took averages within each language group. Whereas native speakers used pitch exactly as predicted on all the intonation features measured, the other language groups differed considerably from the native speakers. In particular, the L+H* pitch accent, used by native speakers to make contrasts in the information structure, was less distinctive among the nonnative speaker groups. For example, the text was constructed to contain a contrast between the rainy weather of Seattle and the sunny weather of other cities, as follows: "In Spring, Seattle is usually wet. Meanwhile, other cities are having sun" (p. 405). In the second sentence, native speakers, on average, increased their pitch by 41 Hz between the accessible word *having* and the contrast word *sun*, a difference that was statistically significant. This happened even though there is normally a declination in pitch throughout an intonational phrase so that without the contrast, the pitch would be lower on *sun*. Among the nonnative groups, the average pitch was lower on *sun* than on *having;* that is, the contrast in the text was not supported by the intonation. There were no significant loudness differences for any of the groups. Figures 9.1 and 9.2 illustrate a typical English speaker and a typical Thai speaker (both men) reading this phrase in the study.

It is of course possible that the oral reading task itself led among the nonnative speakers to a certain stilted style of speech lacking pitch contrasts. Therefore, measurements were made in the description task to compare function words, which were predicted to have no pitch accents, to content words, which were predicted to have H* pitch accents: the pitch of all instances of the verb *to be*, used as an auxiliary or a copula, was compared to that of the following content word. For example, if a subject said, "The sky is blue," the pitch of *is* was compared to that of *blue*. Here again,

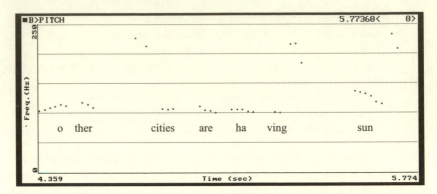

Figure 9.1   A male native speaker of English raises his pitch to make a contrast on *sun*.

on average, the native group made a large statistically significant difference in both pitch (48 Hz) and loudness (3 Db) between content items in the discourse and the preceding function words. The nonnative groups also averaged a slightly higher pitch and loudness on the content words, but the difference was only statistically significant for the Japanese group. Moreover, the pitch distinction was far less pronounced within this group than for the native English speakers: content words were only 13 Hz higher than function words for the Japanese group, compared to 48 Hz for the native English speakers. The loudness difference for the Japanese group was 2 Db, also significant.

Other findings showed a difference between the Thai and Japanese language groups and the Indo-European (Spanish and English) groups at phrase boundaries, which may reflect the historical similarity between

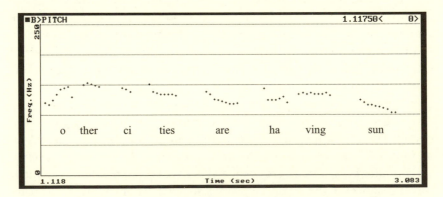

Figure 9.2   For this male Thai speaker of English, *sun* has a lower pitch than *having*.

the latter two groups. Spanish and English groups used low-rising (↗) and plateau (→) pitch boundaries similarly to indicate a connection be-tween phrases within the description task, whereas the Thai and Japa-nese speakers were more likely to end phrases with a low pitch bound-ary (↓), even when the context indicated that the subsequent phrase was a closely related one. For Spanish and English speakers, the per-centage of low boundaries in the description was 13% and 12%, respec-tively, of all phrase boundaries; for the Japanese and Thai speakers, these percentages were 44% and 47%. Figures 9.3 and 9.4 show English and Thai speakers, both men, uttering closely related phrases in the picture description task. In these excerpts, the English speaker uses plateau (→) and low-rising boundaries (↗) while the Thai speaker's pitch bound-aries are low (↓):

> ENGLISH   ... looking down↗ on a→ public square↗ in an old part of
> a- of a city↗ and it possibly could be winter time↗ ...
>
> THAI   In this picture it is very crowded↓ and it look very busy↓ I
> think it has a good economy↓ because ...

The majority of the Thai speakers also used a low pitch boundary (↓) at the end of a yes/no question in the oral reading passage whereas the other three groups used a high (↑). Finally, to measure paratones, two sentences with similar structure were included in the oral reading passage, one in paragraph-medial and the other in paragraph-initial position, so that the pitch range in the two environments could be compared. Spanish and English speakers both used paratones; that is, they averaged a significantly broader pitch range on the paragraph-initial sentence than on the paragraph-medial one. For English speakers, the average difference was

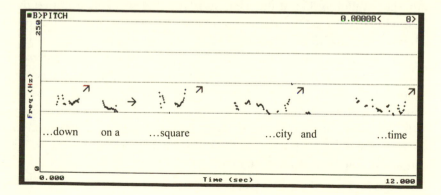

Figure 9.3 A male native speaker of English uses rising (↗) and plateau (→) pitch boundaries to connect his phrases in a description of a city scene.

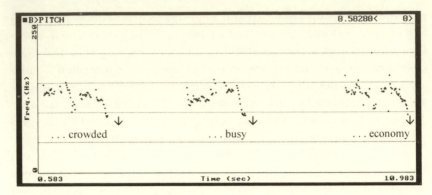

Figure 9.4   A male Thai speaker of English uses low pitch boundaries (↓) between phrases in his description.

22 Hz and for Spanish, 29 Hz. However, the Japanese and Thai groups did not distinguish the paragraph shift in this manner.

In a similar study, Hewings (1995a) analyzed the intonation of four Greek, four Korean, and four Indonesian speakers of English as a second language and twelve native speakers of British English. Subjects read scripted dialogues that the nonnative speakers had had the opportunity to practice in advance. Although Hewings used Brazil's (1985) model of intonation, whereas my 1994 study used Pierrehumbert's (1980), it is possible to recognize similarities between the two studies. One similar result was that although the native and nonnative speakers agreed in their choice of pitch boundaries in many instances, there was an important class of exceptions: at certain connective junctures, the majority of the native speakers used rising pitch boundaries whereas the nonnative groups used "falling," or in this model, low pitch boundaries (↓). The nonnative result was parallel to that of the Thai and Japanese speakers in my study. Hewings's interpretation of this pitch boundary is, however, slightly different from mine: in Brazil's model, an intonational phrase with a rising tone, called a "referring tone," is used to refer to what is already shared in the common ground between the speaker and the hearer. Thus, for Hewings, this intonation is socially affiliative, but for me, a rising pitch boundary is attitudinally neutral; it merely suggests an interdependency with what is to follow. The native speakers in Hewings's study tended to use this tone in situations such as the following (p. 257) where the script contained a marker of disagreement or contention:

s   It might be difficult to work there.
l   Yes, it can be difficult, but in my experience students are
    happiest in University accommodation.

After L's utterance of the word *difficult*, the majority of native speakers used a rising pitch boundary, which according to Hewings, softened the impact of the disagreement, while the nonnative speakers were more likely to select a low boundary. Moreover, Greek, Korean, and Indonesian language groups were about equal in the frequency with which they selected the low boundary in these environments.

Hewings (1995b) describes an almost identical study with a focus on Indonesian speakers of English. Again, speakers took parts in reading a prepared script of a dialogue, and the pitch boundaries at junctures between intonational phrases were tabulated. In phrases where native speakers used rising pitch boundaries, the Indonesians used low pitch boundaries in 69% of the cases (p. 34). Other findings included the Indonesians' tendency to use shorter intonational phrases than those of the native English speakers. Hewings attributes this to the fact that, because the intonation contour reflects a preplanned unit of speech (Beattie, 1983; Levelt, 1989), those struggling with a foreign language would face a higher cognitive load and therefore plan shorter speech units. Finally, Hewings reports that the Indonesians were more likely to place the final pitch accent near the end of an intonational phrase, whereas the native speakers placed it earlier in the phrase. To understand this last result in terms of my intonation model, it would necessary to analyze each accent placement individually in terms of the information structure of its phrase. Was there evidence, for example, that native speakers were placing their pitch accents to reflect a contrast in the text, while Indonesians were not? An analysis of the information structure of the dialogues could lead to a better understanding of why the two language groups differed in this regard.

To summarize so far, these studies have focused on the prosody of nonnative speakers of English from particular language backgrounds and attempted to identify features that distinguish nonnative from native speech. In particular, we saw a higher use of low pitch boundaries at connective junctures among nonnative speakers from Thai, Japanese, Indonesian, Korean, and Greek language backgrounds, whereas Spanish and English groups were more prone to use rising and plateau boundaries. Spanish and English groups similarly used paratones at topic shifts. We have seen additional evidence that pitch distinctions were generally exploited more by native speakers than nonnative speakers to make contrasts and to distinguish content from function words. Spanish speakers were similar to the other nonnative groups on these features. Because descriptions of nonnative speech reveal different pitch patterns from one language background to another, one may conclude that intonational features cannot necessarily be considered universal.

In studies that focus on interactional discourse, Gumperz highlights the role of prosody in what he refers to as "contextualization cues," through which the participants in conversation negotiate the nature of an interaction—its meaning, goals, level of formality, and so forth. I discuss his 1992 analysis, just one of several treatments of cross-cultural communication Gumperz conducted over the years (Gumperz, 1971; Gumperz, 1982; and others). This study concentrated on a rather unsatisfactory encounter between an Indian student and an English academic advisor. Gumperz documented how differences between certain prosodic cues used by these two speakers led to continued misinterpretations as both became more and more frustrated. One characteristic of Indian English is a tendency to end phrases with low pitch boundaries. This may have been interpreted by the advisor as a signal that the student was finished speaking—the student later complained of being continually interrupted before he had a chance to get to his main point. In addition, sequences of two or more words were distinguished by "a combination of slow tempo, staccato enunciation, and, sometimes, increased loudness" (p. 238). In Gumperz's transcripts, these heavily accented chunks tended to be located at the ends of phrases. This accent pattern may have had the effect of obscuring contrasts to the advisor: instead of a single stressed syllable of a contrasted word being associated with L+H* pitch accent, as it would be in British English, several syllables in a row had heavy accents. For example, in the first two lines of the following exchange (p. 242), the Indian student (D) strongly emphasizes the last few words (I use Gumperz's transcription symbol of italics to represent the heavily accented sequences[3]):

D   hmm I'm not *insulting you*↓
     I just hm   ⎡feeling *sorry for myself*↓
L   ⎣no, I didn't say you were↓
     but exactly↘
     why are you feeling so sorry for <u>YOURSÉLF</u>?

According to Gumperz's analysis, the advisor (L) interprets D's stress on the whole phrase "sorry for myself" to be contrastive on the single word *myself.* This leads her to conclude that D is emphasizing his *personal* feelings (he *himself* was offended). Since prosody has different language-specific structural properties, participants in a cross-cultural interaction may derive different conclusions about the intended meanings. Moreover, since prosody also conveys emotional meaning, mismatches in prosodic cues can result in misinterpretation of attitude; what was a structural pattern in Indian English was interpreted as a negative emotional stance by the British English speaker.

Another study of mismatched intonational cues (Pickering, 1999) done in the United States concerns the importance of key in classroom interactions between Chinese teaching assistants (ITAs) and American students. By way of background, it is a common practice in U.S. universities for graduate students, many of whom speak English as a second language, to teach undergraduate classes. Because nonnative speech in the classroom setting has been perceived as problematic by the undergraduates (Bailey, 1984), many universities have developed special programs, tests, workshops, and other materials to help ITAs communicate more effectively in American classrooms. In the following two excerpts from chemistry classes, Pickering (pp. 124–128) compares the use of key in similar contexts by teaching assistants, one a native speaker of English from the United States, and the other a Chinese speaker of English. Both cases involve a response to a student who gives an incorrect answer in reference to chemical procedures. (USTA = American TA; S = student; student responses are not coded for prosody):

Native Speaker:

1	USTA	→ What <u>ABÓUT</u> how would we TEST for NH <u>FOUR</u>
2		specifically?
3	S1	Heat it.
4	USTA	→ well if you REMÉMBER that didn't <u>WORK</u> too well
5		→ we had to do SOMEthing other than just <u>HEAT</u> it.
6	S2	Put hydrogen peroxide in it.
7	USTA	↳ YEAH.

Recall from chapter 2 that mid key (→) indicates simply an additive stance toward the prior utterance. Thus, according to Pickering, following the incorrect response given in line 3, the teacher invites further student contributions by maintaining a mid key in lines 4 and 5. Following the correct response in line 6, the teacher indicates a satisfactory closure of the exchange with the low key (↳) affirmation *yeah* in line 7.

Such conventionalized but subtle uses of pitch level can be particularly problematic for nonnative speakers and can lead to miscommunication in cross-cultural interaction. In the following similar exchange from a parallel class taught by a Chinese ITA, key choices made by the teacher contribute to a problematic interaction (ITA = Chinese TA):

Nonnative Speaker:

1	ITA	↗ WHAT's the → SÉCOND <u>STEP</u>?
2	S1	It depends on if you have Na in the sample or not in
3		the flame test. If you have Na then you can't tell if you
4		have potassium so you have to do a solution test for

```
5         potassium.
6    ITA   ↱ DIRÉCTLY THEN? ((pause)) ↱ you MEAN ↱ HERE
7         you want to → PREPÁRE SOLÚTION ↳ NOW
8         → RIGHT?
9    S1   ((silent beat)) ↳ Yeah. ((flat tone, low voice))
```

The student's incorrect response in lines 2–5 (that the second step is to do a solution test) is met with a high key (↱) question from the ITA, "directly then?" When the student does not respond, the ITA rephrases the question again with a high key and directs the student to agree through the use of a mid key confirmation marker, "right?" Pickering analyzes this as disconcerting to the student whose hesitant, minimal response in the last line indicates his intimidation. As we have seen, for English speakers, a high key response can convey a contrast in attitude with respect to the prior contribution. Although this response did not necessarily have this value for the nonnative speaker, it apparently sounded harsh to the native speaker student.

Davies and Tyler (1994), in another analysis of an ITA dialogue with an American native speaker undergraduate student during an office conference, document the confusion generated by mismatches between lexicogrammatical and prosodic cues. The following example (p. 211) is taken from an exchange in which the nonnative speaker ITA (T) is interrupted by the student (S), indicating a communication problem. The sequence shows the same pattern of low pitch boundary at a phrase boundary in mid-utterance as found in Hewings (1995a, 1995b) and Wennerstrom (1994):

```
T   oh ah I think it's a not very serious problem↓ ((pause))
S   OH haha    ⎡ hahaha it feels very serious
T              ⎣ because ah
```

In the first line T ends a clause with a low pitch boundary and a pause, which to a native speaker signals "finality" of the clause with respect to any subsequent contribution. At that point, S begins to speak, thinking the turn complete. However, immediately thereafter, T continues with the conjunction *because*, indicating that his actual intention was to complete his turn with a dependent clause. The result is overlapping speech in which T is cut short. Tyler (1992) and I (2000b) have found similar mismatches of prosodic cues prior to interruptions.

Findings such as these that identify prosody as a factor in interactional problems between speakers from different cultural backgrounds point to directions for teaching and research. In the language classroom, Clennell (1997) suggests that "consciousness raising activities" that focus attention on those aspects of prosody not found in the learners' native languages be developed. Indeed, many of the pronunciation textbooks mentioned earlier in this chapter take exactly this approach to the teaching of English, centering activities on meaningful components of English prosody that differ from those of other languages. Interactive studies are also useful in increasing our general understanding of the subtleties of cross-cultural communication, which go well beyond grammar and vocabulary.

Accent and Comprehensibility Studies

This category of research involves the effects of nonnative speakers' prosody on raters' perceptions of their ability to be understood. One methodology to study this topic has been to have native speaker judges rate nonnative speaker discourse for comprehensibility, accentedness, and other measures of language production, and then to analyze the characteristics of the speech itself. An important study in this genre is by Anderson-Hsieh, Johnson, and Koehler (1992), who analyzed 60 oral reading passages by male nonnative speakers of English at a range of levels of proficiency and from a variety of language backgrounds. The pronunciation of each speaker was rated on a 7-point scale and the speech was then analyzed for accuracy in three categories: segments, syllable structure, and prosody, including stress, rhythm, phrasing, and intonation. The researchers found that, of the three variables, prosody had the highest correlation with the pronunciation scores (p. 545). Once again, this reinforces the notion that prosody is crucial to communicative competence in second-language learners.

I (1998) also considered how prosody contributed to the comprehensibility ratings of 20 Chinese ITAs in the delivery of a 10-minute lecture in English. Although the details of the study are presented in chapter 5, I mention it again here because it represents a tabulation of raters' assessments of nonnative speech. The lectures were scored on a scale of 0–3 by three raters for "English production," a holistic score that included pronunciation, prosody, fluency, and grammar. Audiotapes of the lectures were measured on a CSL machine so that the intonation associated with particular classes of items in the discourse—the H* pitch accent for new information, the L+H* pitch accent on contrasts, the connective low-rising pitch boundary between closely related phrases, and the paratone at topic shifts—could be measured and averaged. The statistically significant finding on a multiple regression analysis was that the use of paratones coincided with higher ratings: the more a subject's pitch changed at topic shifts, the higher the rating in English production.

Hahn (1999) studied the effect of the placement of primary word stress on ratings of English lectures delivered by a nonnative speaker. A group of 90 undergraduates listened to one of three versions of an identical lecture. One version had native-like stress placement, a second version had primary stresses reflecting nonnative usage, and the third version had a monotonous pitch with little primary stress. The first version, rated significantly higher on a measure of communicative effectiveness, was also more easily processed and understood. On written tests of their recall of the main content of the lecture, students who heard the first version scored higher than those who had heard the other versions.

Another methodology for studying the effect of prosody on judgments of accentedness was employed by Munro (1995), who asked raters to judge filtered speech of native speakers of Canadian English and nonnative speakers from a Mandarin Chinese background. The filtering process allowed listeners to hear only the prosodic features, including rate of speech, pause placement, intonation, and word stress; the segmental features were not distinguishable. Raters assigned an "accent" rating on a 4-point scale to filtered and unfiltered speech of speakers from both language groups engaged in narrative and sentence-reading tasks. Even in the filtered condition, raters could identify nonnative accents by the prosody. Temporal variables were a factor in these judgments of accent: Munro reports that rate of speech, measured in number of syllables per second, was significantly lower among the nonnative speakers. In the narrative task, the average rate for native speakers was 3.4 syllables per second and for nonnative speakers, 2.5 (also see Munro & Derwing, 1994).

This result is supported by other studies of tempo, including Anderson (1993), Anderson-Hsieh and Koehler (1988), and Derwing and Munro (1997). Anderson measured tempo in terms of rhythmic intervals as the time in seconds between stressed syllables. In her study, 60 nonnative speakers from Japanese, Chinese, and Korean language backgrounds were rated by 14 linguistically naïve listeners on a measure of "intelligibility" in an oral reading task. Of those 60, the 18 lowest and highest rated speakers were classified, respectively, as least and most intelligible. The tempo of their speech and that of 18 native speakers was then measured for the study. Anderson found that native speakers spoke the most rapidly with the smallest time between rhythmic beats, the least total speaking time, and the fewest total stressed syllables. The nonnative speakers' speech rate was correspondingly slower on all three measures, with those rated as least intelligible having the slowest tempo. However, speech rate does not *determine* comprehensibility: Derwing and Munro found that 10 out of the 26 native speaker judges in their study perceived faster rates of nonnative speech to be *less* comprehensible; and Anderson-Hsieh and

Koehler report that in heavily accented speech, faster rate *detracted* from native speaker comprehension, whereas in less accented, more fluent speech, rate did not have this effect. In addition, native speakers perceived certain samples of heavily accented speech as faster even though they were in fact of the same rate as that of less accented speakers. "It may be," suggest Derwing and Munro (p. 14), "that rate sometimes serves as a general scapegoat for perceived comprehension difficulties, whether it is the direct cause or not."

In sum, the studies in this category all indicate that prosody—intonation, word stress, rate of speech, and rhythm—is an important component in native speakers' judgments of nonnative speakers' comprehensibility and accentedness, although it is not always clear how each particular prosodic variable weighs into these judgments. When measures based on native speaker ratings are used to make important decisions about employment, admission to universities, and other opportunities, prosody can make a crucial difference in the lives of nonnative speakers faced with "gatekeeping" oral assessments of their speech.

Fluency Studies

The role of prosody in nonnative speaker fluency has also been a question of interest. Educational Testing Service included fluency as a subscore in the 1985 version of the Test of Spoken English (TSE) and Spoken English Assessment Kit (SPEAK) tests along with separate scores for comprehensibility, pronunciation, and grammar. Reprinted below is the fluency rating scale from the SPEAK test:[4]

SPEAK TEST SCORING KEY—FLUENCY

0   Speech is so halting and fragmentary or has such a nonnative flow that intelligibility is virtually impossible.

1   Numerous nonnative pauses and/or a nonnative flow that interferes with intelligibility.

2   Some nonnative pauses but with a more nearly native flow so that the pauses do not interfere with intelligibility.

3   Speech is as smooth and as effortless as that of a native speaker.

These descriptions refer to less fluent speech as "halting and fragmentary" and as having "numerous pauses," whereas fluent speech is described as "smooth," "effortless," and as having "native flow." Such descriptions, no doubt created to encourage test raters to think holistically in their judgments of fluency, apparently correspond to prosodic features. The terms "halting" and "fragmentary" refer to length and frequency of pauses and their placement in relation to the intonation contour and the syntax. In contrast, "smooth" and "flow" refer to a lack of interruption in the intonation contour. "Effortless" probably refers to rate of speech, as well as appropriate pause placement. Thus, without using the technical terms for prosody, this test indirectly asks raters to take pauses, rate of speech, stress, and intonation into account in their judgments of nonnative speaker fluency.

Indeed, empirical studies provide evidence of the importance of temporal features in perceptions of fluency. Freed (2000) found that rate of speech, calculated as the number of nonrepeated semantic units per minute, and the number of pauses in the speech stream were both important in rater judgments of fluency in oral interviews of Americans studying French. This result is confirmed in other studies in which temporal variables such as average pause length (Riggenbach, 1991; this chapter), frequency of pauses (Hedge, 1993), and rapidity of speech (Crystal & Varley, 1993), correlated with measures of fluency.

Two additional studies, Isaac (1997) and Wennerstrom (2000b) specifically considered intonation's influence on fluency ratings. Both studies found that not only the length and placement of a pause but also the shape of the pitch boundary prior to it played a role in raters' judgments of fluency. Thus, it was not longer utterances or shorter pauses per se that led to a perception of fluent speech but instead the ability to speak phrasally rather than word by word, using appropriate pitch boundaries to show the interdependency among phrases. Even in the presence of a long pause, a speaker could signal the intention to continue through intonation without detracting from fluency ratings. For example, the following excerpt (Corpus 4) from a Swiss speaker of Italian was rated as highly fluent by three raters who applied the criteria for rating the SPEAK test (presented earlier in this chapter) to tape recordings of naturally occurring conversations. On a scale of 0–3, the Italian speaker's fluency score was 2.9, even though in certain environments he paused for as much as 1–2 seconds. Lengthy pauses may be noted near the end of the following excerpt in which the speaker discusses Swiss prisons with a female American friend ("in there" in the first line refers to "in prison"):[5]

1	NNS	↱You got ÉVERYTHING IN THERE↓
2		You got a TEEVÉE::::::→
3		you can have a- (.3) VCR::::→
4		you can have a:::→ (.4) ⁺ÉVERYTHING⁺↓ (.9)
5		You just (.6) y- you DON'T have the FRÉEDOM to go
6		OUT↓ (.6)
7	NS	uuh=
8	NNS	=SÓMETIMES you can even bring your→ your WIFE-

9		(.3) ɪɴ ᴛʜᴇʀᴇ↓ (.6)
10	ɴs	mm hmm=
11	ɴɴs	=So::→ (.8) It's COMPLÉTELY DÍFF(H)RENT↓ (.5)
12	ɴs	huh=
13	ɴɴs	=↳DÍFFERENT STYLE↓ (1.5)
14		↳OK↓⇑ what do you THINK abou:::t→ (1.6)
15		the ÁCTUAL:::→ (1.0) PÓLITICS of
16		the STATES→ (.7)
17		a:::s::→ (2.0) GUÁRDIANS of the WORLD↓ (.5)
18	ɴs	huh huh umm I see it as being . . .

The nonnative speaker introduces a major topic shift in line 14 from prisons to the politics of the United States. His pauses during the topic introduction are preceded by plateau pitch boundaries (→), as shown in figure 9.5. Thus, the intonational phrases from lines 14–17 are presented as continuing parts of a whole, conveying an impression of thoughtfully formulating the topic rather than struggling to express himself.

In contrast, a woman from Japan who was rated 1.7 out of 3.0 in fluency has shorter but more frequent pauses. Her pattern is to associate H* pitch accents with almost every word and to place a sharply rising pitch boundary after each pitch accent as shown in this excerpt (from Corpus 4). She is discussing her plan to show pictures of modern Japan to American schoolchildren:

ɴɴs   . . . not only WORDS↗ (.4) I can SHOW↗ (.4) the (.4)
PÍCTURES↗ (.6) HELPED↗ (.8) STÚDENTS↗ to un-
HELP- (.5) STÚDENTS↗ (.2) UNDERSTÁND the- (.4)
JÁPANESE CÚLTURE↓

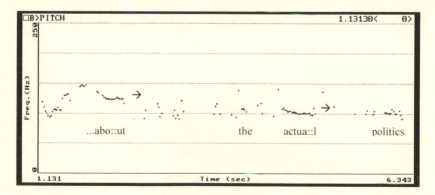

Figure 9.5   Long pauses in this highly fluent nonnative speaker's dialogue are preceded by plateau (→) pitch boundaries.

As figure 9.6 shows, the words *pictures, helped,* and both utterances of *students* have H* pitch accents and occupy their own intonational phrases, ending with sharply rising pitch boundaries followed by a pause. Because H* pitch accents in English are used to add new information to the discourse, and because rising pitch boundaries can function to request confirmation that a listener is following, the combination of these two could lead a listener to evaluate every word as a new idea. The effect is to obscure the main point of the discourse because every word seems to be singled out as worthy of comment. In fact, the nonnative speaker was continually interrupted in this conversation.[6]

Finally, the relationship between the syntactic clause and the prosodic features that surround it has been considered in definitions of fluency. Pawley and Syder (1975, 2000) introduced the "one-clause-at-a-time constraint"; that is, native speakers encode utterances in chunks no larger than one independent clause, representing a focus of consciousness. Thus, in nonnative speech, clause-internal pauses are more likely to be perceived as disruptive to fluency than pauses at clause boundaries. Indeed, in Freed's (2000) study, wherein the number of pauses was found to correlate with ratings of fluency, only "dysfluent-sounding" pauses were tabulated. These were mainly midclause pauses, distinct from the more predictable pauses at clause junctures that would be expected in native speech.

To summarize, temporal features—rate of speech and length and location of pauses—significantly affect judgments of nonnative speaker fluency. However, the surrounding intonation and syntax may also make a difference in how pauses affect fluency. I return to this topic in the sample analysis of this chapter by Riggenbach, who considers fluency in

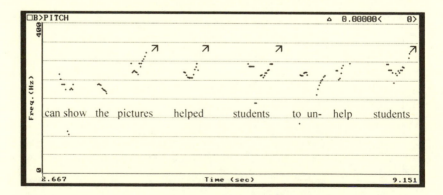

Figure 9.6 Single words occupy intonational phrases ending with rising pitch boundaries (↗) in the conversation of this nonnative speaker from Japan.

the context of conversation. Riggenbach argues that discussions of non-native speaker fluency should properly take interactive phenomena—turn-taking, repair, latches, and overlaps—into account.

Acquisition Studies

The studies so far have all focused on learners' interlanguage at some stage of the acquisition process, but little is known about how second-language prosody is acquired. Regarding grammar acquisition, Krashen (1981) has proposed the Monitor Model, which, simply stated, distinguishes two modes of adult language development: the conscious learning of grammar rules and the unconscious acquisition of an "interlanguage" as the learner's grammatical system develops toward that of the target language. Lack of consistency in grammatical production can be attributed to the fact that the learned rules can be used to "monitor" the acquired system, given sufficient time and motivation to focus on form. In contrast to grammar, prosody is usually acquired unconsciously, without explicit teaching of rules. Despite the recent increase in ESL textbooks that address prosody, the quantity of instructional materials is still miniscule relative to what exists for grammar. For most learners, only an acquired system of prosody would be in evidence, with no learned system to monitor acquired forms. Thus, the acquisition of prosody could provide a testing ground for unconscious language development over time. At the early stages, one would expect that prosodic features of the native language would simply transfer into English. However, because many adult learners clearly do acquire a good facility with English prosody, it is evident that changes can occur in the developing system over time.

Indeed, some scholars have found that transfer of the prosodic features of the first language to the target language does not predict all of the patterns in learners' development. Wenk (1985), in a study of French speakers acquiring English, found developmental stages in the acquisition of stress patterns. At an intermediate stage, the subjects produced interlanguage patterns that were somewhere between the French and English norms for stress alignment. Juffs (1990) measured word stress and sentence-level pitch accent in an oral reading task by Chinese speakers of English and found that the majority of errors were associated with word stress. He also found errors due to strategies such as the placement of a heavy stress on every word and consistent sentence-final pitch accent assignment. This may have been an attempt by speakers to articulate each word clearly, an artifact of pedagogical approaches that emphasize careful pronunciation, resulting in slow, word-by-word speech. Juffs's findings may also be related to Hewings's (1995b) conclusion that Indonesian speakers' short phrases were due to the higher cognitive demand of speaking a second language. In any case, these studies indicate that transfer alone does not explain nonnative speakers' acquisition of prosody, for the intermediate stages reveal patterns characteristic of neither the native nor the target languages.

My (1998) study of Chinese speakers of English, mentioned earlier in the chapter, also has implications for the acquisition of intonation. Certain subjects did not display the same acquisition patterns as the majority, despite their common language background. For example, some subjects consistently used the low-rising pitch boundary ($\nearrow$) to link closely related phrases together yet did not consistently use L+H* pitch accents to make contrasts. However, other subjects displayed the opposite pattern, using intonation to make contrasts but not to connect phrases. In short, there was no evidence that all speakers acquired components of the intonation system in the same order, for, even at the same level of English, speakers used different combinations of intonational morphemes.

Another line of inquiry with regard to nonnative speaker prosody is the effect of instruction on acquisition. Gilbert (1980) and Neufeld and Schneiderman (1980) investigated the role of practice in the acquisition of native-like intonation patterns. In Gilbert's study, subjects listened to filtered English utterances in which only the prosody was accessible and then mimicked the intonation with kazoos. Similarly, in Neufeld and Schneiderman's study, learners of English practiced intonation itself without knowing the meaning of what they were uttering. Both studies found a positive result in ultimate language acquisition from oral and aural practice of intonation, which suggests that being attuned to the prosody of a target language at early stages of acquisition could influence eventual progress toward native-like speech.

In synthesis, we have only a sketchy understanding of the nature of the acquisition of prosody. Findings indicate that the prosodic forms in interlanguage result not only from transfer of first-language prosody but possibly from developmental stages or articulation strategies. Moreover, there appears to be a good deal of variation in how English prosody is acquired even among speakers within a single language group, let alone from one group to another. The studies reviewed here reflect a "form-oriented" view of acquisition (Bardovi-Harlig, 1999)—that is, the methodologies involve measuring some aspect of interlanguage prosody and comparing it to that of the target language. Another possible set of methodologies, however, could be developed out of a "meaning-oriented" (Bardovi-Harlig) approach, whereby evidence would be sought for how certain ideas, typically conveyed through prosody in English, were expressed in the interlanguage. For example, one could determine if lexical or grammatical devices were being used to express the concept of "contrast" and then factor in the role of intonation. Considering the complexity of acquisition, it is probably wise to think of these studies as pioneering attempts to test methodologies and establish which problems merit further study. In the section that follows, I suggest possible areas for future research that build on previous work.

Unresolved Issues

The following are several topics for further research on prosody in the discourse of language learners. Because English is the focus of this volume, the issues are framed around the discourse of nonnative speakers of that language. However, there is ample room for studies of the acquisition of prosody in other languages as well. It has been suggested that one's prosody does not merely transfer from the first language but that there are intermediate stages of development toward the target language. Some aspects of prosody are perhaps more easily acquired, or even universally accessible. These are all unanswered questions.

A word of caution is in order for studies of prosody in nonnative discourse: In the analysis of audio- or videotapes of nonnative speech, it is important not to divorce tapes from transcripts during analysis. Although this is good advice in any analysis of oral discourse, it is especially important in nonnative speech, where the prosodic characteristics may not fall neatly into the same categories of native speech. Thus, even if written transcripts are coded with prosodic information, they may miss the details and therefore skew research results.

How Do Language Learners Acquire the Prosody of a Second Language?

To fully understand the acquisition of prosody, one might obtain samples of natural speech from the same speaker at different stages of language development. Interactional data could be used or special discourse tasks could be designed to elicit particular functions usually expressed in English through prosody (such as contrast, topic division, or the linking together of phrases). One option would be to do this type of analysis at the beginning, middle, and end of a course of language study that included the explicit teaching of prosody to determine the effects of the pedagogy. It would also be interesting to study the acquisition of prosody in the absence of instruction. As I noted earlier, prosody tends to be acquired unconsciously without any "monitoring" with learned rules. The study of the development of prosodic features over time could lead not only to information about the acquisition of prosody but to a better understanding of "natural" language acquisition as a process.

What Is the Relationship Between Prosody and Listening Comprehension for Nonnative Speakers?

Undoubtedly, the processing of prosody contributes to listening comprehension (Cutler, Dahan, & van Donselaar, 1997), yet so far much of the research in second-language listening has focused on comprehension of lectures as measured by tests on content (Chaudron & Richards, 1986; Flowerdew, 1994) or on discrete-point listening tasks (see Richards, 1983). Another avenue, however, would be to use discourse analysis methods to assess the understanding of nonnative listeners. Brown's (1995) intriguing study of the listener's point of view in interactions suggests a new methodology to investigate second-language listening. Using conversation analysis methods, Brown was able to draw conclusions at each point of an interaction about the listener's mental representation of spatial and temporal relationships between various referents introduced into the discourse by another speaker. As we have seen in previous chapters, intonation interacts with information structure, indicating which referents are assumed to be already assessable, added, foregrounded, or contrasted with a previous referent. Therefore, by analyzing the intonation of nonnative listener responses to native speakers, one could draw conclusions about how the resulting mental representation was constructed. This methodology could be applied to analyze listening comprehension in general or to study prosodic factors specifically.

What Is the Relationship Between Prosody and Interactional Trouble in Cross-Cultural Interactions?

As mentioned earlier in this chapter, studies by Gumperz (1992), Pickering (1999), and Davies and Tyler (1994) relied on a careful scrutiny of tapes and transcripts of native- and nonnative speaker conversations with a focus on problematic exchanges. This type of labor-intensive microanalysis has usually been undertaken in case studies; to establish validity, there is a need for more studies that replicate these individual findings in other contexts. Such projects could be undertaken by identifying rough spots in interaction, such as interruptions, frequent repairs, and topic discontinuity, traceable to a prosodic source. After identifying such instances, one could analyze the surrounding text for evidence of the prosody's contribution to the interactional trouble. In addition, participants in the discourse could be interviewed after the fact to determine where one speaker's understanding differed from another's intended meaning.

What Can Interlanguage Data Tell Us about the Universal Aspects of Prosody?

Another possibility for research on second-language prosody is prosodic universals. It would be useful to investigate second-language data from English, whose prosodic features are fairly well studied, to compare the prosody of speakers from different first-language backgrounds. Those features of English acquired most easily by speakers might be candidates for prosodic universals. I remarked on this briefly in 1994, upon discovering that speakers from all four of the language backgrounds I studied, English, Thai, Japanese, and Spanish, associated a → plateau intonation boundary with hesitation sounds such as *uhh* or *ahh*. At the time, I was so absorbed in looking for cross-linguistic *differences* in intonation that I did not consider this an interesting result. It now strikes me, however, that the intonation on hesitation sounds would be a fairly easy feature to look for in other languages as a possible linguistic universal.

Another possibility would be to look for paralinguistic universals of prosody in the emotional or pragmatic realm. Again, this could be done as a conversation analysis or by asking listeners to identify emotions in the discourse of speakers of another language with which they were not familiar. If these judgments were made in response to audiotapes, the emotion expressed through body language could be factored out. This concentration on communication universals could offer a refreshing alternative to the more traditional focus on errors and miscommunications in studies of cross-cultural communication.

How Do the Prosodic Systems of Other Languages Compare to English?

I mention this topic last, although it is in some sense the most obvious way to understand what people from various linguistic backgrounds confront as they learn English. Studies such as Fernald et al. (1989), comparing the intonation of mothers talking to infants in a variety of native languages, reveal certain intonation patterns common to several languages. In deciding to confine the scope of this volume largely to English prosody, I have left out many excellent studies of the prosodic systems of other languages. To mention just a few, I refer the reader to Hirst and DiCristo's (1998) anthology, *Intonation Systems: A Survey of Twenty Languages*, as well as Shen (1990) for Chinese intonation; Beckman and Pierrehumbert (1986) for Japanese intonation; and Kjellen (1995) for

Swedish intonation and rhythm. However, as these studies are mainly in the phonological tradition, they tend to rely on constructed examples to illustrate the key aspects of prosody. Nor do all attempt to discuss the interpretation of prosodic features. Therefore, there is a great need for studies that analyze prosodic meaning in natural discourse data in other languages. Such research could lead to further conclusions about language transfer, language acquisition, and language universals.

Sample Analysis

The sample analysis for this chapter is provided by Heidi Riggenbach, a conversation analyst who specializes in second-language discourse. She is also the editor of an anthology, *Perspectives on Fluency* (Riggenbach, 2000). The following brief analysis is a good example of how prosody, in this case hesitation phenomena and rate of speech, can be analyzed in the context of natural interaction to shed light on a complex question in second-language research: what is fluency? The analysis consists of excerpts drawn from a larger study (Riggenbach 1989, 1991). Of interest for this chapter on the prosody of second-language discourse is the qualitative microanalysis of the conversations themselves, as Riggenbach attempts to determine which features, in the context of interaction, contribute to rater judgments of what constitutes fluent versus nonfluent speech.

Hesitation Phenomena in Second-Language Fluency*

For nonnative speakers who want or need to participate in an English language speech community, an understanding of that speech community's conversational "norms" may be helpful. Specifically, a consciousness of the micromechanics involved in the claiming and yielding of turns may contribute to the acquisition of associated oral skills. Learners of English often claim that they "cannot get a word in" when speaking with native speakers of English (more specifically, North Americans), or that native speakers speak too much or too quickly to allow them to claim a turn. It appears that, for these learners, it is beneficial, for example, to learn to predict when a speaker's turn is nearing possible completion— to recognize "turn construction units" (as in Schegloff, 1979) so as to enable more efficient turn-taking and thus more participative conversation (Riggenbach, 2000).

*This section was contributed by Heidi Riggenbach.

Related to this is native speakers' perception about nonnative speakers' fluency level: in the speech of learners who repair and hesitate frequently or at the "wrong" places—in the middle of a clause rather than at the end—the "juncture point" is often judged to be "choppy" or disfluent (Ejzenberg, 2000; Pawley & Syder, 2000; Riggenbach, 1991). In contrast, nonnative speakers of a language are considered fluent when there is "ease of communication," which, from another perspective, amounts to speech that is "smooth," "lacking unnatural pauses," relatively fast-paced and up to tempo (Fiksdal, 2000; Kopenon & Riggenbach, 2000).

Initially a large number of audiotaped dialogues, contributed by language learners as part of an ESL course assignment, were rated for fluency level by 12 ESL instructors on a 7-point open-ended scale, with "very fluent" on one end of the scale, "very nonfluent" on the other end. These ratings were used to identify three learners at the top and bottom of the scale. These six subjects' speech samples were then examined microanalytically for various fluency/disfluency markers such as hesitation phenomena (filled and unfilled pauses); repair (repetitions, restarts); and rate of speech. Quantitative analyses revealed statistically significant differences between the fluent and nonfluent groups. A Mann-Whitney U test/Wilcoxon rank sum (significant at $p < .05$) suggests that learners' use of hesitation features—specifically unfilled pauses—may be salient in determining the fluency level of speakers. The other statistically significant difference between high and low fluency groups was rate of speech, although one nonfluent subject's speech rate was more in line with that of the fluent speakers. Thereafter, these, and other features associated with traditional notions of fluency, were examined in context to determine, in each case, just how they might have contributed to judgments about that subject's fluency level.

In this qualitative phrase of the analysis, it was found that, simply put, pauses in speech were considered native-like if they occurred at juncture points, such as clause boundaries, or in isolation, that is, not grouped with other pauses or other fluency-related features (such as repairs). In contrast, nonfluent-sounding pauses occurred with or close to other pauses or repairs, or at points other than clause or phrase boundaries, where they tended to contribute to what is often described as choppy-sounding rather than smoothly flowing speech.

An example of an interactive segment that reveals why a "very nonfluent" learner was characterized as such is the following. The language learner (LL), "Wanda," a native speaker of Chinese, has just described to her native speaker (NS) classmate and conversation tutor of 5 weeks a "typical" U.S. classroom, where students come and go as they please. The native speaker replies (<< = slower tempo):

```
 1     NS    It's very hard, it's very difficult (.) to concentrate (.) on
 2            what the teacher is teaching (.) when people co::me
 3            and go:
 4            ⌈and the door opens and closes an- an so on.
 5     LL    ⌊Mm-hm
 6     NS    So (.) I agree with you that it's very strange. What
 7            class (.) is this, can I ask?
 8     LL    Umm:: (.8) a class- uh (.5) is happened-uh- in my
 9            English class
10     NS    Uh-huh=
11     LL    =And the um: (1.0) my:: music class.=
12     NS    =In your music class ⌈also? Hmm
13     LL                        ⌊Yeah.
14    (1.0)
15     NS    Huhh. Uh-are you taking classes where this does not
16            happen?
17    (1.2)
18     NS    <<Do you have any classes (.) that you are in (.) where
19            the students do (.) stay? And don't get up and go?
20     LL    Uh- yeah.
21            (.5)
22     NS    Which class?
23            (1.3)
24     LL    Uhh:: (3.5) Uh: (.5) well-our- (.) analysis class.
```

A close examination of this entire conversation segment reveals that more than half of the language learner's turns are backchannels or contain backchannels (such as "Mm-hm"), which do not necessarily contribute to the impression of fluency as compared to more substantive "content" turns. This segment is also characterized by a large number of questions from the native speaker, in contrast to few attempts on Wanda's part to ask questions of the native speaker interlocutor, even when clarification or restatement is necessary. For example, in line 15 the native speaker asks Wanda: "Are you taking any classes where this does not happen?" This is followed by a gap of 1.2 seconds, in which Wanda could have asked for clarification. Instead, the native speaker must restate her question, this time in "foreigner talk" style—slower rate of speech, more detail, parsing, and stress to emphasize key words. At this point, in line 20, Wanda understands of the question (with her "Uh-yeah"), but she doesn't provide further information until after the prompt "Which class?" This sequence is an example of the kind of work that the native speaker, rather than the language learner, must do to keep the conversation moving forward, and it also suggests reasons for the characterization of this language learner as "very nonfluent."

In contrast, the following conversation excerpt illustrates a language learner who was considered "very fluent." The language learner (LL) "Sherry," also a native speaker of Chinese, is discussing with her American friend of three months, a native speaker of English (NS), the discomfort she would feel if she were to give a party:

```
 1   LL   if (.) if I'm inviting people from: (.) for example from
 2         school, from work, an' y'know my old friends and then
 3         they don't know each other then (.4) I 'ave got the
 4         added task of y'know (.4)
 5   NS   In   ⌈troduce-
 6   LL        ⌊uh- introducing one to another.
 7   NS   Yea ⌈h. (Tha-)
 8   LL        ⌊An' you don't know whether they will mix and
 9         they will talk or whether it will be a flop.
10   NS   Yeah, I know, I know. That's always
11         ⌈That's always
12   LL   ⌊The fear. (.4)
13   NS   Yeah (.7)
```

Perhaps because the micropauses and pauses in lines 1–3 occur either in isolation or at clause boundaries, they are not markedly disfluent-sounding; Sherry maintains her turn, her regular rhythm, and her rate of speech. The lexical filler "y'know" in line 4, followed by a pause, may be the motivation for the collaborative completion supplied by the native speaker: collaborative completions—when one speaker supplies a word or phrase to complete the sentence for another—can also demonstrate alignment between interlocutors, because one speaker aids the other by offering a candidate turn-completion unit. In this case, the native speaker supplies the word "introduce" (line 5), which Sherry accepts, overlapping with a repetition in the native speaker's midturn.

Another collaborative completion, this one supplied by Sherry, provides further evidence of the cooperative nature of this conversation excerpt and further evidence of the characterization by raters of this language learner as "very fluent." Here, in line 10, Sherry is perhaps tipped off, consciously or unconsciously, by the native speaker's disfluencies—the repetition of "I know" and the repetition of "That's always," the latter synchronized with her collaborative completion in line 12.

The impression that the language learner's contributions to this conversation are usually natural and "native-like" is substantiated by written comments from the raters of her speech sample: "The speaker's speech is very smooth and she talks pretty fast"; "Initiates conversation readily"; "Her conversational ability is quite good. The only problem that keeps her from being a 7 (the highest on a 7-point scale with "very fluent" as 7, and "very nonfluent" as 1) is a lack of sandhi variations/reductions—the blending together of word boundaries that nonnative speakers almost never truly acquire."

This analysis demonstrates that the type and number of hesitation and repair features learners use do contribute to perceptions of their fluency level. It also suggests that fluency is a complex phenomenon. In order for there to be fluency, different conditions have to be met—some proficiency in grammar, pronunciation, and vocabulary, as well as a display of "smoothness," both within a learner's own speech and across turns, in two or multiparty dialogue. Nonfluency, on the other hand, can arise from a deficiency in any one of these areas: the inability to produce a given grammatical structure may be the first link in a chain of disfluencies that may as easily have begun with a comprehension lapse, a pronunciation problem, or a motivation for precision in word choice. Thus, an interesting direction that emerges from this study is to explore not only what constitutes fluency but also what constitutes nonfluency.

Chapter Conclusion

There is no question that second-language educators and researchers are becoming more aware of the importance of prosody in communication and the difficulty it may present to language learners. The ESL pronunciation books and teacher education books have recently begun to devote large sections to stress, intonation, rhythm, and other topics of prosody in response to this new priority.

Researchers have focused on characterizing the difficulties that nonnative speakers face with English prosody by comparing native to nonnative speakers' prosody in discourse contexts. In interaction, mismatches between native speaker expectations and prosodic structure transferred into English from another language have been shown to result in miscommunications. Studies have also employed various language assessment measures to quantify raters' perceptions of nonnative speech in terms of its accent, fluency, or overall comprehensibility. Statistical methods have then been applied to determine how speakers' prosody correlates with other measures of English proficiency. By looking at nonnative speakers at different levels of proficiency, researchers have addressed questions of how prosody is acquired. Findings suggest that prosody has an influence on native speaker perception of comprehensibility, accent, and fluency beyond the segmental, grammatical, and lexicosemantic structure of the discourse. It also appears that some prosodic aspects of language can gradually be acquired by nonnative speakers, though individuals follow different acquisition routes.

Nevertheless, further research involving prosody in the discourse of second-language learners is needed. The acquisition of prosody could be better understood through longitudinal interlanguage studies and comparisons between first- and second-language prosody. The role of prosody in both production and listening could be further explored through analyses of the interaction between native and nonnative speakers. Future research could focus not only on difficulties in the use of prosody by nonnative speakers but also on possible universal aspects of prosody that enhance communication between people from different language backgrounds.

Finally, Riggenbach's sample analysis has provided an example of a discourse-based research project on second-language speech in which prosody, in conjunction with other features, was taken into account. Her analysis of the turn-taking patterns of two nonnative speakers of English, one rated very fluent and the other very nonfluent, leads to new insights about the interdependency among various linguistic features in the complex process of communication. This analysis reinforces the main theme of this chapter: in the study of nonnative speaker discourse, the message conveyed by the prosody is not to be ignored.

10

CONCLUSION

In Lecture 6 of the collection *How to Do Things with Words*, Austin refers to "tone of voice, cadence, emphasis" as among the "more primitive devices in speech" (1962, pp. 73–74) for which syntax and the lexicon provide more explicit alternatives. This view has unfortunately tended to dominate language-related fields throughout their history. Prosody has been considered the extra flourish, the nuance, not what is said but the way it is said, a side issue beyond the scope of mainstream analyses. In this volume I have tried to make the case that prosody deserves more central attention. Without variation in prosody, speech would not only be very flat and uninteresting but would lack large components of meaning.

In defending this position, my method has been to investigate many examples of natural discourse in which an aspect of prosody performs a function that would not be accomplished by virtue of the lexicogrammatical structure alone. In addition, I have brought together the writings of others whose experimental research shows the many contributions of prosody to discourse meaning and organization. I have also included sample data analyses, the details of which demonstrate their authors' motivations and methodologies. I hope that these provide a sense of the variety of possible applications of prosodic analysis of spoken discourse and the feasibility of conducting further research.

There is no doubt that similar observations about prosody have been made before by other discourse analysts. Indeed, most major treatments of spoken discourse have included references to prosodic effects. Many discourse analysis books include coding systems for prosodic variables. Atkinson and Heritage (1984), Brown (1995), Coulthard and Montgomery (1981), Eggins and Slade (1997), Gumperz (1982), Schiffrin (1994), Tannen (1984a), and Tsui (1994) all have special tables or appendices devoted to the prosodic coding of texts. However, there has been a tendency for discourse analytic treatments of prosody to arise as byproducts of other investigations rather than as part of a systematic basis of inquiry. For example, Schiffrin (1987) set out to examine all cases of discourse markers in a corpus of conversation to discover their functional patterns. In so doing, she also uncovered interesting subcategories for most discourse markers whose function varied depending on their intonation. Thus, Schiffrin's book includes a good deal of information about intonation but only as it pertains to discourse markers.

Although such investigations have led to noteworthy insights, there is naturally some inconsistency in the aspects of prosody covered and in coding. By bringing together many of the discoveries of other discourse analysts into one volume, and categorizing them within a framework of prosodic phonology, I hope that it will be more feasible for others to include prosody as a central part of discourse analysis in the future. What follows is a brief summary of the major themes about prosody's contribution to discourse meaning that I hope have been communicated here.

Prosody Is Compositional

The term "prosody," which includes the variables of pitch, volume, and duration, covers a broad spectrum of phenomena. It includes a phonological intonation system, a rhythmic basis for the alignment of speech in time, and a variety of expressive options. Moreover, the intonation system itself involves four subsystems: pitch accents are associated with lexical items to indicate how the speaker intends those items to cohere within the information structure of the discourse; final pitch boundaries reflect the hierarchical organization of the discourse—how listeners are to interpret an utterance in relation to what follows; key conveys the speaker's stance at the onset of a new intonational phrase in relation to the prior; and paratones indicate the topic status of a new constituent. Although this complexity has led some analysts to throw up their hands at the whole subject, I have argued that it is not too difficult to tease apart the functions of prosody, depending on the kind of analysis one wishes to conduct.

This task is made easier by my interpretational model in which the intonational units are smaller than those in many other models. This framework allows the researcher to separate the contribution of pitch accents from that of the boundaries in an analysis. Likewise, the placement of an intonational unit in the text can be discussed separately from the degree of emphasis it receives and the loudness, pitch, and voice quality with which it is delivered. Finally, the timing of speech—the rate, the rhythm, the pause length, and the pause placement—can also be analyzed independently. In sum, many phenomena work together under the complex umbrella of prosody to contribute to the communication process.

Prosody Is Cohesive

Given a group of utterances in context, it is usually possible to determine whether they form a coherent whole. Part of this determination involves identifying the cohesion among the utterances and this includes their prosody. This book probably devotes more page space than most to the topic of low pitch and its role in cohesion. Because I view this as an understudied phenomenon, I have tried throughout the book to feature examples of how low pitch contributes to interpretation. I can little resist one more (constructed example):

> STUDENT   If you WON the LÓTTERY↗ would you STILL KEEP
> your JOB as a PROFÉSSOR↑
> PROFESSOR   ↑Are you KÍDDING↗ I wóuldn't éven fínish téaching this
> CLASS!↓

The L* pitch accents in the middle of the last utterance indicate that the idea of "quitting one's teaching job" is in the air by the time the professor gets the floor. The disagreement comes only in how soon he or she would begin to sprint for the parking lot. Low pitch adds an additional layer of cohesion to this discourse.

Cohesion is also reflected in contrasts, for which L+H* pitch accents are a signal. In the previous example, the idea is evoked through cultural schema that a professor who quits might do so at the end of an academic term, or perhaps not at all, as educational jobs are thought to have their own rewards beyond the financial. The second utterance soundly refutes any thoughts that the job might be enjoyable—if it weren't for the paycheck, this professor would not stay another minute. The cohesion achieved in the sharp contrast between the expectation set up in the first utterance and the reality expressed in the second is reinforced by the L+H* pitch accent on the word *class.* The quitting would not be eventual but immediate—within the time span of the next hour.

Another type of cohesion comes from the pitch boundaries, which provide connections between one constituent and the next. In the lottery example, the high-rising pitch boundary after the student's utterance reinforces the interdependency within the dialogue—the first utterance awaits the second for the interpretation to be complete. Moreover, high key (↑) in the professor's response reinforces the nature of the conjunctive link between the two turns—it is at odds with the expectation projected in the student's question. Finally, although not shown in this example, we have seen how speakers can use pitch range and pause length to indicate whether topic-sized constituents are interrelated. In this way, prosodic cues can function as discourse markers that reinforce cohesion, even at the topic level.

Prosody Is Interactional

If metaphors are any reflection of social organization (as claimed by Lakoff & Johnson, 1980), examining metaphors having to do with interaction will be instructive for our understanding of prosody. Consider the following metaphors for successful and unsuccessful conversation:

Successful conversation	*Unsuccessful conversation*
in synch	out of synch
in tune	out of tune
a harmonious conversation	a discordant conversation
he didn't miss a beat	we were off our stride
on the same wave length	on a different wave length

These metaphors suggest that, at some level, speakers of English associate a smoothly running conversation with pleasant, rhythmic music. This may not be too far from the reality: rhythm underlies the phonology of spoken language, providing a steadying force. Pitch accents tend to be aligned rhythmically, even across speakers, when talk is proceeding smoothly. Variation in rhythm conveys information about the interaction as well—it has been claimed that broken rhythm indicates a shift of gears, or an interactional problem.

In addition to the rhythm, other prosodic cues underlie a speaker's ability to anticipate the completion of another's turn. Often participants do not attempt to take the floor in midturn even when there is a pause but instead latch on almost immediately at the turn's end. This acute sensitivity to the other's speech evidently involves a combination of judgments about the syntax, the lexical coherence, the gestures, pragmatic factors, and certainly the prosody: the rate of speech and the placement and shape of the pitch boundaries. For example, the extension of a pitch boundary into a long plateau prior to a pause can convey the intention to keep the floor, whereas a low boundary, whose final lengthening can be perceived before the end of the turn, indicates that it is on its way to completion slightly prior to the actual cessation of the speech. Another feature of interactional genres of discourse is the prosodic indication of each speaker's ever-changing stance toward the conversation. The tone concord between the end of one participant's turn and the onset of the next indicates how closely each speaker's contribution is integrated with the prior one—is the speaker diverging attitudinally with what has come before? The stance is indicated in the choice of key—how low or high in the pitch range to begin each new utterance. In short, interaction involves participants' continual processing of and responding to each other's prosodic cues.

Prosody Is Expressive

The word "infinite" surely applies to the number of possibilities available for speakers to express themselves beyond the basic intonation and rhythmic systems—the pregnant pause, the angry shout, the scornful hoot, the high-pitched expletive—all involve variations in timing, pitch, volume, and voice quality to display one's point of view. Although, traditionally, researchers of intonation have tended to dismiss these expressive aspects of prosody as uninteresting because they are outside the phonological realm, they may in fact be quite interesting to ethnographers. Part of understanding a culture is understanding genres of discourse and the norms and rules governing the speech within each genre. I have argued that the expressive functions of prosody need to be analyzed in a description of a culture's ways of speaking. Expressive prosody is important, for speakers manipulate their prosody, making certain aspects of a text more prominent than others, in accord with their emotional priorities.

In the study of culture, then, one could ask what aspects of a text are associated with prosodic extremes. We have seen examples in this volume wherein evaluative speech, and particularly quoted speech, was uttered with higher-than-average pitch. In this sense, the prosody of a text can be said to reflect its author's values and can therefore provide an important analytical focus. At the level of the speech community, one can also ask in what circumstances prosodic extremes are sanctioned. For example, it is considered normal in many societies for women to use a very high pitch when interacting with babies, but are men sanctioned to do so? This is an example of how pitch variation and voice quality can depend on the genre, setting, participants—and, in this case, their gender—surrounding a speech event. Prosodic analysis could be more widely used in studies of discourse and social behavior because the prosody with which something is expressed may reflect a speaker's, and even a society's, attitude toward it.

To conclude, discourse analysts need not shy away from the investigation of prosody. On the contrary, discourse-analytic approaches to the study of prosody are exactly what is needed today as we move toward more global and diverse networks of social interaction and increasing technological resources to promote language contact. Although phonologists and phoneticians have gone a long way in the investigation of prosody, their research goals have generally led them to rely on idealized speech samples out of context. They have usually placed a low priority on extended discourse beyond the level of the single utterance. The challenge is now for discourse analysts to apply the work on prosody in theoretical linguistics to meet their own research goals. Prosody is essential to the understanding of spoken language as it naturally occurs in social contexts. It is part of what makes extended texts coherent. It gives voice to human emotions so that, rather than monotonous robots, we are creative musicians in the symphony of communication that forms the basis of our lives as social beings.

APPENDIX

Description of Discourse Data Corpora

Throughout this volume, I use many examples of discourse to illustrate various functions of prosody. Below are the corpora of discourse data from which examples are drawn. For each corpus, information is provided about the circumstances under which the data were collected; the genre, topic, and purpose of the speech situation; the participants' genders, ages, social groups, relationships to each other; and any other relevant information. Each corpus is assigned a number, referenced in the examples throughout the book.

Not included among these descriptions are the data corpora used in the sample analyses contributed by guest authors, which are described within the analyses themselves. Nor are excerpts drawn from published data described here, but the original source is cited in each case. Finally, there are a few constructed examples used in the volume, as indicated.

Corpus 1: Academic Lectures

Three lectures were given by faculty at the University of Washington to create a videotape and textbook (Wennerstrom, 1991) for the training of international teaching assistants whose native languages were not English. The purpose of these materials was to provide examples of well-organized lectures delivered by native speakers so that students could study their linguistic and organizational structure. The lectures were all videotaped in 1987. The "students" included friends of the author, English teachers, and workers from the media center where the videotaping was done. Thus, the audiences can be described generally as Americans with at least some college education but no specific background in the topics of the lectures. All lecturers and students were speakers of Standard American English. All three lectures were about 30 minutes long and were given spontaneously, using notes.

1-A

Lecture 1-A was given by a male professor in the statistics department. He was an American from Boston of about 40 years of age. There were five students in the class taking notes. Outside of a few questions and answers, there was little classroom interaction in the lecture. The topic of the lecture was a mathematical one: the derivative. The lecturer provided an overview of the topic with examples, including several mathematical formulas and graphs drawn on the blackboard.

1-B

Lecture 1-B was given by a female lecturer in statistics of about 40 years of age, from Chicago. The topic of the lecture was an introduction to the concept of correlation. The lecturer gave a handout with four graphs on it that had also been drawn in advance on the blackboard. The lecture was organized around the four graphs, which were covered one after another. There were four students in the class taking notes. Outside of a few questions, there was little interaction during this class.

1-C

Lecture 1-C was an interactive class session with discussion and brainstorming. The lecturer was a female from Kentucky of about 35 years of age. The topic was international marketing. The lecturer organized her class around a series of general brainstorming questions about factors that could influence marketing a product overseas. Throughout the interactions, she wrote the students' contributions on the blackboard in a branching diagram. The atmosphere was quite informal as the participants bantered ideas about. There were five students in this class. The initials in the transcripts are of the following genders:

D = the lecturer; woman

B = man

J = man

K = woman

R = woman

Corpus 2: Group Conversation about Nepal

Corpus 2 was an informal conversation that took place in the mid-1980s, among five close friends, two men and three women. About 45 minutes of the conversation was audiotaped. Four of the five participants were two married couples and the fifth was a single woman. All were graduate students at a major university in the United States, in their early thirties, whose dialect was Standard American English. Three were actually in the field of discourse analysis and were recording the conversation to use for analysis purposes. For this reason, the participants were accustomed to being recorded and were not inhibited in their speech. The atmosphere was casual with lots of joking and storytelling. A range of topics was covered, but many of the examples are drawn from a segment about a trip to Nepal that two members of the group, a married couple, had recently taken. The initials in the transcripts correspond to the following genders and marital relationships:

T = man

C = woman; T and C were married to each other

S = woman

R = man; S and R were married to each other

M = woman

Corpus 3: Menopause Interviews

This corpus consists of three informal "conversational" interviews of women in different stages of menopause. The data were collected in 1996 as part of an ethnographic study of menopause and humor (Wennerstrom, 2000a). Participants were women in their 40s and 50s who volunteered to contribute to an informal small-group discussion of the topic. All were speakers of Standard American English. There were four to five participants present at each interview, including me; my role was to introduce questions and direct the discussion. All participants were from the same workplace and therefore knew each other already. The atmosphere was quite relaxed and informal for all three interviews.

Corpus 4: Cross-Cultural Conversations

This is a corpus of conversations between native and nonnative speakers of English. The conversations were collected in 1993–94 as part of an assignment in different sections of an advanced English as a second language (ESL) conversation class in the United States: students were to taperecord themselves in conversation with a native speaker outside of class, transcribe a portion of the tape, and discuss the transcript in class. (These tapes have been retranscribed because the students themselves were not experienced in transcription.) The students were from various countries. All were in the United States on a temporary basis to study English in a large private language school affiliated with a major university. All had been in the country for less than one year and were between the ages of 18 and 35. Their level of English proficiency ranged from intermediate to high. The native speakers in the conversations varied a good deal: some were close friends of the ESL students; others were host parents, landlords, neighbors, fellow church members, teachers, and volunteer tutors. The conversations ranged from very informal to very stiff and formal in some cases when the student did not know the interlocutor well. The particular circumstances of each conversation and the genders of the participants are indicated in the text for each example.

Corpus 5: Oral Narratives about "My Parents' Mistake"

Corpus 5 consists of personal narratives told orally by members of a discourse analysis graduate seminar in 1992. All students were between 25 and 40 years of age and were native speakers of American dialects of English. Their assignment was to tell a story on the topic of "mistakes my parents made in raising me," which would later be analyzed as part of a unit on narrative structure. The stories were told in small groups huddled around a tape recorder. Each person took a turn to tell a personal narrative, so the stories were largely monologues with occasional input from others in the group. There was a certain amount of nervousness in these stories because the students had only just met in one previous class period. Because the tapes were collected in a noisy room, they contain a lot of extraneous noise, which I have tried to edit out of the figures as much as possible. The genders of the storytellers and their topics are given with the examples in each case.

Corpus 6: Oral Narratives from Nonnative Speakers of English

This is a group of stories told by nonnative speakers of English in an advanced ESL conversation class from 1993 to 1994. Some of the storytellers were the same speakers as in Corpus 4. Again, they were from various countries and at intermediate to advanced levels of English proficiency. This time they had another class assignment: to tell a personal story about a time in their past when they were either embarrassed or scared. They told the stories in small groups to each other and then made tapes of the stories at home. These narratives vary in spontaneity: some of the stories were told conversationally to a listener (one can hear the responses on the tapes), but others were told with the speaker sitting alone with a tape recorder. Also, the students had practiced the stories at least once before taping them. The genders of the storytellers and their topics are given with the examples in each case.

GLOSSARY

Abstract An initial element in a narrative, often a brief summary, indicating that the narrative is about to be told.

Acoustic Having to do with the physical properties of sound.

Amplitude The amount of air pressure in a sound wave, which is heard as the loudness.

Anaphor An element of a text, such as a pronoun, whose interpretation depends on a previous element, called the "antecedent."

Anecdote A story whose purpose is to draw a specific reaction from listeners (as defined by Eggins and Slade, 1998).

Antecedent With respect to an anaphor, the previously mentioned element in a text upon which its interpretation depends.

Antonymy A semantic relationship between lexical elements of opposite meaning.

Auditory Having to do with the sense or organs of hearing.

Backchannel A short conversational response, usually intended to encourage a speaker to continue, such as "yeah" or "uh huh."

Baseline The low end, or "floor," of a speaker's pitch range, which declines gradually throughout the intonational phrase.

Beat insertion The addition of extra time between stressed syllables in order to make rhythmic intervals a more consistent duration.

Birmingham school   A branch of discourse analysis started at the University of Birmingham that focuses on the organizational and prosodic structure of interactional exchanges.

Boundary tone   A unit of pitch associated with the beginning or end of a larger intonational constituent, such as an intonational phrase.

Coda   A concluding element of a narrative that often links the narrative back to the present interaction.

Code switching   Changing from one language or dialect to another during an interaction.

Coherence   The extent to which a text makes sense as a whole.

Cohesion   A semantic relationship among items in a text.

Collocation   A semantic relationship among elements of a text based on their association within a common mental schema, as for example, *rain* and *umbrella.*

Commissive speech act   A speech act that commits the speaker to an obligation, as in an offer, promise, or threat.

Complicating actions   The main events of a narrative's plot.

Concord breaking   A response (usually disharmonious) in which the pitch range at the termination of an utterance by one speaker is met by a different pitch range onset (key) by another.

Contextualization cue   A verbal or nonverbal signal, often recognized implicitly, that aids in the interpretation of language in a given context.

Conversation analysis   A branch of discourse analysis in which informal conversation is studied in detail in order to understand the underlying social organization of the culture that produced it.

Declination   The gradual lowering of the median pitch from the beginning to the end of the intonational phrase.

Deixis   The aspects of language having to do with relationships in time, space, and point of view, as for example, *you, now, then, here,* and *there,* which can be interpreted only with reference to the spatiotemporal orientation of the speaker.

Directive speech act   A speech act that directs the hearer to do something, as in a question, request, or demand.

Discourse analysis   The study of actual language in use.

Discourse marker   A unit of language that conveys information about the organization of discourse, as for example, *oh, well,* and *you know.*

Ellipsis   The omission of a constituent whose referent is obvious in context.

Eurhythmy   The overall rhythmic balance of strong and weak elements in a constituent of speech.

Evaluation   A linguistic expression of assessment, opinion, priority, or point of view.

Face Positive social value in interaction.

Felicity conditions Conditions that must hold in order for a speech act to have an intended illocutionary force.

Final lengthening The lengthening of the duration of the final syllable(s) of an intonational phrase.

Flap For English, the consonant produced by a quick, light contact between the tongue and the alveolar ridge, as in the middle of the word *water*.

Focus The part of an utterance that is new, contrastive, or otherwise not available from context.

Foot The unit of language that occupies one rhythmic interval.

Fundamental frequency (F_0) The lowest of the simultaneous frequencies of speech, perceived as the pitch.

Generative phonology A branch of phonology in which the sound system of a language is considered to be composed of internalized abstract elements from which actual speech sounds are "generated" by the interaction of phonological and phonetic principles and constraints.

Genre A type of discourse with a set of conventional linguistic features, as in a sermon, lecture, or anecdote.

Grammaticalization The gradual (historical) incorporation of a linguistic element into the grammar of a language.

Iconic Having a basis in real-world phenomena. Intonation is sometimes said to have an iconic relationship with the real-world phenomenon of getting attention with a high-pitched noise.

Illocution The intended communication of an utterance.

Implicature The unstated information that is part of the interpretation of an utterance.

Information structure The organization of discourse into units of meaning, often categorized as new versus given.

Interlanguage The language system of a second-language learner with respect to a target language.

Intonation The pitch of the voice during speech.

Intonational phrase The basic prosodic constituent of speech containing an initial key, at least one pitch accent, and a final pitch boundary.

Key The relative placement of the pitch in a speaker's range at the onset of an utterance, which conveys the speaker's stance with respect to the prior utterance.

Latch A direct connection between one turn and the next with no intervening pause.

Lexical cohesion The semantic relationships among lexical items in a text.

Locution The literal meaning of an utterance, based on its lexicogrammatical structure.

Macro-marker   A paragraph-level discourse marker that indicates a major organizational transition.

Metrical grid   A system of representation of the rhythmic structure of a constituent of speech.

Metrical phonology   A branch of phonology in which the rhythmic structure is considered the basis for other phonological processes.

Monitor model   A theory of language learning in which there is a gradually developing, unconscious "acquired" system and a conscious "learned" system. The learned rules can be used to "monitor" the acquired system.

Mora   A unit of syllable weight, usually the size of a short vowel.

Nuclear pitch accent   The most important pitch accent of an intonational phrase, often called the "focus."

Orientation   The setting or background for a narrative.

Paralanguage   Those gradient aspects of language, such as the degree of loudness, the height of pitch, pause length, and vowel duration, that vary for expressive and pragmatic reasons.

Paratone   The expansion or contraction of pitch range to indicate a topic-level transition in discourse.

Performance features   In oral narratives, the sounds, gestures, and lexicogrammatical manipulations that enhance the telling of the story.

Perlocution   What actually happens in the real world as a result of a speech act.

Phoneme   An abstract minimal unit of sound in a language that can distinguish meaning, as in /p/ vs. /b/ in *pig* and *big*.

Pitch   How high or low we hear a sound to be, depending on the frequency of repetition of the sound wave.

Pitch accent   A unit of intonation associated with the stressed syllables of lexical items that play a role in the information structure of the discourse.

Pitch accent association   The process by which pitch accents become manifest on the stressed syllables of salient items in the discourse (Selkirk, 1984).

Pitch boundary   The unit of intonation associated with the ends of intonational phrases, indicating the interdependencies among such phrases.

Pitch reset   At the onset of each new intonational phrase, the reestablishment of a higher pitch in the speaker's range relative to the end of the previous phrase.

Prominence   The degree to which a constituent, such as a syllable, can be heard to stand out from others due to pitch, loudness, or duration.

Prosody   The pitch, timing, and volume of speech.

Queclarative   A question used as an opposite assertion.

Reference   The aspect of language having to do with how entities in the real world are represented in discourse.

Representative speech act A speech act that represents some state of affairs, as in a statement.

Resolution The outcome or ending of a narrative.

Rhythm In speech, a pattern of stressed elements (beats) aligned at regular intervals in time.

Rhythm rule A postlexical phonological rule that realigns word stress so that the overall metrical pattern of a phrase will be rhythmically balanced.

Ripping A grammatical change in which an element moves to initial position (Hopper & Traugott, 1993).

Run-on The phenomenon of continuing without pause from one intonational phrase to the next (Eggins and Slade, 1998)

Rush-through The phenomenon of continuing without pause from one intonational phrase to the next with an increase in tempo (Schegloff, 1992).

Schema An abstract, idealized mental representation of a commonly experienced situation.

Segmental phonology The study of the vowels and consonants of a language.

Sentence A syntactically defined linguistic constituent with at least one independent clause consisting of a subject and a finite verb.

Speech act An action performed in the real world through the use of language.

Stress The degree of energy or prominence of a syllable, which may be manifest as higher pitch, increased volume, or longer duration.

Stress clash The juxtaposition of two stressed elements in close proximity within an intonational constituent.

Stress-neutral affix An affix that does not change the stress of its root word.

Stress-timed language A language for which the stressed syllables of lexical units tend to align rhythmically.

Subordinacy A semantic relationship in which one constituent is in a subclass of another, as *cat* is subordinate to *animal.*

Substitution A placeholding lexical element, such as *one* or *do*, which represents another lexicogrammatical constituent.

Superordinacy A semantic relationship in which one constituent is in a general category that includes another, as *animal* is superordinate to *cat.*

Syllable weight The "size" of a syllable, determined by the number of vowels and consonants it contains and their length.

Syllable-timed language A language for which syllables tend to be rhythmically aligned.

Synonymy A semantic relationship between lexical items of similar meaning.

Systemic functional linguistics A branch of linguistics in which systems of grammar are derived from how language functions in human interaction.

Tempo   The duration of the intervals in a rhythmic sequence; the rate of speech.

Termination   The relative placement of the pitch in a speaker's range at the end of an utterance.

Tone concord   A response (usually harmonious) in which the pitch range at the termination of an utterance by one speaker is met by a similar pitch range onset (key) by another.

Topic shading   A gradual transition from one topic to another (Schegloff, 1990).

Transition relevance place   In conversation, a potential point of turn shift, usually indicated by syntactic or prosodic cues to completion.

Trochaic   Having a rhythmic pattern in which the strong beat begins the rhythmic interval.

Utterance   A constituent of speech delineated by its discourse properties, as in a turn, speech act, or functional unit.

Voice quality   Variations in sound vibration during speech that produce effects such as breathy, creaky, or whispered voice.

West Coast functional linguistics   A branch of linguistics (developed mainly at universities on the West Coast of the United States) whose proponents look to real-world phenomena common to the human experience to explain the regularity of grammars of the world.

NOTES

CHAPTER 1

1. Although a detailed explanation of the transcription coding system of this volume is given in chapter 2, for now we can consider the words in capital letters to have a high pitch on their most stressed syllables (indicated with an accent mark for multisyllabic words), the underlined capital letters to indicate a steeply rising "contrastive" pitch (also on the stressed syllable of the word in question), and tiny capital letters to indicate a lower pitch. The downward arrow symbol (↓) shows that the intonation at the end of the phrase falls to the bottom of the speaker's pitch range.

2. Sperber and Wilson (1995) make a similar argument about this category of sentences (pp. 211–212).

3. Thanks to Alicia Wassink for this anecdote.

CHAPTER 2

1. Brazil, Coulthard, and Johns (1980) cite Sweet (1906) for the origin of the term "key." Hymes (1974) also uses the term to describe the "tone, manner, or spirit" of a speech act (p. 57).

2. This observation comes from Richard Wright, in personal communication (1998).

3. ToBI stands for Tone and Break Index. Tone refers to pitch accents and boundary tones, whereas break index refers to a system to quantify the junctures between prosodic constituents in relative terms.

4. Cinque (1993), Levelt (1989), Selkirk (1984), and others argue that a broad focus at the level of the utterance as a whole "percolates" down through the syntax, resulting in a high pitch on the stressed syllables of the main arguments of the entire sentence. I would respond that, for discourse analysts, such a reliance on syntactic structure can become unwieldy.

5. I take full responsibility for the opinion, argued in more detail in Wennerstrom (1997), that the meaning ascribed to deaccent by Ladd (1980) overlaps that which has been attributed to L* pitch accent by Pierrehumbert and Hirschberg (1990). However, Pierrehumbert, Hirschberg, and Ladd have all stated in personal communication that deaccent is simply the lack of a pitch accent. This would relegate deaccented items to the status of function words, which have no pitch accents and whose pitch is therefore determined by their relationship to surrounding tones according to phonetic principles. My view, based mainly on the fact that low pitch carries too much meaning to be a nonentity, is more in line with Werth (1984) and Chafe (1994).

6. Pierrehumbert (1980) included a phrase-initial high or low boundary tone—seemingly similar to Brazil's key. However, by 1990, Pierrehumbert and Hirschberg had dropped this tone from their inventory.

7. I believe that paratones and key are actually the same phenomenon. They are both constituent-initial pitch range shifts that indicate the degree of continuity, or lack of it, between two units. I leave the details of this proposal to be worked out by others, however.

CHAPTER 4

1. A comprehensive survey of the literature on cognition and discourse exists in Tomlin, Forrest, Pu, and Kim (1997).

2. Although Halliday and Hasan emphasize the importance of intonation in information structure, the primary unit of intonation in Halliday (1967a) is a clause-sized contour. Thus, his model does not allow for the one-to-one mapping of meaningful tones to particular lexical items and utterance boundaries.

3. In classroom discussions, students may tentatively offer new ideas with L* pitch accents and high-rising boundaries, allowing the teacher to confirm that the items are to be added to the discourse.

4. I use the term L* *pitch accent* where Ladd uses the term *deaccent.*

5. It is not always possible to distinguish pronouns with L* pitch accents from those with no pitch accent. If the latter occur in the vicinity of another item with L* pitch accent, they will be low pitched anyway because of a phonetic interpolation process.

CHAPTER 5

1. A similar case can be found in Schiffrin (1987), p. 76.

2. This information comes from Tench, (1990) who provides a thorough overview of the history of paratone studies.

3. Dialogues are reprinted from *Language and Speech, Vol. 25,* Part 4, September–December 1982, with kind permission of Kingston Press Ltd., London.

4. The perception study involved filtering and other manipulations of the discourse data to determine whether listeners could perceive topic shifts by prosodic features alone, which they were shown to be able to do.

5. On the SPEAK Test, a standardized test of speaking comprehensibility (Educational Testing Service, 1985), scores ranged from 150–220.

6. I'd like to thank Soohee Kim (1999) in personal communication for this idea.

7. PLIB was written by Ken Whistler of Dr. LST: Software using mainframe software written by Mark Liberman of AT&T Bell Labs and based on a hardware recipe provided by John McCarthy of U. Mass. I am grateful to Tony Woodbury and Robin Queen for access to PLIB at the University of Texas Dept. of Linguistics. See McLemore (1991) for an example of PLIB use with female speakers. For use of the Signalyze™ program, I am grateful to Joel Sherzer and Johnathon Loftin in the Linguistic Anthropology Lab at the University of Texas.

8. Male informants were chosen for diversity. They ranged in age from 22 to 80. They were Black, Hispanic, and Anglo. Five different men were used for each subtype. Comparison was also made with pitch contours of women. The pitch contours for women using the discourse marker *Anyway*$_3$ followed identical patterns, with simply higher values. For women, the highs and lows were in the area of 263–192–208 Hz, showing an average drop of 76 Hz and an average rise of 18 Hz.

9. In this model, equivalent to L*↓.

10. H*↓ in this model.

11. L+H*↗ or L+H*↓ in this model.

CHAPTER 6

1. The figure has been reproduced electronically with permission from Chicago Linguistic Society. This figure and the examples were originally published in *Papers from the Tenth Regional Meeting of CLS*.

2. This figure is reproduced electronically with kind permission from Ivan Sag and Mark Liberman.

3. This figure is reproduced electronically with kind permission from Ivan Sag and Mark Liberman.

4. Geluykens uses the term "queclaratives" in this study to refer to statements used as questions. However, I will confine the term to Sadock's sense: questions used as opposite assertions.

5. However, some of the contexts Eaton has constructed seem to be above the head of a typical 7-year-old. For example, the shopping dialogue provided here would not be clear to the 7-year-old with whom I happen to live at this writing because he rarely shops, and moreover, he likes the look and feel of a penny. Yet, I believe he understands and uses sarcasm in contexts pertinent to his own affairs.

6. *Language* 61: 748 (1985). Used by permission of Linguistic Society of America.

7. Quoted material and examples used by permission of Linguistic Society of America.

8. Jackendoff uses Bolinger's (1965) model of intonation, in which whole contour shapes correspond to meaningful units.

9. For Martinich, "tone" has to do with lexical meaning rather than anything prosodic, as in the choice between a rude swear word and a milder alternative.

10. Credit for this idea goes to Suzanne LePeintre (in personal communication, 1997).

11. Gaines's "rising intonation" is equivalent to the low-rising ($\nearrow$) pitch boundary of this model; his "falling intonation" is equivalent to the low ($\downarrow$) pitch boundary.

12. All excerpts are from *The People of the State of California vs. Orenthal James Simpson, #BA097211*, Reporter's Transcript of Proceedings, Vols. 79–80, February 1–2, 1995.

CHAPTER 7

1. Reprinted from *Language and Speech*, Vol. 41, Parts 3 and 4, July–December 1998, with kind permission of Kingston Press Ltd., London.

2. To the best of my ability, I have converted Schegloff's original transcription coding to match mine in this and a second transcript later in the chapter, as follows: his underlining of initial segments to indicate stress = my capital letters for H* pitch accents; his reference in the text to "nuclear stress" = my L+H* pitch accent; his comma for continuing intonation = my partially falling ($\searcher$) pitch boundary; his period for final intonation = my low ($\downarrow$) boundary; and his question mark for rising intonation = my high-rising ($\uparrow$) boundary.

3. Reprinted from *Language and Speech*, Vol. 41, Parts 3 and 4, July–December 1998, with kind permission of Kingston Press Ltd., London.

4. This is not to be confused with Halliday's (1994, p. 306) use of the term "tone concord," which refers to a sequence of two identically constructed intonation contours, often found in paratactic expansions (e.g., an elaboration, enhancement, or extension to a first clause).

5. Both the figure and the transcript excerpt are reprinted from *Language and Speech*, Vol. 41, Parts 3 and 4, July–December 1998, with kind permission of Kingston Press Ltd., London.

CHAPTER 8

1. Ching (1982) reports a parallel case of high-rising pitch boundaries used to topicalize a noun phrase in an orientation to a longer sequence to make sure the recipient is following.

2. The plus symbols used in many of my examples for "higher-than-usual" pitch reflect this specific top-10% calculation from Wennerstrom (1997). However, for many purposes, an analyst should be able to identify pitch extremes in relative terms.

3. Reprinted from Journal of Pragmatics, Vol. 22, Margaret Selting, Emphatic speech style—with special focus on the prosodic signalling of emotive involvement in conversation, Pages 375–408, Copyright (1994), with permission from Elsevier Science.

4. The rhythm of the second utterance was shown in figure 3.4.

5. I have adapted Tannen's transcription symbols from p. xix as follows: her accent mark (é) is my H* pitch accent in capital letters; her CAPS for "very emphatic stress" is my plus (+); her high bracket [⌈] for "high pitch on the phrase" is my high key (↱); and my mid key (→) represents a return to a normal range.

6. This is the same speaker described earlier in the chapter as having a "deadpan" style.

CHAPTER 9

1. Here the term "accent" is used to refer not to "pitch accent" but to the cluster of phonological features associated with nonnative speech, as in "foreign accent."

2. Model 6095–97, Kay Elemetrics, Pine Brook, New Jersey.

3. In addition, I have made the following adjustments to Gumperz's transcription system: his falling pitch (//) is my low (↓); his slight fall (/) is my partial fall (↘); his (=) for overlapping speech is my bracket ([); and his capital letters for extra prominence is my underlined capitals for L+H* contrastive pitch accent.

4. SPEAK materials selected from SPEAK® Test Rater Training Kit, 1985. Reprinted by permission of Educational Testing Service, the copyright owner. Note: this version of the SPEAK test has been discontinued since a 1996 revision. The revised SPEAK test yields a single holistic score for communicative competence, which includes functional competence, sociolinguistic competence, discourse competence, and linguistic competence. Permission to reprint SPEAK materials does not constitute review or endorsement by Educational Testing Service of this publication as a whole or any other questions or testing information it may contain.

5. Part of the excerpt is analyzed in Wennerstrom (2000b), pp. 119–120.

6. Additional data from the same speaker are analyzed in Wennerstrom (2000b), pp. 121–123.

BIBLIOGRAPHY

Abrahams, R. (1970). *Positively black.* Englewood Cliffs, NJ: Prentice Hall.

Acton, W. (1998). Directed motion in pronunciation instruction. *Journal of Communication and International Studies 5,* 47–64.

Allen, G., & Hawkins, S. (1980). Phonological rhythm: Definition and development. In O. Yeni-Komshian (Ed.), *Child phonology* (pp. 227–256). New York: Academic Press.

Anderson, P. (1993). *Defining intelligibility parameters: The secrets of sounding native.* Paper presented at the TESOL Annual Convention, Atlanta, GA, March 1993.

Anderson-Hsieh, J., & Koehler, K. (1988). The effect of foreign accent and speaking rate on native speaker comprehension. *Language Learning 38*(4), 561–605.

Anderson-Hsieh, J., Johnson, R., & Koehler, K. (1992). The relationship between native speaker judgments of nonnative pronunciation and deviance in segmentals, prosody, and syllable structure. *Language Learning 42* (4), 529–555.

Archer, D. (1993). *The human voice: Exploring vocal paralanguage* [videotape]. Santa Cruz: University of California.

Atkinson, J., & Heritage, J. (Eds.). (1984). *Structures of social action: Studies in conversation analysis.* Cambridge: Cambridge University Press.

Auer, P. (1996). On the prosody and syntax of turn-continuations. In E. Couper-Kuhlen & M. Selting (Eds.), *Prosody in conversation* (pp. 57–100). New York: Cambridge University Press.

Auer, P., Couper-Kuhlen, E., & Müller, F. (1999). *Language in time: The rhythm and tempo of spoken interaction.* New York: Oxford University Press.

Austin, J. (1962). *How to do things with words* (2nd ed.). Cambridge, MA: Harvard University Press.

———. (1970). Performative utterances. In J. Urmson & G. Warnock (Eds.), *Philosophical papers* (2nd ed., pp. 233–252). Oxford: Oxford University Press.

Bailey, K. (1984). The "foreign TA problem." In K. Bailey, F. Pialorsi, & J. Zukowski/Faust (Eds.), *Foreign teaching assistants in U.S. universities* (pp. 3–15). Washington, DC: National Association for Foreign Student Affairs.

Bamberg, M. (Ed.). (1997). *Oral versions of personal experience: Three decades of narrative analysis* [Special issue]. *Journal of Narrative and Life History 7*, 1–4.

Bardovi-Harlig, K. (1999). From morpheme studies to temporal semantics: Tense-aspect research in SLA. *Studies in Second Language Acquisition 21* (3), 341–382.

Bartlett, F. (1932). *Remembering: A study in experimental and social psychology.* Cambridge: Cambridge University Press.

Bauman, R. (1986). *Story, performance, and event.* Cambridge: Cambridge University Press.

Bauman, R., & Sherzer, J. (Eds.). (1989). *Explorations in the ethnography of speaking* (2ⁿᵈ ed.). Cambridge: Cambridge University Press.

Beattie, G. (1983). *Talk: An analysis of speech and nonverbal behavior in conversation.* Milton Keynes: Open University Press.

Beckman, M., & Ayers, G. (1994). *Guidelines for ToBI labeling,* Version 2. Ms. and accompanying speech materials. Columbus: Ohio State University.

Beckman, M., & Pierrehumbert, J. (1986). Intonational structure in Japanese and English. *Phonology Yearbook 3*, 15–70.

Biber, D. (1994). *Dimensions of register variation: A cross-linguistic comparison.* Cambridge: Cambridge University Press.

Bing, J. (1985). *Aspects of English prosody.* New York: Garland.

Blum-Kulka, S. (1997). *Dinner talk: Cultural patterns of sociability and socialization in family discourse.* Mahwah, NJ: Lawrence Erlbaum.

Bolinger, D. (1965). *Forms of English: Accent, morpheme, order.* Cambridge, MA: Harvard University Press.

———. (1978). Intonation across languages. In J. Greenberg (Ed.), *Universals of human language: Phonology* (pp. 471–524). Palo Alto, CA: Stanford University Press.

———. (1986). *Intonation and its parts.* Palo Alto, CA: Stanford University Press.

———. (1989). *Intonation and its uses.* Palo Alto, CA: Stanford University Press.

Bradford, B. (1988). *Intonation in context: Intonation practice for upper-intermediate and advanced learners of English.* New York: Cambridge University Press.

Brazil, D. (1975). *Discourse intonation I.* Discourse Analysis Monograph 1. Birmingham: University of Birmingham English Language Research.

———. (1978). *Discourse intonation II.* Discourse Analysis Monograph 2. Birmingham: University of Birmingham English Language Research.

———. (1985). *The communicative value of intonation.* Discourse Analysis Monograph 8. Birmingham: University of Birmingham English Language Research.

———. (1997). *The communicative value of intonation in English.* London: Cambridge University Press.

Brazil, D., & Coulthard, M. (1979). *Exchange structure.* Birmingham: English Language Research.

Brazil, D., Coulthard, M., & Johns, A. (1980). *Discourse intonation and language teaching.* London: Longman.

Briggs, C. (1997). Sequentiality and temporalization in the narrative construction of a South American cholera epidemic. In M. Bamberg (Ed.), *Oral versions of personal experience: Three decades of narrative analysis* [Special issue]. *Journal of Narrative and Life History, 7* (1–4), 169–184.

Brown, G. (1977). *Listening to spoken English.* London: Longman.

———. (1995). *Speakers, listeners and communication: Explorations in discourse analysis.* New York: Cambridge University Press.

Brown, G., Currie, K., & Kenworthy, J. (1980). *Questions of intonation.* London: Croom Helm.

Brown, G., & Yule, G. (1983). *Discourse analysis.* Cambridge: Cambridge University Press.

Brown, J., Donelan-McCall, N., & Dunn, J. (1996). Why talk about mental states? The significance of children's conversations with friends, siblings, and mothers. *Child Development 67* (3), 836–849.

Brown, P., & Levinson, S. (1978). Universals in language usage: Politeness phenomena. In E. Goody (Ed.), *Questions and politeness: Strategies in social interaction* (pp. 56–310). London: Cambridge University Press.

———. (1987). *Politeness: Some universals in language usage.* Cambridge: Cambridge University Press.

Bruner, J. (1986). *Actual minds, possible words.* Cambridge, MA: Harvard University Press.

Bülow-Møller, A. (1990). The notion of coercion in courtroom questioning. In *Proceedings from Nordfest Conference.* Espoo, Finland: Abo Academy.

Carrell, P. (1982). Cohesion is not coherence. *TESOL Quarterly 16* (4), 479–488.

Celce-Murcia, M. Brinton, D., & Goodwin, J. (1996). *Teaching pronunciation: A reference for teachers of English to speakers of other languages.* New York: Cambridge University Press.

Chafe, W. (1970). *Meaning and the structure of language.* Chicago: University of Chicago Press.

———. (1980). The deployment of consciousness in the production of a narrative. In W. Chafe (Ed.), *The pear stories: Cognitive, cultural, and linguistic aspects of narrative production* (pp. 9–50). Norwood, NJ: Ablex.

———. (1988). Linking intonation units in spoken English. In J. Haiman & S. Thompson (Eds.), *Clause combining in grammar and discourse* (pp. 1–27). Amsterdam: John Benjamins.

———. (1994). *Discourse, consciousness, and time: The flow and displacement of conscious experience in speaking and writing.* Chicago: University of Chicago Press.

echoic memory

Chaudron, C., & Richards, J. (1986). The effect of discourse markers on the comprehension of lectures. *Applied Linguistics 7* (2), 113–127.

Ching, M. (1982). The question intonation in assertions. *American Speech 57* (2), 95–107.

Chomsky, N. (1971). Deep structure, surface structure, and semantic interpretation. In D. Steinberg & L. Jacobovits (Eds.), *Semantics: An interdisciplinary reader in philosophy, linguistics, and psychology* (pp. 183–216). London: Cambridge University Press.

Chomsky, N., & Halle, M. (1968). *The sound pattern of English.* New York: Harper and Row.

Chun, D. (1988). The neglected role of intonation in communicative competence and proficiency. *Modern Language Journal 72* (3), 295–303.

Cinque, G. (1993). A null theory of phrase and compound stress. *Linguistic Inquiry 24*, 239–297.

Clark, H. (1992). *Arenas of language use.* Chicago: University of Chicago Press.

Clennell, C. (1997). Raising the pedagogic status of discourse intonation teaching. *English Language Teaching Journal 51* (2), 117–125.

Coulthard, M., & Montgomery, M. (Eds.). (1981). *Studies in discourse analysis.* London: Routledge & Kegan Paul.

Couper-Kuhlen, E. (1986). *An introduction to English prosody.* Baltimore: Edward Arnold.

———. (1992). Contextualizing discourse: The prosody of interactive repair. In P. Auer & A. Di Luzio (Eds.), *The contextualization of language* (pp. 337–364). Amsterdam: John Benjamins.

———. (1993). *English speech rhythm: Form and function in every-day verbal interaction.* Amsterdam: John Benjamins.

———. (1996). Intonation and clause combining in discourse: The case of "because." *Pragmatics 6* (3), 389–426.

Couper-Kuhlen, E., & Selting, M. (Eds.) (1996). *Prosody in conversation.* New York: Cambridge University Press.

Cruttendon, A. (1986). *Intonation.* Cambridge: Cambridge University Press.

———. (1997). *Intonation* (2nd ed.) Cambridge: Cambridge University Press.

Crystal, D. (1969). *Prosodic systems and intonation in English.* Cambridge: Cambridge University Press.

Crystal, D., & Varley, R. (1993). *Introduction to language pathology* (3rd ed.). London: Whurr.

Cutler, A., Dahan, D., & van Donselaar, W. (1997). Prosody in the comprehension of spoken language: A literature review. *Language and Speech 40* (2), 141–201.

Cutler, A., & Pearson, M. (1986). On the analysis of prosodic turn-taking cues. In C. Johns-Lewis (Ed.), *Intonation in discourse* (pp. 139–156). San Diego: College-Hill Press.

Danet, B., Hoffman, K., Kermish, N., Rafn, H., & Stayman, D. (1976). An ethnography of questioning in the courtroom. In R. Shuy & A. Shnukal (Eds.), *Lan-*

guage use and the uses of language (pp. 222–234). Washington, DC: Georgetown University Press.

Dauer, R. (1993). *Accurate English: A complete course in pronunciation.* Englewood Cliffs, NJ: Prentice-Hall Regents.

Davies, C., & Tyler, A. (1994). Demystifying cross-cultural (mis)communication: Improving performance through balanced feedback in a situated context. In C. Madden & C. Myers (Eds.), *Discourse and performance of international teaching assistants* (pp. 201–220). Alexandria, VA: TESOL.

Derwing, T., & Munro, M. (1997). Accent, intelligibility, and comprehensibility: Evidence from four L1s. *Studies in Second Language Acquisition 19* (1), 1–16.

Dretske, F. (1972). Contrastive statements. *Philosophical Review 81,* 411–437.

Dry, H. (1983). The movement of narrative time. *Journal of Literary Semantics 12,* 19–53.

Ducrot, O. (1980). *Let mots du discours.* Paris: Les Editions de Minuit.

Duncan, S. (1972). Some signals and rules for taking speaking turns in conversations. *Journal of Personality and Social Psychology 23* (1), 283–292.

Eaton, R. (1988). Children and sarcasm: A psycholinguistic study. *Journal of Literary Semantics 17* (2), 122–148.

Educational Testing Service. (1985). *Speaking proficiency English assessment kit* [Training manual]. Princeton, NJ: Educational Testing Service.

Eggins, S., & Slade, D. (1997). *Analysing casual conversation.* London: Cassell.

Ejzenberg, R. (2000). The juggling act of oral fluency: A psycho-sociolinguistic metaphor. In H. Riggenbach (Ed.), *Perspectives on fluency* (pp. 287–313). Ann Arbor: University of Michigan Press.

Erickson, F. (1984). Rhetoric, anecdote, and rhapsody: Coherence strategies in a conversation among Black American adolescents. In D. Tannen (Ed.), *Coherence in spoken and written discourse* (pp. 45–154). Norwood, NJ: Ablex.

———. (1992). They know all the lines: Rhythmic organization and contextualization in a conversational listing routine. In P. Auer & A. Di Luzio (Eds.), *The contextualization of language* (pp. 365–397). Amsterdam: John Benjamins.

Erickson, F., & Shultz, J. (1982). *The counselor as gatekeeper: The social interaction of interviews.* New York: Academic Press.

Feldman, C. (1991). Oral metalanguage. In D. Olson & N. Torrance (Eds.), *Literacy and orality* (pp. 47–65). Cambridge: Cambridge University Press.

Feldman, C., Bruner, J., Kalmar, D., & Renderer, B. (1993). Plot, plight, and dramatism: Interpretation at three ages. *Human Development 36,* 327–342.

Fernald, A., Taeschner, T., Dunn, J., Paponsek, M., DeBoysson-Bardies, B., & Fukui, I. (1989). A cross-language study of prosodic modification in mothers' and fathers' speech to preverbal infants. *Child Language 16,* 477–501.

Ferrara, K. (1997). Form and function of the discourse marker "anyway": Implications for discourse analysis. *Linguistics 35,* 343–378.

Fiksdal, S. (1990). *The right time and pace.* Norwood, NJ: Ablex.

————. (2000). Fluency as a function of time and rapport. In H. Riggenbach (Ed.), *Perspectives on fluency* (pp. 128–140). Ann Arbor: University of Michigan Press.

Fleishman, S. (1997). The "Labovian model" revisited with special consideration of literary narrative. In M. Bamberg (Ed.), *Oral versions of personal experience: Three decades of narrative analysis* [Special issue]. *Journal of Narrative and Life History 7* (1–4), 159–168.

Flowerdew, J. (1994). *Academic listening: Research perspectives.* New York: Cambridge University Press.

Ford, C., & Thompson, S. (1996). Interactional units in conversation: Syntactic, intonational, and pragmatic resources for the management of turns. In E. Ochs, E. Schegloff, & S. Thompson (Eds.), *Interaction and grammar* (pp. 134–184). Cambridge: Cambridge University Press.

Fox, A. (1973). Tone-sequences in English. *Archivum Linguisticum 4*, 17–26.

Fox, B. (1987). *Discourse structure and anaphora.* New York: Cambridge University Press.

Freed, B. (2000). Is fluency, like beauty, in the eyes (and ears) of the beholder? In H. Riggenbach (Ed.), *Perspectives on fluency* (pp. 243–265). Ann Arbor: University of Michigan Press.

Freeman, M. (1993). *Rewriting the self: History, memory, narrative.* London: Routledge.

French, P., & Local, J. (1986). Prosodic features and the management of interruptions. In C. Johns-Lewis (Ed.), *Intonation in discourse* (pp. 157–180). San Diego: College Hill.

Gaines, P. (1998). *Cross purposes: A critical analysis of the representational force of questions in adversarial legal examination.* Unpublished doctoral dissertation, University of Washington, Seattle, WA.

Garfinkel, H. (1967). *Studies in ethnomethodology.* Englewood Cliffs, NJ: Prentice-Hall.

Geluykens, R. (1987). Intonation and speech act type: An experimental approach to rising intonation in queclaratives. *Journal of Pragmatics 11*, 483–494.

Gilbert, J. (1980). Prosodic development: Some pilot studies. In S. Krashen & R. Scarcella (Eds.), *Issues in second language research* (pp. 110–117). Rowley, MA: Newbury House.

————. (1984). *Clear speech* [Student's book]. New York: Cambridge University Press.

————. (1993). *Clear speech: Pronunciation and listening comprehension in North American English* (2nd ed.) [Student's book]. New York: Cambridge University Press.

Givón, T. (1983). Topic continuity in discourse: An introduction. In T. Givón (Ed.), *Topic continuity in discourse: A quantitative cross-language study* (pp. 1–42). Philadelphia: John Benjamins.

Goffman, E. (1967). *Interaction ritual.* New York: Pantheon Books.

————. (1981). *Forms of talk.* Philadelphia: University of Pennsylvania Press.

Goldsmith, J. (1990). *Autosegmental and metrical phonology.* Cambridge, MA: Basil Blackwell.

Good, D., & Butterworth, B. (1980). Hesitancy as a conversational resource: Some methodological implications. In H. Dechert & M. Raupach (Eds.), *Tempo-*

ral variables in speech: Studies in honour of Frieda Goldman-Eisler (pp. 145–152). The Hague: Mouton.

Goodwin, C. (1981). *Conversational organization: Interaction between speakers and hearers.* New York: Academic Press.

Goodwin, C., & Heritage, J. (1990). Conversation analysis. *Annual Review of Anthropology 19*, 283–307.

Grant, L. (1993). *Well said: Advanced English pronunciation.* Boston: Heinle and Heinle.

Grice, P. (1961). The causal theory of perception. *Proceedings of the Aristotelian Society, Supplementary Vol. 35*, 121–152.

———. (1975). Logic and conversation. In P. Cole & J. Morgan (Eds.), *Syntax and semantics: Vol. 3, Speech acts* (pp. 41–58). New York: Academic Press.

Grosz, B., & Hirschberg, J. (1992). Some intonational characteristics of discourse structure. *Proceedings of the International Conference on Spoken Language Processing 1992*, Banff, 429–432.

Gumperz, J. (1971). *Language in social groups.* Palo Alto, CA: Stanford University Press.

———. (1982). *Discourse strategies.* Cambridge: Cambridge University Press.

———. (1992). Contextualization and understanding. In A. Duranti & C. Goodwin (Eds.), *Rethinking context* (pp. 229–252). New York: Cambridge University Press.

Gunter, R. (1966). On the placement of accent in dialogue. *Journal of Linguistics 2*, 159–179.

Günthner, S. (1996). The prosodic contextualization of moral work: An analysis of reproaches in "why"-formats. In E. Couper-Kuhlen & M. Selting (Eds.), *Prosody in conversation* (pp. 271–302). New York: Cambridge University Press.

Gussenhoven, C. (1984). *On the grammar and semantics of sentence accents.* Dordrecht: Foris.

Hagen, S., & Grogan, P. (1992). *Sound advantage.* New York: Prentice-Hall.

Hahn, L. (1999). *Native speakers' reaction to non-native stress in English discourse.* Unpublished doctoral dissertation, University of Illinois, Urbana-Champaign, IL.

Hahn, L., & Dickerson, W. (1999). *Speechcraft: Discourse pronunciation for advanced learners.* Ann Arbor: University of Michigan Press.

Halle, M., & Vergnaud, J. (1987). *An essay on stress.* Cambridge, MA: MIT Press.

Halliday, M. (1967a). *Intonation and grammar in British English.* The Hague: Mouton.

———. (1967b). Notes on transitivity and theme in English (Parts 1–3). *Journal of Linguistics 3* (1), 37–81; *3* (2), 199–244; *4* (2) (1968), 179–215.

———. (1985). *An introduction to functional grammar.* London: Edward Arnold.

———. (1994). *An introduction to functional grammar* (2nd ed.). London: Edward Arnold.

Halliday, M., & Hasan, R. (1976). *Cohesion in English.* London: Longman.

Hayes, B. (1984). The phonology of rhythm in English. *Linguistic Inquiry 15*, 33–74.

———. (1995). *Metrical stress theory: Principles and case studies.* Chicago: University of Chicago Press.

Hedge, T. (1993). Key concepts in ELT (Fluency). *English Language Teaching Journal 47* (3), 275–276.

Hellermann, J. (1997). *Rhythm and the intonation unit.* Paper presented at the American Association of Applied Linguistics annual convention, Orlando, FL, March 1997.

Heritage, J. (1984). A change-of-state token and aspects of its sequential placement. In J. Atkinson & J. Heritage (Eds.), *Structures of social action: Studies in conversation analysis* (pp. 299–345). Cambridge: Cambridge University Press.

Hewings, M. (1995a). Tone choice in the English intonation of non-native speakers. *International Review of Applied Linguistics 33* (3), 251–265.

———. (1995b). The English intonation of native speakers and Indonesian learners: A comparative study. *Regional English Language Conference Journal 26* (1), 27–46.

Hinds, J. (1977). Paragraph structure and pronominalization. *Papers in Linguistics 10*, 77–99.

Hirschberg, J., & Litman, D. (1987). Now let's talk about "now": Identifying cue phrases intonationally. *Proceedings of the Twenty-fifth Annual Meeting of the Association for Computational Linguistics*, Stanford, CA.

Hirst, D., & Di Cristo, A. (Eds.). (1998). *Intonation systems: A survey of twenty languages.* Cambridge: Cambridge University Press.

Hopper, P., & Traugott, E. (1993). *Grammaticalization.* Cambridge: Cambridge University Press.

Hu, H. (1944). The Chinese concepts of face. *American Anthropologist 46*, 45–64.

Hymes, D. (1974). *Foundations of sociolinguistics: An ethnographic approach.* Philadelphia: University of Pennsylvania Press.

Isaac, A. (1997). *Critical factors in native speaker perceptions of nonnative speaker fluency.* Paper presented at the American Association of Applied Linguistics annual convention, Orlando, FL, March 1997.

Jackendoff, R. (1972). *Semantic interpretation in generative grammar.* Cambridge, MA: MIT Press.

Jefferson, G. (1984). Transcript notation. In J. Atkinson & J. Heritage (Eds.), *Structures of social action: Studies in conversation analysis* (pp. ix-xvi). Cambridge: Cambridge University Press.

———. (Ed.). (1995). *Harvey Sacks: Lectures on conversation.* Vols. I and II. Oxford: Blackwell.

Johnstone, B. (1996). *The linguistic individual: Self-expression in language and linguistics.* New York: Oxford University Press.

Juffs, A. (1990). Tone, syllable structure and interlanguage phonology: Chinese learners' stress errors. *International Review of Applied Linguistics 28* (2), 99–117.

Kaisse, E. (1985). *Connected speech: The interaction of syntax and phonology.* Orlando, FL: Academic Press.

———. (1987). Rhythm and the cycle. In *Papers from the 23rd Annual Regional*

Meeting of the Chicago Linguistics Society (pp. 199–209). Chicago: Chicago Linguistics Society.

Kintsch, W. (1988). The role of knowledge in discourse comprehension: A construction-integration model. *Psychology Review 95* (2), 163–182.

Kirshenblatt-Gimblett, B. (1989). The concept and varieties of narrative performance in East European Jewish culture. In R. Bauman & J. Sherzer (Eds.), *Explorations in the ethnography of speaking* (2nd ed., pp. 283–308). Cambridge: Cambridge University Press.

Kjellen, O. (1995). *Svensk prosodi i praktiken: Instruktioner och övningar i svenskt uttal, speciellt språkmelodin* (9th ed.). Uppsala: Hallgren & Fallgren.

Klatt, D. (1975). Vowel lengthening is syntactically determined in a connected discourse. *Journal of Phonetics 3*, 129–140.

Kopenon, M., & Riggenbach, H. (2000). Overview: Varying perspectives on fluency. In H. Riggenbach (Ed.), *Perspectives on fluency* (pp. 5–24). Ann Arbor: University of Michigan Press.

Krashen, S. (1981). *Second language acquisition and second language learning.* New York: Pergamon.

Kreidler, C. (1997). *Describing spoken English: An introduction.* New York: Routledge.

Küntay, A., & Ervin-Tripp, S. (1997). Narrative structure and conversational circumstances. In M. Bamberg (Ed.), *Oral versions of personal experience: Three decades of narrative analysis* [Special issue]. *Journal of Narrative and Life History 7* (1–4), 113–120.

Kutik, E., Cooper, W., & Boyce, S. (1983). Declination of fundamental frequency in speakers' production of parenthetical and main clauses. *Journal of the Acoustical Society of America 73* (5), 1731–1738.

Labov, W. (1972). *Language in the inner city.* Philadelphia: University of Pennsylvania Press.

———. (1997). Some further steps in narrative analysis. In M. Bamberg (Ed.), *Oral versions of personal experience: Three decades of narrative analysis* [Special issue]. *Journal of Narrative and Life History 7* (1–4), 395–415.

Labov, W., & Waletzky, J. (1967). Narrative analysis: Oral versions of personal experience. In J. Helms (Ed.), *Essays on the verbal and visual arts* (pp. 12–44). Seattle: University of Washington Press.

Ladd, R. (1980). *The structure of intonational meaning.* Bloomington: Indiana University Press.

———. (1984). English compound stress. In D. Gibbon & H. Richter (Eds.), *Intonation, accent and rhythm: Studies in discourse phonology* (pp. 253–266). Berlin: De Gruyter.

———. (1996). *Intonational phonology.* Cambridge: Cambridge University Press.

Lakoff, G., & Johnson, M. (1980). *Metaphors we live by.* Chicago: University of Chicago Press.

Lakoff, R. (1975). *Language and women's place.* New York: Harper and Row.

Lehiste, I. (1975). The phonetic structure of paragraphs. In A. Cohen & S. Nooteboom (Eds.), *Structure and process in speech perception* (pp. 195–203). Berlin: Springer.

———. (1980). *Phonetic characteristics of discourse.* Tokyo: Acoustical Society of Japan.

Levelt, W. (1989). *Speaking: From intention to articulation.* Cambridge, MA: MIT Press.

Levinson, S. (1983). *Pragmatics.* Cambridge: Cambridge University Press.

Liberman, M. (1975). *The intonation system of English.* Doctoral dissertation, Massachusetts Institute of Technology, Cambridge, MA. [Published by Garland Press, New York, 1979].

Liberman, M., & Prince, A. (1977). On stress and linguistic rhythm. *Linguistic Inquiry 8,* 249–336.

Liberman, M., & Sag, I. (1974). Prosodic form and discourse function. In *Papers from the Tenth Regional Meeting of the Chicago Linguistic Society* (pp. 416–427). Chicago: Chicago Linguistics Society.

Linde, C. (1993). *Life stories.* New York: Oxford University Press.

Local, J. (1992). Continuing and restarting. In P. Auer & A. Di Luzio (Eds.), *The contextualization of language* (pp. 273–296). Amsterdam: John Benjamins.

———. (1996). Conversational phonetics: Some aspects of news receipts in everyday talk. In E. Couper-Kuhlen & M. Selting (Eds.), *Prosody in conversation* (pp. 177–230). New York: Cambridge University Press.

Local, J., & Kelly, J. (1986). Projection and "silences": Notes on phonetic and conversational structure. *Human Studies 9,* 185–204.

Longacre, R. (1976). "Mystery" particles and affixes. In S. Mufwene et al. (Eds.), *Papers from the Twelfth Regional Meeting of the Chicago Linguistics Society* (pp. 468–475). Chicago: Chicago Linguistics Society.

———. (1981). A spectrum and profile approach to discourse analysis. *Text 4,* 337–359.

———. (1983). *The grammar of discourse.* New York: Plenum.

Mann, W., & Matthiessen, C. (1991). Functions of language in two frameworks. *Word 42* (3), 231–249.

Mann, W., & Thompson, S. (1989). Rhetorical structure theory: A theory of text organization. In L. Polanyi (Ed.), *The structure of discourse.* Norwood, NJ: Ablex.

———. (1992). Relational discourse structure: A comparison of approaches to structuring text by "contrast." In S. Hwang & W. Merrifield (Eds.), *Language and context: Essays for Robert E. Longacre* (pp. 19–46). Arlington, TX: Summer Institute of Linguistics and the University of Texas.

Martin, J. (1992). *English text: System and structure.* Amsterdam: John Benjamins.

Martinich, A. (1984). *Communication and reference.* New York: Walter de Gruyter.

McClave, E. (1994). Gestural beats: The rhythm hypothesis. *Journal of Psycholinguistic Research 23* (1), 45–66.

McCrum, R., Cran, W., & MacNeil, R. (1986). *The story of English.* London: BBC Publications.

McLemore, C. (1991). *The pragmatic interpretation of English intonation: Sorority speech.* Unpublished doctoral dissertation, University of Texas at Austin.

Menn, L., & Boyce, S. (1982). Fundamental frequency and discourse structure. *Language and Speech 25* (4), 341–383.

Mishler, E. (1986). *Research interviewing: Context and narrative.* Cambridge, MA: Harvard University Press.

Morley, J. (1991). The pronunciation component in teaching English to speakers of other languages. *TESOL Quarterly 25* (3), 481–520.

———. (1993). *Rapid review of vowels and prosodic contexts.* Ann Arbor: University of Michigan Press.

Müller, F. (1996). Affiliating and disaffiliating with continuers: Prosodic aspects of recipiency. In E. Couper-Kuhlen & M. Selting (Eds.), *Prosody in conversation* (pp. 131–176). New York: Cambridge University Press.

Munro, M. (1995). Nonsegmental factors in foreign accent: Ratings of filtered speech. *Studies in Second Language Acquisition 17,* 17–34.

Munro, M., & Derwing, T. (1994). Evaluations of foreign accent in extemporaneous and read material. *Language Testing 11,* 253–256.

———. (1995). Foreign accent, comprehensibility and intelligibility in the speech of second language learners. *Language Learning 45,* 73–97.

Myers-Scotton, C. (1997). *Duelling languages: Grammatical structure in codeswitching.* New York: Oxford University Press.

Nespor, M., & Vogel, I. (1986). *Prosodic phonology.* Dordrecht: Foris.

———. (1989). On clashes and lapses. *Phonology 6,* 69–116.

Neufeld, G., & Schneiderman, E. (1980). Prosodic and articulatory features in adult language learning. In R. Scarcella & S. Krashen (Eds.), *Issues in second language research* (pp. 105–109). Rowley, MA: Newbury House.

Nootebaum, S., & Terken, J. (1982). What makes speakers omit pitch accents: An experiment. *Phonetica 39,* 317–336.

Ochs Keenan, E., & Schiefflin, B. (1976). Topic as a discourse notion: A study of topic in the conversations of children and adults. In C. Li & S. Thompson (Eds.), *Subject and topic* (pp. 459–489). New York: Academic Press.

Pawley, A., & Syder, F. (1975). Sentence formulation in spontaneous speech. *New Zealand Speech Therapists' Journal 30* (2), 2–11.

———. (2000). The one-clause-at-a-time hypothesis. In H. Riggenbach (Ed.), *Perspectives on fluency* (pp. 163–199). Ann Arbor: University of Michigan Press.

Pennington, M. (1996). *Phonology in English language teaching.* New York: Longman.

Pennington, M., & Richards, J. (1986). Pronunciation revisited. *TESOL Quarterly 20* (2), 207–225.

The People of the State of California vs. Orenthal James Simpson, #BA097211, Reporter's Transcript of Proceedings, Vols. 79–80, February 1–2, 1995.

Peterson, C., & McCabe, A. (1983). *Developmental psycholinguistics: Three ways of looking at a child's narrative.* New York: Plenum.

Pickering, L. (1999). *The analysis of prosodic systems in the classroom discourse of NS and NNS teaching assistants.* Unpublished doctoral dissertation, University of Florida, Gainesville, FL.

Pierrehumbert, J. (1980). *The phonology and phonetics of English intonation.* Unpublished doctoral dissertation, Massachusetts Institute of Technology, Cambridge, MA.

Pierrehumbert, J., & Hirschberg, J. (1990). The meaning of intonational contours in discourse. In P. Cohen, J. Morgan, & M. Pollack (Eds.), *Intentions in communication* (pp. 271–311). Cambridge, MA: MIT Press.

Pike, K. (1945). *The intonation of American English.* Ann Arbor: University of Michigan Press.

———. (1954). *Language in relation to a unified theory of structure of human behavior.* Glendale, CA: Summer Institute of Linguistics.

PLIB. Phonology Lab in a Box. Dr. LST: Software, 545 33rd Street, Richmond, CA 94804.

Polanyi, L. (1985). *Telling the American story.* Norwood, NJ: Ablex.

Polanyi, L., & Scha, R. (1983). The syntax of discourse. *Text 3,* 261–270.

Prince, E. (1981). Toward a taxonomy of given-new information. In P. Cole (Ed.), *Radical pragmatics.* New York: Academic Press.

Prince, G. (1982). *Narratology: The form and functioning of narrative.* Janua linguarum. New York: Mouton.

Richards, J. (1983). Listening comprehension: Approach, design, procedure. *TESOL Quarterly 17* (2), 219–239.

Riggenbach, H. (1989). *Nonnative fluency in dialogue versus monologue speech: A microanalytic approach.* Unpublished doctoral dissertation, UCLA, Los Angles, CA.

———. (1991). Toward an understanding of fluency: A microanalysis of nonnative speaker conversations. *Discourse Processes 14,* 423–441.

———. (1999). *Discourse analysis in the language classroom, Vol. I, The spoken language.* Ann Arbor: University of Michigan Press.

———. (Ed.). (2000). *Perspectives on fluency.* Ann Arbor: University of Michigan Press.

Roach, P. (1994). Conversion between prosodic transcription systems: "Standard British" and ToBI. *Speech Communication 15,* 91–99.

Rochemont, M., & Cullicover, P. (1990). *English focus constructions and the theory of grammar.* Cambridge: Cambridge University Press.

Rubin, D. (1995). *Memory in oral traditions: The cognitive psychology of epic, ballads, and counting-out rhymes.* New York: Oxford University Press.

Sacks, H., Schegloff, E., & Jefferson, G. (1974). A simplest systematics for the organization of turntaking for conversation. *Language 50* (4), 696–735.

Sadock, J. (1974). *Toward a linguistic theory of speech acts.* New York: Academic Press.

Sag, I., & Liberman, M. (1975). The intonational disambiguation of indirect speech acts. *Papers from the 11th Regional Meeting of the Chicago Linguistic Society,* 487–497.

Sankoff, G., & Laberge, S. (1984). On the acquisition of native speakers by a language. In J. Baugh & J. Sherzer (Eds.), *Language in use: Readings in sociolinguistics* (pp. 305–316). Englewood Cliffs, NJ: Prentice Hall.

Schaffer, D. (1983). The role of intonation as a cue to turn-taking in conversation. *Journal of Phonetics 11,* 243–257.

Schegloff, E. (1979). The relevance of repair for syntax-for-conversation. In

T. Givón (Ed.), *Syntax and semantics, Vol. 12, Discourse and syntax* (pp. 261–286). New York: Academic Press.

———. (1982). Discourse as an interactional achievement: Some uses of "uh huh" and other things that come between sentences. In D. Tannen (Ed.), *Analyzing discourse: Text and talk* (pp. 71–93). Georgetown: Georgetown University Press.

———. (1990). On the organization of sequences as a source of "coherence" in talk-in-interaction. In B. Dorval (Ed.), *Conversational organization and its development* (pp. 51–77). Norwood, NJ: Ablex.

———. (1998). Reflections on studying prosody in talk-in-interaction. *Language and Speech 41* (3–4), 235–263.

Schiffrin, D. (1987). *Discourse markers.* Studies in Interactional Sociolinguistics, Vol. 5. Cambridge: Cambridge University Press.

———. (1994). *Approaches to discourse.* Cambridge, MA: Blackwell.

Scheutze-Coburn, S., Shapley, M., & Weber, E. (1991). Units of intonation in discourse: A comparison of acoustic and auditory analyses. *Language and Speech 34* (3), 207–234.

Schwenter, S., & Traugott, E. (1994). Grammaticalization workshop presented at New Ways of Analyzing Variation, Stanford University, October 1994.

Searle, J. (1969). *Speech acts.* New York: Cambridge University Press.

———. (1975). Indirect speech acts. In P. Cole & J. Morgan (Eds.), *Syntax and semantics, Vol. 3, Speech acts* (pp. 59–82). New York: Academic Press.

———. (1979). Metaphor. In A. Ortony (Ed.), *Metaphor and thought* (pp. 92–123). Cambridge: Cambridge University Press.

Selkirk, E. (1984). *Phonology and syntax: The relation between sound and structure.* Cambridge, MA: MIT Press.

Selting, M. (1994). Emphatic speech style—With special focus on the prosodic signalling of heightened emotive involvement in conversation. *Journal of Pragmatics 22,* 375–408.

———. (1996). Prosody as an activity-type distinctive cue in conversation: The case of so-called "astonished" questions in repair initiation. In E. Couper-Kuhlen & M. Selting (Eds.), *Prosody in conversation* (pp. 231–270). New York: Cambridge University Press.

Selting, M., & Couper-Kuhlen, E. (1996). Introduction. In E. Couper-Kuhlen & M. Selting (Eds.), *Prosody in conversation* (pp. 1–10). New York: Cambridge University Press.

Shen, X. (1990). *The prosody of Mandarin Chinese.* University of California Publications in Linguistics, Vol. 118. Berkeley: University of California Press.

Signalyze™. August 1994 version.

Snow, C. (1991). Building memories: The ontogeny of autobiography. In D. Cicchetti & M. Beeghly (Eds.), *The self in transition: Infancy to childhood* (pp. 213–242). Chicago: University of Chicago Press.

Sperber, D., & Wilson, D. (1995). *Relevance: Communication and cognition* (2nd ed.). Oxford: Blackwell.

Stein, D. (1985). Discourse markers in Early Modern English. In R. Eaton,

O. Fischer, W. Koopman, & F. van der Leek (Eds.), *Papers from the 4th International Conference on English Historical Linguistics* (pp. 283–203). Amsterdam: John Benjamins.

Stenstrom, A. (1986). A study of pauses as demarcators in discourse and syntax. In J. Aarts & W. Meijs (Eds.), *Corpus linguistics II: New studies in the analysis and exploitation of computer corpora* (pp. 203–218). Amsterdam: Rodopi.

Strawson, P. (1952). *Introduction to logical theory.* New York: John Wiley & Sons.

Sweet, H. (1906). *A primer of phonetics.* Oxford: Clarendon Press.

Swerts, M. (1997). Prosodic features at discourse boundaries of different strength. *Journal of the Acoustical Society of America 101*, 514–521.

Swerts, M., & Geluykens, R. (1994). Prosody as a marker of information flow in spoken discourse. *Language and Speech 37* (1), 21–43.

Tannen, D. (1984a). *Conversational style.* Norwood, NJ: Ablex.

———. (1984b). Spoken and written narrative in English and Greek. In D. Tannen (Ed.), *Coherence in spoken and written discourse* (pp. 21–41). Norwood, NJ: Ablex.

Tappan, M. (1997). Analyzing stories of moral experience: Narrative, voice, and the dialogical self. In M. Bamberg (Ed.), *Oral versions of personal experience: Three decades of narrative analysis* [Special issue]. *Journal of Narrative and Life History 7* (1–4), 379–386.

Tench, P. (1990). *The roles of intonation in English discourse.* Frankfurt am Main: Peter Lang.

———. (1991). The stylistic potential of intonation. In W. van Peer (Ed.), *The taming of the text* (pp. 50–82). London: Routledge.

———. (1996). *The intonation systems of English.* London: Cassell.

Terken, J., & Hirschberg, J. (1994). Deaccentuation of words representing "given" information: Effects of persistence of grammatical function and surface position. *Language and Speech 37* (2), 125–145.

Thompson, S. (1994). Aspects of cohesion in monologue. *Applied Linguistics 15* (1), 58–75.

Tomlin, R. (1987). Linguistic reflections of cognitive events. In R. Tomlin (Ed.), *Coherence and grounding in discourse* (pp. 455–480). Amsterdam: John Benjamins.

———. (1997). Mapping conceptual representations into linguistic representations: The role of attention in grammar. In J. Nuyts & E. Pederson (Eds.), *With language in mind* (pp. 162–189). Cambridge: Cambridge University Press.

Tomlin, R., Forrest, L., Pu, M., & Kim, M. (1997). Discourse semantics. In T. van Dijk (Ed.), *Discourse as structure and process* (pp. 63–111). London: Sage.

Toolan, M. (1988). *Narrative: A critical linguistic introduction.* London: Routledge.

Tsui, A. (1994). *English conversation.* Oxford: Oxford University Press.

Tyler, A. (1992). Discourse structure and the perception of incoherence in ITAs' spoken discourse. *TESOL Quarterly 26* (4), 713–729.

Uhmann, S. (1992). Contextualizing relevance: On some forms and functions of speech rate changes in everyday conversation. In P. Auer & A. Di Luzio (Eds.), *The contextualization of language* (pp. 297–336). Amsterdam: John Benjamins.

———. (1996). On rhythm in everyday German conversation: Beat clashes in assessment utterances. In E. Couper-Kuhlen & M. Selting (Eds.), *Prosody in conversation* (pp. 303–365). New York: Cambridge University Press.

Underhill, R. (1988). Like is, like, focus. *American Speech 63*, 234–246.

Van Dijk, T. (1982). Episodes as units of discourse. In D. Tannen (Ed.), *Analyzing discourse: Text and talk.* Washington, DC: Georgetown University Press.

Walker, A. (1987). Linguistic manipulation, power, and the legal setting. In L. Kedar (Ed.), *Power through discourse.* Norwood, NJ: Ablex.

Ward, G., & Hirschberg, J. (1985). Implicating uncertainty: The pragmatics of fall-rise intonation. *Language 61* (4), 747–776.

Wenk, B. (1985). Speech rhythms in second language acquisition. *Language and speech 28* (2), 157–175.

Wennerstrom, A. (1991). *Techniques for teachers: A guide for nonnative speakers of English.* Ann Arbor: University of Michigan Press.

———. (1992). The paratone: An intonational marker of English discourse organization. Unpublished master's thesis, University of Washington, Seattle, WA.

———. (1993). Focus on the prefix: Evidence for word-internal prosodic words. *Phonology 10*, 309–324.

———. (1994). Intonational meaning in English discourse: A study of nonnative speakers. *Applied Linguistics 15* (4), 399–420.

———. (1997). *Discourse intonation and second language acquisition: Three genre-based studies.* Unpublished doctoral dissertation, University of Washington, Seattle, WA.

———. (1998). Intonation and second language acquisition: A study of Chinese speakers. *Studies in Second Language Acquisition 20* (1), 1–25.

———. (2000a). Is it me or is it hot in here? Menopause, identity, and humor. *HUMOR: International Journal of Humor Research 13* (3), 313–331.

———. (2000b). The role of intonation in second language fluency. In H. Riggenbach (Ed.), *Perspectives on fluency* (pp. 102–127). Ann Arbor: University of Michigan Press.

———. (2001) Intonation and evaluation in oral narratives. *Journal of Pragmatics 33* (8), 1183–1206.

Wennerstrom, A., & Siegel, A. (2001). Keeping the floor: Prosody, syntax, and discourse structure. Manuscript submitted for publication.

Werth, P. (1984). *Focus, coherence and emphasis.* Breckenham, Kent: Croom Helm.

Wolfram, W. (1991). Dialects of American English. Englewood Cliffs, NJ: Prentice-Hall Regents.

Wolfson, N. (1982). *CHP: The conversational historical present in American English narrative.* Cinnarinson, NJ: Foris.

Wong, R. (1987). *Teaching pronunciation: Focus on English rhythm and intonation.* Englewood Cliffs, NJ: Prentice-Hall Regents.

Young, D. (1991). Projection and deixis in narrative discourse. In W. van Peer (Ed.), *The taming of the text* (pp. 20–49). London: Routledge.

Yule, G. (1980). Speakers' topics and major paratones. *Lingua 52*, 33–47.

INDEX